What The Press Is Writing About "Our Hawaii"

"The McDermotts share their island favorites in a wonderfully readably narrative style—a very personal selected listing that will whet your appetite before you go and be a handy reference on the dash of your rental car once you arrive."

Seattle P.I.

"...the real beauty (of Our Hawaii) is being guided through the islands by local residents. Out-of-the-way sites, restaurants and stores are described which a casual travel writer would never find. The McDermotts have avoided the pitfalls of cliche travel writing . . . (bringing) the people, places and happenings alive."

The Garden Island

"The personal approach takes the reader on a factual, often light-hearted and humorous journey as the writers record their experiences while ferreting out and recording the unusual as well as some of the well known points of interest through the major Hawaiian islands." *Hawaii Tribune Herald*

"They tell people about experiences—the wonderful mule ride they took, or the best golf course they played, or the quaint little candy shop that makes fudge that no one should miss."

The Portland Oregonian

"The book is geared for visitors ... Aloha Airlines bought copies to make available to first-class passengers."

Honolulu—Advertiser

First Published 1985
Orafa Publishing Company, Inc.
1314 So. King Street, Suite 1064
Honolulu, Hawaii 96814
U.S.A.

© **1985 John & Bobbye McDermott**

Library of Congress Cataloging in Publication Data

John and Bobbye McDermott
Our Hawaii
Includes Index
1. Hawaii—Description and travel—1985-Travel Experience Books. II. Title
85-61324

ISBN: 0-912273-12-7

Typeset by Crossroads Press, Hawaii
Printed by Rose Printing Company, Florida

Previous books by John & Bobbye McDermott
  HOW TO GET LOST AND FOUND IN NEW ZEALAND
  HOW TO GET LOST AND FOUND IN FIJI
  HOW TO GET LOST AND FOUND IN TAHITI
  HOW TO GET LOST AND FOUND IN THE COOK ISLANDS
  HOW TO GET LOST AND FOUND IN AUSTRALIA
  HOW TO GET LOST AND FOUND IN CALIFORNIA
   AND OTHER LOVELY PLACES
  HOW TO GET LOST AND FOUND IN NEW JAPAN

COVER DESIGN BY JOHN WHYLAND

How to Get Lost and Found in
OUR HAWAII

By John & Bobbye McDermott

ORAFA Publishing Co., Inc.
Honolulu, Hawaii, U.S.A.

OUR HAWAII

"Solid advice and a good read," wrote the initial previewer of the *Our Hawaii* book. "Going through Hawaii, island by island, with the McDermotts is like going on a trip through the home country of a dear friend."

The McDermotts spare no feelings in guiding would-be travelers to Hawaii's best, away from the worst, what not to miss like Lappert's Hula Pie Ice Cream on Kauai, and what to avoid like luaus in general and street hustlers in particular.

Hawaii is composed of six principal islands and what the authors devote to each island is in ratio to what they feel each island has to offer the visitor.

Much space, for example, is devoted to the district of Waikiki in the city of Honolulu, because, as the McDermotts explain, it is the flagship of the Hawaii visitor industry and has more to offer than all of the other destination areas put together.

Favorite places to eat, places to stay, unique adventures and experiences are part of the potpourri on the menu the writers set before the reader.

One of the most delightful parts of *Our Hawaii* is the humorous, never-too-serious approach to the subject maintained by the authors. It *is* a good read.

Curled up before a Mainland fireplace or as a pocket reference while traveling in the Hawaiian islands, *Our Hawaii* will prove to be one of your most enjoyable companions.

LIST OF MAPS

The Islands of Hawaii   viii ix

Oahu   xviii

Molokai   67

Maui   77

Hawaii   114

Kauai   172

Waikiki Shopping   215

Honolulu Shopping   217

Maps by John Whyland

(Note: Excellent detailed maps of each island including specific strip maps for driving are available free of charge throughout Hawaii in give-away tourist publications and at rental car offices.

To Charles Tuckman,
legal counsel, literary critic
and frustrated editor, who made
so many good things happen in
our lives.

CONTENTS

PREFACE
Happiness Is Hawaii   xi

1. WAIKIKI
It's Still Wicky Wacky Woo   1
Where We Go To Eat   9
Action After Dark   17
The Missionaries   32
Day of Infamy   37
Tour To The East   41
The Little Circle Tour   48
The Circle Island Tour   53

2. MOLOKAI
People & Mules   65

3. MAUI
Two Islands   75
East Maui: Pretty Resorts, Bad Condos   86
Lahaina: Royalty & Whales   91
Everybody Loves Hana   101

4. THE BIG, BIG ISLAND
Hilo & Environs   115
Waterfalls and Volcanoes   126
Two Scenes: Refuge & Murder   133
Kailua-Kona   138
The Shoreline Trail   143
The Greening Of Kohala   154
Waimea: Horse Heaven   161
The Big Island Backwater   168

5. KAUAI
The Motion Picture Island   173
Plantation Life Of Yesterday   179
Tour To The West   182
Action At Poipu   192
Tour To Hanalei   198

6. THE LADY NAVIGATOR'S SHOPPING SECRETS   213

7. AROUND THE ISLANDS   250

Acknowledgments   254

Index   255

The Birth of Hawaii

The Hawaii archipelago started millions of years ago far to the northwest when a rupture in the Pacific plate allowed molten lava to spurt through weakened "hot spots" on the ocean floor, 15,000 feet down. The resultant volcanoes piled lava on top of lava until individual mountains were built high enough to break through the ocean's surface to become islands.

Kauai

The first principal island in this geological progression, coming from northwest to southeast in what is now the state of Hawaii, was Kauai. Lihue is its capital. Its mother volcano is Mt. Waialeale. Kauai's satellite sister is the small island of Niihau.

Oahu

The next island to surface was Oahu, 100 miles southeast of Kauai. Honolulu is today the capital of the county of Oahu and the state of Hawaii. The district of Waikiki on the south shore is the flagship of the visitor industry. The lava that created Oahu came from two mountain chains forming separate arms, the Waianae Range to the west and the Koolau Mountains to the east.

Maui

Twenty miles east by southeast of Oahu is a cluster of islands: Molokai, Lanai, and Maui, together comprising Maui County. The capital city of the county is Wailuku.

Maui once was two islands and you can see the division plainly today. In attitude, as well as in physical respects, it is still two islands. The mother volcano of West Maui was Puu Kukui, elevation 5,788 feet. The traditional capital of West Maui is Lahaina.

East Maui is home of mighty Haleakala, elevation 10,023 feet, the largest volcanic crater in the world. On the slopes of this awesome mountain are the Wailea/Kihei resort areas. On the east tip of the island is the quiet beauty of Hana.

Southeast of Maui is the uninhabited island of Kahoolawe.

Hawaii—The Big Island

Last among the developed islands— and youngest—is the Big Island of Hawaii where active volcanoes are still creating land. Five principal volcanoes have created twice as much land on the Big Island as there is on all of the other islands combined: Mauna Kea and Mauna Loa, both over 13,000 feet, Hualalai, Kohala and Kilauea. The capital of the island is Hilo, still an agrarian town. Across the island on the west side of Mauna Loa is Kona, and another world.

Twenty miles southeast of the Big Island, beneath the ocean, is another volcano, Loihi, meaning long, now measuring 13 miles long and 8 miles wide. It is estimated that as early as the year 2020, Loihi can stick its head above the surface of the Pacific—probably complete with condominiums and real estate offices.

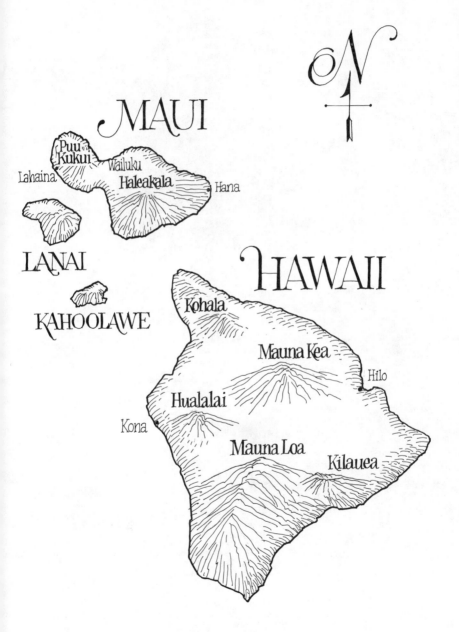

Preface

HAPPINESS IS HAWAII

Welcome to our town. Welcome to our state.

Hawaii and its six principal islands are kissed by many blessings. An ideal climate. An abundance of beaches and mountains. Plentiful water and rich land.

Best of all, its homogeneous people reflect the heavenly abundance. They smile. They are at ease. They are generous.

One of our greatest pleasures as Hawaii-based travel writers, frequently abroad, is to return to the warmth of our friends in Hawaii.

Now, after writing seven books about other countries in the Pacific, the Lady Navigator and I have come back to Diamond Head to write about home. We luxuriate at the opportunity.

We look forward to sharing our secrets. What we do in Hawaii. What our friends do. What we tell our visiting relatives and travel writing buddies to do.

In our other books we have been the outsiders going into a new country to explore, ask questions, seek out adventures.

But now we are the insiders with the insiders' knowledge. Our hope is to help the visitor find the ultimate pleasure of these magical islands through suggestions and tips and snippets of advice. Just as important, we would like to add to the visitor's understanding of the character of this most unusual potpourri of islands in the Pacific.

Millions of people have received their first impressions of Hawaii by reading Michener's *Hawaii,* a good book. Full of information and a fine feeling of the islands. But it must be remembered that *Hawaii* is fictionalized fact and is sometimes misleading in light of today's Hawaii.

If you want a more substantive background of the islands, get Gavin Daws' *Shoal of Time,* and/or Edward Joesting's *Hawaii, An Uncommon History.* Both are excellent reference books that you may find in your local library or, better still, buy copies to add as new treasures to your own library.

To save asking a million questions, buy *Ronck's Hawaiian*

Almanac, a pocket-sized handbook of useful statistics and solid, basic information.

My first encounter with Hawaii began in 1951, after spending two years in Paris and one year in Geneva.

My first job was with an advertising public relations agency in Honolulu which was involved in a fund-raising project for a local Japanese hospital. I spent much of my first month at Kuakini Hospital.

It was an eye-opening education. After the broad-beamed, hairy-legged, bath-on-Saturday maidens of Switzerland, the petite, delicate beauty of the sweet-scented Hawaiian-Japanese nurses almost put me into surgery with a chronic case of gaping mouth.

They brought in such strange things to eat for lunch. Rice rolled in brown seaweed (sushi). Delicious Chinese morsels wrapped in soft-white dough (dim sum). Raw fish to dip in soy sauce (sashimi). Bits of smoked pork (char su). Containers filled with noodles in a spicy fish broth (saimin). These and other items on the broad menu of Oriental foods found in Hawaii became another joy of residency.

Spurred by knuckle-headed ambition, I left this corner of paradise after a year and went to New York to pursue a writing career in the theater, for television ... dreams of fame, scads of money. I ended up in another advertising agency.

When the sleet was blowing at gale speed horizontally onto my dirty window overlooking scrungy Manhattan, my mind instantly shifted to the white sand beaches of Waikiki.

Even worse was summertime. The humidity and the heat rose from the black streets in nearly visible waves around the relentless clock. Waves. What I dreamed of were the frothy white-topped waves in incredible shades of blue to green as they curled toward shore in front of the Outrigger Canoe Club, and the cooling tradewinds that played pattycake with the overhead palm fronds.

It took a couple of years of the Big Apple to prove that the Little Pineapple had more to offer and I moved back to Hawaii, never to stray again.

I returned happily to my old company as copy chief and creative director, gradually taking on more responsibilities until one day I eventually became the manager and owner of the largest advertising agency in Hawaii. It wasn't the career of a playwright on

Broadway, but it wasn't bad.

But, after twenty years, it still wasn't enough and I left this cozy economic nest to pursue a career as a travel writer.

Meanwhile, the Lady Navigator, who had arrived from Texas on a vacation and never left, had created the largest public relations company in Hawaii. She took a leave of absence from her company and eventually sold it to follow me around the world becoming the editor, shopping authority and rewrite specialist on our series of seven *How to Get Lost and Found* travel experience books on Pacific destinations.

When we headed our own companies, we both had major travel accounts which gave us the opportunity to go everywhere in the islands, meet everybody and do everything, to watch and become part of the growth of the islands. For example, when I first came to Hawaii in 1951, there were 50,000 annual visitors. Now there are over five million. Quite a change.

The meteoric rise in tourism was matched by facilities and services.

Aloha Airlines, then one of my clients, was flying DC3s. A criterion of stewardess employment was the ability to play the ukulele and entertain the passengers. After all, the 214-mile flight to Hilo took the best part of two hours.

The airline graduated from DC3s to jet-prop Friendship Fokkers, then to BAC 111 jets and then to a fleet of Boeing 737s.

Sheraton, another client, took over the Royal Hawaiian and the Moana hotels from the Matson Navigation Company, and over the next two decades exploded as a major force in Hawaii and across the Pacific, opening new hotels everywhere.

I remember when Laurance Rockefeller opened the Mauna Kea Beach Hotel with a room rate for two, breakfast and dinner included, of $36 per day. And when the Sheraton Waikiki Hotel opened, the advertised rate was $18.

But that type of reminiscence will remind us of real estate we should have bought twenty years ago and we'll all break out into tears—again. (I sold a big old beachhouse in Kailua for $92,000 that recently re-sold for $1.5 million.)

Few visitor facilities were available on the Neighbor Islands. The Big Island had the Hilo Hotel and the old wooden Naniloa on the waterfront in Hilo, and the Kona Inn in Kona. Nothing existed on Maui except the Pioneer Inn at Lahaina. The favorite retreat among locals was the new Coco Palms on Kauai where the indefatigable and innovative Grace Buscher created instant Hawaiiana customs—among them the loin-clothed, torch-bearing beachboys running through the coconut grove at dusk, lighting kerosene tiki torches.

On Kauai I remember a taxi driver taking me to the airport and refusing any money. "Aloha," she said.

And a revered bank manager friend on Maui whose home was swept away by a tidal wave. For weeks thereafter whenever he went to his car there would be a shirt, clothes for the kids, fresh fruit, vegetables. "Aloha—we care," his friends were saying.

We recently came back from Kauai and the Lady Navigator, prepping for her chapter on shopping hints, saw a local lady with cartons of Kauai cookies she had read about but couldn't find. Soon she was in conversation with the lady, nibbling on a cookie, and the local lady was adamant that the Lady Navigator take a carton. "Aloha," she was saying.

Yes, my friend, the aloha spirit still lives in Hawaii. The spirit is one which expresses love. You say aloha when you greet a person and when you say goodbye. You express aloha when you give because you want to give.

The easiest way to find the aloha spirit in Hawaii is to have it yourself. If you smile, if you have a heart filled with love, you'll quickly find smiles and love in return.

You'll find the islands are one big love boat where you can have any kind of vacation you want.

There is sun to send you home with a tan. (But do be careful. Don't spoil your glorious holiday by trying too hard, too fast and getting, instead, an inglorious, painful sunburn.)

There is water to soothe your jangled nerves. To swim in, surf on, snorkel and scuba under. Water to fish in. Big fish. Small fish. To sail or cruise on. There is pure water to drink—so pure that it will almost make you give up the Mai Tais. Almost.

Sweet air to breathe and food and drink from every great world cuisine—plus local specialties you must try.

And there is romance. People fall in love with Hawaii ... and in Hawaii. It is where singles become pairs and pairs, newly acquainted and old acquaintances, become lovers.

Much of your good time in Hawaii will depend on you. Be

happy and Hawaii will meet you more than half way.

Our plan is to add to your happiness by not writing a guide book with endless lists of restaurants and hotels. We refer you to Bob Bone's *Maverick Guide of Hawaii* or Fisher's *Annotated Guide to Hawaii*.

But we will tell you about our favorite food haunts and places to stay, and take you along with us on recommendable adventure trips on every island.

We will introduce you to some of our favorite characters.

We'll tell you where to stop to photograph. *1P* is a place from which to take a picture that you will show to the family when you get back home. A *2P* stop could produce photos you'll want to show the camera club, and *3P* stops are don't-you-dare-miss-it viewpoints likely to yield pictures you'll enter into photo contests. Sometimes, in my enthusiasm, I have added 4P and 5P shots but they are impossible.

You should be aware of the highway markers—the red and yellow Hawaiian warrior posted by the Hawaii Visitors Bureau—pointing to reliable places of interest.

A word of confession. We thought that we knew every corner of Hawaii and had had every experience and knew everybody. Not so. Six months of new research uncovered delightful country we'd never seen, happy adventures that we had never experienced, and new friends who made the experiences even sweeter.

So this is our Hawaii. We want you to enjoy it as much as we do ... and, who knows, you, too, may never leave.

NEEDED WARNINGS
AND NEEDED WORDS

Prices destroy travel books before they are printed.

We checked all prices—and telephone numbers—before publication and they were valid at the time of printing in 1985. As a seasoned traveler, you know there will be changes.

Constant changes in the travel industry are one reason we always use a travel agent. Gertrude Berger, our beautifully efficient travel agent, has the latest airline prices and schedules—a monumental task—and can lock up hotel room reservations and car rentals in times of conventions and seasonally busy periods.

1. Use a travel agent when coming to Hawaii.

2. Learn a few Hawaiian words.

Our everyday conversations are sprinkled with Hawaiian words which are part of our vocabulary. The most common words pertain to direction, food and feelings.

Mauka (mau-kah) is towards the mountains.

Makai (mau-kye) is towards the sea. In Honolulu we have localisms for east and west.

Diamond Head is towards east, that is, in the direction of Diamond Head. (If we are beyond Diamond Head, we say *Koko Head.)*

Ewa is west. (Ewa, pronounced eh-va, is a plantation town in west Oahu.)

Pau (pow) means finished. A waitress will come to your table and ask, "All pau?"

Hana means work. Another expression you'll hear is *Pau Hana* A time to play, drink together.

Racially, a Caucasian is referred to as a *haole* (how-lee). A visitor or a newly arrived resident is called a *Mainland haole*. Chinese are *pakes* (Pah-kay). A Japanese is called a *Buddhahead* but not out loud, and only to his face if he is a very close friend. Then you say, "You dumb Buddhahead." And he replies, "You dumb haole."

Hapa means half. *Hapa-haole*, half white.

Heiau (hey-ee-ow) is a Hawaiian temple.

Huhu is angry. *Pilikia* (pee-lee-key-ah) means trouble. "She give me so much pilikia that I get all huhu."

Keiki (kay-kee) is a baby. *Kane* (con-ee) is a man. *Wahine* (vah-hee-knee) is a woman. Many public restrooms, especially in bars, are so marked.

Aloha means hello, goodbye, I love you. *Mahalo* says thank you.

Nui (new-ee) means big. *Manini* (mah-knee-knee) means little, as in cheap.

Puka (poo-ka) is hole and *pupu* is an hors d'oeuvre.

Ono is good. *Pilau* (pee-lao) is bad.

Shaka! means great. *Shaka brah* means, " Good going, brother!" which is said while rattling a raised clenched fist but with the little finger and thumb extended.

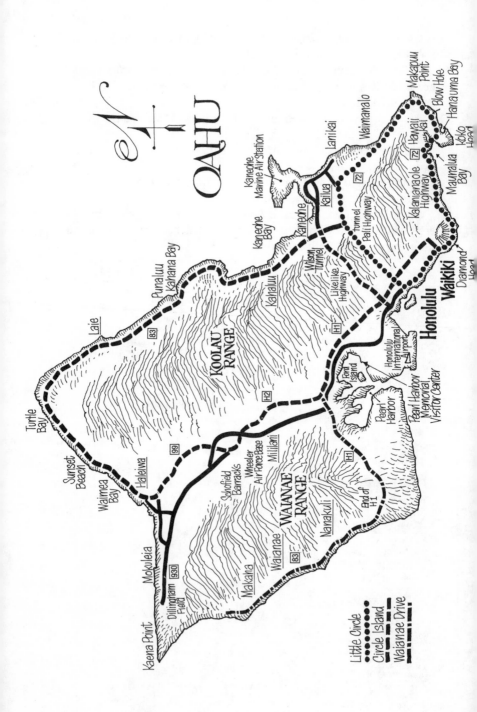

1. Waikiki—
It's Still Wicky Wacky Woo

Let me give you the inside skinny about Waikiki.

There is a local tendency to snub the state's biggest asset.

"I *never* go to Waikiki anymore."

The attitude rubs off on a number of return visitors.

"We skip Waikiki and go straight to the Neighbor Islands."

Balderdash.

Waikiki is where the action is. Where the best eating is with the most variety in cuisine and price. Where the best shopping is. Where the best dancing is. Where the most girl-meets-boy heat is.

And for accommodations there are 33,000 rooms. Penthouse or pad. Apartment or guesthouse. Name your mattress and your price.

Nothing on the Neighbor Islands comes remotely close to "the legendary Waikiki."

The choice is dependent on the objective of the visitor.

If the person lives a life of frantic, minute-by-minute, telephone-call-to-telephone-call, appointments back-to-back with conferences, emergency meetings, questions, deadlines ... sure. Go to a Neighbor Island, drop your socks, kick your shoes in the corner, fill a glass with ice, pour a beverage, and recover.

The Neighbor Islands offer perfect locations for the restorations of frazzled bodies and minds.

But for those who want to taste the best of the resort life where life and laughter come in large bunches, then you have to be in Waikiki.

Yes, of course, it has changed. Once upon a time, long ago, Waikiki *was* Hawaii—and that meant you stayed at the Matson's Royal Hawaiian Hotel or the Moana—and you had money. Matson ships and Matson hotels were designed for the well-to-do. Bring-your-own-limousine crowds.

Since that time the world has changed and travel now is a right-of-life for everyone. And everyone can afford to come to Waikiki.

Mind you, the Royal Hawaiian is still there in all of its pink glory and doing more business than it ever has in its half century. And practically next door the rebuilt Halekulani, an old-time favorite, is bringing in new and oldtimers for $145 a day for a garden view room and $250 a day for an ocean view room.

Waikiki still has a lot of snob appeal.

Best of all, it has action appeal for everybody.

The surf-and-sand action is here with surfboards, windsurfing, boogie boards, body surfing, snorkeling and scuba diving.

Don't like the ocean? Every hotel has at least one swimming pool. With a pool bar for those who want to get wet inside.

The zoo and the aquarium and tennis courts are in Waikiki's Kapiolani Park. A municipal golf course is just across the Ala Wai Canal.

Shopping is everywhere in Waikiki. The Ala Moana Center with 155 shops is a long stroll or a short bus ride away.

Culture? A bus or taxi from Waikiki will take you to the Honolulu Academy of Arts, to the Bishop Museum or to hear the Honolulu Symphony, a highly respected regional orchestra. Yes, there is even a short but established opera season.

A stream of stage shows flows through Honolulu. Concert artists, rock stars, ballet troupes, country-music greats— they all draw large local audiences in Hawaii's capital.

Waikiki has discos, ballroom dancing, comics, local and imported acts and a hundred bars.

Whatever your pleasure, you'll find it in Waikiki— including lots of people to talk to.

If you want to talk to someone for more information, the Hawaii Visitors Bureau maintains information booths at all airports, the Ala Moana Center, the Royal Hawaiian Shopping Center, and on the 8th floor of the Waikiki Business Plaza, across the street from the Royal Hawaiian.

Over the last decade Waikiki has had its share of bad publicity if only because its growth from a simple, social resort area with much glamour appeal to a major, highrise destination area has attracted "another Miami beach" type of feature stories.

True, it is not the calm, low-key, no-taller-than-a-palm-tree resort of yesterday and national media have delighted in cheap headlines dealing with "Problems in Paradise." There are street walkers. (At least they have been shunted from Kalakaua Avenue to Kuhio Avenue, one street over. That's some progress.) There are also sidewalk solicitors for boat rides, time-share condominiums and hokey luaus.

Street vendors are a nuisance and there is action in the courts to get them off the streets.

We tell our friends that the best way to get rid of them is to boycott whatever they are hustling. Like dinner cruises.

Visitors with money attract thieves everywhere in the world. Careless visitors attract even more thieves. I remember reading about an Australian lady who had her purse snatched and she was carrying $6,000 *in cash*. That's just dumb.

How serious is crime in Hawaii? Worried about our reputation, I went to talk to Major Allen L. Perry of the Crime Prevention Bureau where I learned that Honolulu, out of 18 cities of comparable size, is at the bottom of the list: 17th in burglaries, 18th in robberies.

"Tell the visitors just to use their heads. You'll be doing us a favor," he said.

You are advised not to lock your car, including the trunk—it is too easy to break in—and never leave valuables in the car.

Take precautions about locking your rooms. (There are now safes in most rooms which have dramatically reduced break-ins.)

Use your head. Don't walk on the beach at night. Don't get drunk and pick up a lady of the evening. Don't wear your wallet outside of your pants. That kind of thing. You are safer than you are at home.

Waikiki and How It Grew

If you look at a map of the district of Waikiki, you see that, in effect, it is a peninsula created by the Ala Wai Canal dredged in 1920 as a rainstorm run-off ditch which starts at the end of the Ala Wai Golf Course on its east boundary and empties into the ocean at the Ala Wai Yacht Harbor on the west. The coral from the canal was used to fill in the duck ponds which dotted this lowland.

The peninsula abuts Kapiolani Park in the foreground of Diamond Head which is where we live.

When Waikiki was the playground of royalty and estate holders, it was served by a mule-pulled streetcar from downtown Honolulu. Local sports came out to surf and paddle outrigger canoes.

By the time the streetcar line was electrified, the beach had acquired a few hotels and the Outrigger Canoe Club. Duke

Kahanamoku of the Olympics fame was part of the scenery.

Today, between the Ala Wai Yacht Harbor and Diamond Head, on any given day, there are 60,000 visitors, 16,000 residents and another 30,000 employees. There is a lot of body heat.

To sample the flavor of today's beach scene we moved the couple of blocks into Waikiki. Five days at the Sheraton Waikiki and then four days at the Ilikai, and a long weekend at the Hyatt Regency. Later we spent a glorious Saturday and Sunday at the Kahala Hilton which is still one of the outstanding architectural successes in Hawaii and a second home of celebrities.

The public world of Waikiki and Kahala is far apart from the private world of the Honolulu resident.

First of all, we found that we were living among 60,000 lily-white, sunburned but smiling visitors who were having one hell of a good time. Local people, when they are sneering at Waikiki, don't know that.

The happy action is everywhere.

Sheraton Waikiki, for example, is an 1,800-room hotel majoring in conventions, and it boils with activity. Naturally it has a hundred shops, two swimming pools, an ocean front dining room, a steak house, a Polynesian room and the Hanohano Room on the top floor where you can dine and dance in the evening, and on Sunday morning munch the most calorie-loaded, richest, biggest brunch you'll ever see in your life. If you can get in. We tried and couldn't. Loaded with local people and Japanese honeymooners. (I complained about not getting in to John Brogan, the unflappable money-motivated hotel manager, and he just smiled and smiled.)

All the hotels are brimming with the same sort of attractions. You can spend a snappy week's vacation and never leave the hotel.

But you are not going to do that.

You are going to by-pass the swimming pool and head for the beach. You should know that of all the people who come to Waikiki only ten percent of them will get into the ocean. Why? They have never been in the ocean. They don't trust the ocean. They are afraid of waves, sharks, wigglies and wet sand. Silly. Waikiki has a lovely ocean. The water is always in the 70's and is beautifully clear.

Here is the where you find the outdoor action. You can take a catamaran ride or learn to handle a surfboard. A long time pal of ours, Marge Stone, editor of the *Tourist News*, exhorts her readers to "rent a wave."

She privately admits that most visitors will not even attempt a surfboard but she makes a convincing case for every visitor—of any age—to take an outrigger canoe ride. Even the non-swimmer.

"Waikiki is the only place in Hawaii, or in America—and maybe the entire world—for this experience. It is a thrilling ride, surging toward shore down the face of a foaming wall of water, watching the swimmers and surfers scatter, yelling from sheer exuberance."

"To me, waves and surfboards and outrigger canoes are almost as symbolic of Waikiki as Diamond Head. How could you 'do' Hawaii without doing the ocean?"

If you like passive action, we recommend people watching. Some great bodies, handsome kids, funny bodies, unbelievable bathing suits. Guaranteed 2P shots for your camera. Maybe 3P. Greatest in the summer but great any time of year.

Impress your friends with a bit of local knowledge; know the different names for the different parts of Waikiki Beach and the different areas of surf offshore.

Starting at the tip of Diamond Head where the Outrigger Canoe Club is located on a very little beach, from east to west, the individual beaches are Sans Souci, Queen's Surf, Kuhio, Gray's Beach, DeRussy and Duke Kahanamoku.

The principal surfs have traditional names: King's, Queen's, Malihini, Main Break, Populars, Canoe.

Buildings along the way will include the old Natatorium, closed and condemned for many years but still standing . . . then the Waikiki Aquarium.

Next, as you walk down the beachfront is a public facility with modern changing rooms, toilets and showers.

To the left of the facility is a grassy area occupied by families on picnics. On the right will be boys who like to mingle with boys.

At one time a mansion owned by a food product heir stood here, a mansion used by Franklin D. Roosevelt when he came to Honolulu for a military conference during World War II. An elevator was installed for his use.

The city acquired the property, leased the mansion to a night-club owner and subsequently tore it down to erect the beach facility. Gossip said that the building was razed because the lessee refused to contribute to the mayor's campaign fund.

Next is the length of Queen's Surf where blacks and friends often congregate under the banyan tree and beat drums.

Kuhio Beach Park is the long, open beach, usually filled with bodies, that runs parallel to Kalakaua Avenue. Hotels are across the street. The concrete wharf separating the Queen's Beach from Kuhio Beach is a popular body surfing and boogie board surfing area. On the beachwalk is the trellised Kuhio Pavilion where oldtimers gather to play cards and checkers and chess.

Where Kuhio Beach ends, a seawall starts at the Sheraton Waikiki and extends to a spot of sand in front of the Halekulani, known as Gray's Beach. It is our favorite swimming spot in Waikiki because a fresh water spring prevents the growth of coral so there is a nice sandy channel to deep water, and it is cool and invigorating.

The beach in front of the Reef Hotel is a popular gathering place, possibly because the bar is so close at hand and its juxtaposition to Fort DeRussy where there is military parking. Sometimes ukulele music. Most often portable stereo radios from military who hope to find a friend among the feminine sun bathers.

The military beach, next door, at Fort DeRussy is man-made as is the Duke Kahanamoku Beach and lagoon in front of the Hilton Hawaiian Village. Both beaches tend to have sizable coral pebbles underfoot.

Just behind the Fort DeRussy beach is a former coastal gun emplacement, Battery Randolph, built between 1909 and 1911 on former duck marshes. The fortification was equipped with two 14-inch guns with a reach of 14 miles. Never fired in anger. When they were fired in peace, the buildings in downtown Honolulu shook, disturbing the merchants, so they were seldom fired at all. In 1946 the fort was dismantled but the concrete walls were too formidable to knock down. Thirty years later, still intact, the old fort was transformed into a U.S. Army Museum. It is still evolving but is a nostalgic remembrance museum for World War II veterans. A place to browse, recall old buddies, experiences, battles, real and imaginary.

The DeRussy Beach is separated from the Kahanamoku Beach by a pier to service the Hilton fleet of catamarans and other boats.

At one time the Kahanamoku area was occupied by the old Niumalu Hotel with grass shack cottages. The open backwater basin was filled with flotsam of milk cartons and bits of lumber, old coconuts and other debris washed in by the tides.

And then Henry J. Kaiser "retired" to Hawaii and the first toy he picked up was the ancient hotel and twenty acres of ground. In 1955, there was no beach. Only a seawall and a long pier from which guests dived into the ocean.

I came back from New York to work on the new Kaiser Hawaiian Village Hotel. What a man Henry J. was.

He had architects still drawing plans on the back of envelopes while concrete was already being poured. Building approvals and permits were months behind construction that was already in place.

Hotel wings rose, swimming pools proliferated like rain drops, restaurants sprang up, beaches were built, the lagoon created. A radio station and then a TV station were added.

Through all of the frantic madness moved Henry J. Kaiser, pasha-built, serene, smiling benignly, never ruffled.

People came and went through a revolving door of personnel changes.

Once, a large group of employees fired from his radio and TV stations held a Former Kaiser Men Cocktail Party next door at the Tahitian Lanai. Who showed up? Sure. Henry Kaiser. He told them they were all good people, picked up the bar bill and left to the sound of cheers.

And Waikiki and Hawaii were never the same again after Henry Kaiser arrived with his bulldozers.

Today the Hilton Hawaiian Village is a maze of towers containing 2,500 rooms and half a dozen restaurants. An interesting comparison to its next door neighbor, the Waikikian, an intimate, two-story conclave of timber buildings sharing the lagoon.

Sentinel at the western edge of Waikiki is the Ilikai, facing the yacht harbor.

Is Waikiki better than it used to be? It is better than the duck ponds and the mud flats and swamps it once was. Yes, much better.

In pre-Kaiser days the only places to stop off for food or liquid refreshment were the Tropics or Canlis or the Wagon Wheel. Linn's bathing suits were famous and matched aloha shirts and muumuus were considered quite smart at the Waikiki Liberty House.

When the old Moana cottages were demolished to make way for the new International Market Place, a night on the town was Don the Beachcomber's for rum punches and a Polynesian show with Marlene Sai singing the wedding song.

But, today, gad, Waikiki today.

Take the Royal Hawaiian Center fronting the Royal Hawaiian and the Sheraton Waikiki. In this one complex you find more food outlets and shops than used to exist in all of Waikiki in 1955.

We never had such a variety of international restaurants. For example, on the second floor there is Japanese cuisine at Suntory, Chinese at the Great Wok, and Mexican, all conveniently sited next to each other to make your decision easier.

On the first floor a Greek take-away, It's Greek to Me.

Fast-food operations and ice cream parlors abound.

The Lady Navigator is a chocolate ice cream freak, along with several other hundred million Americans. After munching cones throughout Waikiki she declared the North Shore Fudge (street level of the Moana Hotel) the winner but she wanted to substitute the cone from Copenhagen Cones (Royal Hawaiian Center). It was superior to all others, she proclaimed.

In the same search and destroy mission vein, I researched the mai tai but, frankly, I came away from several dozen searches woozy and disappointed.

Generally the Waikiki mai tais are too sweet and too weak.

I like a mai tai with *authority* and not a hint of cloyingness to it. Bartenders want to add orgeat syrup—yuk—and then a dash of whiskey sour mix—yuk—and float the dark rum on top.

For the sake of visitors' happiness, let me share with you my top secret Diamond-Head-Stand-Back-Don't-Let-the-Children-Get-Too-Close Mai Tai.

In a bucket-sized glass full of ice put an ounce and a half of light Bacardi rum, another ounce of Myers dark rum. (If it is a big bucket put two ounces of each.) Fill almost to the top with orange-passion fruit mixture. Processed locally and available at any grocery store. Add a small bit of pineapple juice. A fresh lime. A dollop—and this is most important—of orange curacao. Stir. Add a stick of fresh pineapple if you have it. Ambrosia. Try two for lunch and you'll never leave the islands.

Where We Go to Eat

The telephone rings at home. You answer.

It is a colleague of your once-removed cousin who lives in Omaha, Nebraska.

If you lived in St. Louis, the colleague of your once-removed cousin in Omaha, Nebraska would never, never think of calling you. But, for some reason, because you live in Hawaii, he calls you. He is full of enthusiasm.

He wants to give you warm greetings from your cousin from whom you haven't heard in ten years, and, he wants your advice.

"Where are we going to eat?"

It is the most common question asked by a tourist and we should deal with it immediately.

The standard response to the common question is another common question. "What do you like to eat?"

You know he is thinking: "We'd like to eat what you're eating at your house." He doesn't say it and you don't encourage him because that leads to refrigerator bankruptcy. You refer him to the telephone book and give him one or two of your favorites.

Look in the classified section of the telephone book and you'll find 17 pages of restaurant listings followed by another page and a half of restaurants categorized by nationalities: African, American (what's that?), Brazilian, Chinese, East Indian, French, German, Greek, Hawaiian, Indonesian, Italian, Japanese, Korean, Mexican, Filipino, Polynesian, Portuguese, Russian, Spanish, Thailand.

Eating in Waikiki and the surrounding areas—and drinking—can be anything your stomach can stand. You choose from about 250 eateries in Waikiki alone.

Here are a few of our traditional "let's go out tonight" haunts.

Starting at Diamond Head, we take overseas visitors to the Outrigger Canoe Club for lunch or moonlight dinners or brunch on Sunday. The drawback of the private club is that you have to have someone take you, or know someone who can get you a guest card.

Next door, however, facing the same beach is Michel's on the ground floor of the Colony Surf. Expensive for dinner. But the secret attraction is breakfast because Tom Selleck has his morning omelette at Michel's.

Farther down the beach, next to the old Natatorium, is the New Otani Hotel and the outdoor Hau Terrace. Many years ago, Robert Louis Stevenson came to sit under the old hau tree for inspiration. Today's inspiration, while having lunch, is girl watching. Popular with local people.

For dinner, we have never been disappointed at the Captain's Galley, on the beach in the Surfrider Hotel.

From the Surfrider to Fort DeRussy could be considered the middle of Waikiki and the greatest concentration of restaurants.

We found a new favorite the day we started our experimental Waikiki hotel experience. Sheridan Ing, a quietly brilliant millionaire of Chinese extraction with degrees from M.I.T. and Harvard, steered us to Tony Roma's. We have found that you can trust the Chinese about restaurants and the Irish about bars. Sherry said that Tony Roma's had the best babybacked spareribs in town. He was right. We headed for Tony Roma's our first night in Waikiki. The experience was excellent. The restaurant, for one, is frequented by air crews which tells you that the food is great and the prices reasonable. The waitress also confided that the visitors come between six and eight and the locals come after eight.

The babyback ribs were superb. As soon as I lose another ten pounds I'm going back.

Peter Ueberroth, the hero-leader of the Olympics, now the baseball commissioner, is one of the restaurant's owners, so you know it has to be a winner.

Two of the better eateries are Bagwells 2424 in the Hyatt Regency and the Third Floor in the Hawaiian Regent. Expensive. Of the two, I somehow prefer the Third Floor. Matter of taste. *Honolulu Magazine*, in a readership poll, gave first place to the Third Floor, also. Remarkable, it having been open twelve years. The Maile Room at the Kahala Hilton Hotel ranks in the same class.

Canlis, formerly *the* restaurant, has changed somewhat. The experienced mama-san, kimono-clad corps of waitresses is gone. I ordered a vodka martini from a sweet young boy waiter and it came back gin. The waiter wanted me to test the wine while I was sipping the martini. No. No. No. Warren Stone, a local publisher who speaks with a forked tongue on the golf course, recommended the shrimp salad for lunch, lunch being a new effort by Canlis. Still a favorite with some of a loyal social crowd.

At Kuhio and Seaside you'll find the Waikiki Trade Center. On the second floor is Shelby's, an imaginative, reasonably priced place for dinner (lounge entertainment in the back) and the Grape Escape for lunch on the ground floor, both good spots for the fun and young. In the same building is RoxSan's Cabaret which is on the Lady Navigator's stop-by list.

Two restaurants within hotels not to be ignored are Nick's Fishmarket in the Gateway Hotel and La Mer in the new Halekulani.

At the west end of Waikiki concentrated around the Ilikai Hotel is an excellent group of eating establishments, beginning with the hotel's own prestigious Champeaux's, known for imaginative dishes and fantastic harbor and city views from its perch atop the hotel.

Incidentally, a room in the Ilikai facing the yacht harbor is a joy at sunset. You can sit on the lanai and toast the sun going down behind Barber's Point. Below you are the toys of boys, little white-hulled bobbles, their masts and sails protected by blue canvas covers, tied up at slipside. The air holds a golden softness.

Also take time some morning at dawn and walk the piers of the yacht harbor. Sleek, expensive, gorgeous boats. Beaten-up, scabrous, broken scows. All side by side.

Every tenth boat is for sale.

Look at the pierside bulletin boards and create your own short story. Sails, motors, bikes for sale. Crews wanted.

"Sailing for West Coast mid-May. Need two crew members. Experience not necessary." They'll be old hands when they get there.

"Two hard New Zealanders. Christian. Fit. Good deckhands. Will work hard for passage to West Coast."

"For sail (sic): two one-way air tickets to Denver. Call Carol."

In the early morning you can see live-aboard types departing for work, neatly dressed for a day at a desk or department store counter, leaving behind the shorts-and-barefoot environment. Not bad, contrasting working and leisure lifestyles.

The yacht club on the Ilikai side of the harbor is the Hawaii Yacht club whose members consist largely of those yachties in public slips. The club does not give credit at the bar and bartenders are off-duty service men. Well!

Across the channel is the Waikiki Yacht Club whose members lease the club's private slips, have charge privileges, and whose bartenders are well-known and firmly entrenched. You can appreciate the difference immediately, of course. (These important differences were severely shaken recently when a disgruntled member returned to the club and shot up the premises including a sailing foe who was left punctured but still breathing. The club name was quickly expanded to the Waikiki Yacht and Gun Club, particularly by colleagues across the channel.)

Back to food.

Across from the Ilikai is the Bon Appetit in Discovery Bay, an excellent French dinner establishment, owned and operated by Guy Banal who does all the buying and preparation. Intimate interior but facing the bustle of Ala Moana Boulevard. Sensitively created dishes.

A block inland at Eaton Square are a number of good restaurants. Our favorite is Chez Michel. Michel Martin, the owner, created Michel's in the country where he grew his own vegetables and herbs, then moved to the Colony Surf for several years (the name "Michel's" still exists there) but Mike moved to Eaton Square and his fans followed. Chez Michel's has a nice French ambiance made up of wicker and greenery. It is a romantic place to take pretty ladies to lunch.

The last time I was there for dinner with the Lady Navigator, a very pretty lady, I backed my chair into the ice bucket, blew a bottle of Napa Valley chardonnay over the floor and it was all replaced in a flash with the maitre d's comment that it was a stupid place to put an ice bucket. I love the place.

Also in Eaton Square is an elegant Chinese restaurant, House of Hunan, and a Spanish restaurant, Casa Madrid. Downstairs in a semi-basement is King's Bakery, a branch of the famous bakery on King Street. Locals buy goodies here to take to relatives when visiting the Neighbor Islands. King's Bakery also makes the grandest eclairs in Hawaii.

Around the corner and across the street from the Ilikai is a marvelous Chinese restaurant, the Dynasty Restaurant. Reasonable prices. Get a variety a dishes and enough to take some leftovers back to your hotel refrigerator. The waiters in Hawaii's Chinese restaurants are accustomed to the custom. Nothing tastes better for lunch than cold Chinese food. This Dynasty restaurant is very popular. No reservations. Another operation by the same owners is Dynasty II in Ward Center, but the prices are steeper.

On the waterfront side of the Ilikai Manor, on two levels, is a popular steak and chop house, the Chart House. Nice setting. Reservations make getting in easier.

Where Do We Send Our Cousin's Friend Outside of Waikiki?

"Do you have a car?" we ask the friend of our cousin.

Honolulu's eating experience is greatly expanded with the ability to move outside of Waikiki, particularly for local ethnic favorites.

An excellent example is Kapahulu Avenue, the street that serves as the eastern boundary line for Waikiki. Kapahulu has become, in the last five years, an international bazaar of restaurants.

The first restaurant you come to in a new building is Hee Hing, a standard Cantonese restaurant.

The star of this restaurant row is Keo's, a hot-on-hot Thai restaurant where the hot-on-hot Hollywood celebrities hang out. The food is spicy—like in burning—and is very popular.

Farther along the street, on the left hand side and around the corner (hard to find) is an excellent Filipino restaurant; 1521 is its name and the street number. Highly decorated with mother-of-pearl and ba mboo. Unusual and delectable dishes. *Picadillo*, ginger flavored soup with chopped beef and potatoes. *Chicken in Coco*, chicken cooked in coconut milk and yellow ginger. *Fried Lumia Togue*, fried eggroll of sauted bean sprouts. Garlic fried rice.

Look on the same side of the street for Hawaii Ono. (Ono means good in Hawaiian). Ono Hawaiian food, excellent, cheap. You may have to queue on the sidewalk and wait for a seat, both because it is small and well patronized by the locals.

Continuing up Kapahulu to Winam Street you'll find an Italian spaghetti restaurant, The Stuffed Pepper, and across the street is a Korean restaurant called Barbecue Corner.

The street is filled with fast-food places and ice cream parlors, including White Mountain Ice Cream, one of the new wave places that offers assorted chopped chocolate add-on options. Popular with at least one member of our family.

Nearly at the end of Kapahulu but before the overpass, tucked into a corner of Kilohana Square and worth finding, is JR's Upstairs. There is nothing devious or sinister about this non-Dallas JR who prepares elegant dishes but serves no wine. You may bring your own, however. (Dinner only).

At the end of Kapahulu Avenue turn right to Waialae Avenue to another string of good family eating spots, including two of our reliables for Chinese food and a rare little restaurant you'd never find in a tourist guidebook.

To find our secret restaurant turn left at the McDonald's drive-in, towards the mountains, on Palolo Avenue. Continue until you reach 1827 Palolo, next to a small mom'n'pop market. There is Serendipity Restaurant. A hidden jewel. Take a party of six after reserving the table in the middle. Most of our party had rack of lamb—they said it was delicious—and the others had fish baked in paper— also delicious. Take your own wine. You'll be the only visitor to Hawaii to have found Serendipity. Call first: 735-1543.

Now, down to the business of eating along Waialae Avenue.

At 9th and Waialae is a very small, inexpensive, bring-your-own-wine (beer is better with Chinese food) place called the Hong Kong Menu. Janice, the owner, and her cousin, the chef, are from Hong Kong. Ask for the specialties; some are spicy hot.

King's Garden is in the neighborhood shopping district of Kaimuki. If the proprietor, Wah Duck Young, is working the room, we ask him to order for us, with one exception. We must have our order of sam see cake-fried noodles, a sophisticated chow mein with seven kinds of thinly sliced meats and mixed vegetables.

A tip from my Chinese friends: don't go to Chinese restaurants on Mondays because, traditionally, that is the head chef's day off.

Nearer the center of Kaimuki town, try The Pottery for fresh fish or European dishes. Wolfgang Meyer, proprietor and a sometime tennis partner, enjoys an excellent local trade. A specialty is a cornish game hen stuffed with wild rice and grapes, cooked in a clay pot. You keep the pot! Arnold Palmer always stops in on his frequent forays through Honolulu.

Waialae Avenue becomes Kalanianaole Highway beyond the double decked by-pass alongside Kahala Mall Shopping Center. Pass by the next shopping center, Aina Haina, also. About a mile farther, turn into Niu Valley Center to the Swiss Inn, a very popular owner-chef establishment. Martin Wyss, a former chef at the posh Kahala Hilton Hotel, sets a first class table. Everything is good, but if you lucked into an *osso bucco*, you'd never forget it. The only worthwhile osso bucco in Honolulu. Call first.

Of course there is the Maile Room at the Kahala Hilton, expensive, quietly elegant with elegant dishes. The last time we had dinner there was with Julie Zirbel, the public relations lady, who is also quite a dish.

There are so many good places to eat in Honolulu.

Among your options west of Waikiki is one of our dentist's favorites, the top floor of the Ala Moana Americana Hotel, where Dr. Asahina's investment group dines, having pre-ordered dinner. The floor is now called Nicholas Nickolas' "The Restaurant." A foot bridge links the hotel to Ala Moana Center from the second floor parking deck, a convenience if you are driving.

Locals as well as tourists favor the Chinese food at Patti's Noodle Kitchen in Ala Moana and at the China House Restaurant, built on the off-ramp that connects Ala Moana Center to Kapiolani Blvd. near the Sears corner. Both places are known for their *dim sum*, little Chinese pastry-wrapped yummy morsels. The waitress will recommend what to have. Good take-away place too.

Continuing towards town, just before Kapiolani ends and next to the News Building where the morning *Honolulu Advertiser* and the evening *Star-Bulletin* are edited and printed, is the Columbia Inn, a popular hang-out of hung-over media types and other sporting characters. Reasonable food and boisterous bar.

Jumping over to the waterfront, at Ala Moana and Ward Avenue, stop at Kewalo Basin where fleets of boats stand ready to take you deep-sea fishing or cruising to Pearl Harbor, sailing at sunset, or on charters of your choice.

Adjacent to the take-off piers you'll find Fisherman's Wharf, a long-time favorite. John Dominis, a very classy, very expensive restaurant boasting "a total seafood experience" occupies a portion of the same spit of land but it is reached by an obscure road off Ala Moana a block closer to downtown. (John Dominis was the husband of the last queen of Hawaii, Queen Liliuokalani.)

Ward Warehouse and its companion development, Ward Centre, are directly across the street from Kewalo Basin, each complex confronting you with its multiple and difficult choice of restaurants.

The second floor of Ward Centre is devoted exclusively to a cluster of restaurants to fit any meal mood you have. There's Compadres: Mexican, roomy, no reservations, well done and instantly popular. Developed by the founders of Victoria Station who sold that chain at its peak. You'll like Compadres.

There's a seafood house and the previously mentioned Dynasty II. Andrew's, an Italian restaurant where the pasta is made daily, is next door to Ryan's Parkplace Bar & Grill, a local hang-out for singles and would-be singles. (Another meat market is TGI Friday's, at the corner of Ward and King, opposite the Neal Blaisdell Center, the city auditorium and theater. A health club for local jocks is upstairs.)

I never eat downtown anymore but one of my favorites used to be M's Garden Buffet in the YWCA. It still retains the whiff of old-time Hawaii. You can eat in the courtyard or the high-ceilinged cafeteria. The food is decent and reasonably priced.

A block over on Alakea Street, which borders the West end of the capitol complex, is Yong Sing, excellent for dim sum at lunch.

Another local favorite for lunch is the courtyard of the Honolulu Academy of Arts, opposite Thomas Square. Light luncheons prepared and served by the ladies of the museum in most pleasant surroundings. Reservations in the morning only: call 531-8865. Then look through our local art museum, which is quite good.

Incidentally, Thomas Square is named after Admiral Richard Thomas of the British Navy who "freed" the Hawaiian Islands from the over zealous action of an ambitious British commander. From February to July 1843 the British flag, without the permission of London, flew over the Hawaiian Islands and was not hauled down until Admiral Thomas arrived to straighten out the misunderstanding.

One experience which you mustn't miss, and we deliberately

saved this as a piece de resistance, is a Hawaii "poi lunch" at the Willows on any Thursday.

Irmgard Farden Aluli, a veteran entertainer in her seventies, hosts an informal Hawaiian musical hoe-down so reminiscent of parties of a slower paced era that the locals fill the thatched roof pavilion to entertain and be entertained. You must have reservations.

Irmgard and her family group, Puamana, sing well-known songs they have composed. (Farden is a name with a long musical heritage in Hawaii.) Old-time performers come on stage and entertain spontaneously. So much talent and so many laughs. The eyes come alive, the faces beam and the hips flow. Just like yesterday. Visitors and kamaainas alike get so emotionally charged up that the place is filled to overflowing with happy tears.

For luncheons or dinners, The Willows is popular with local people, particularly for its curried dishes and "mile high" lemon pie. The setting among meandering ponds filled with golden fish, a sunny courtyard filtered by palm fronds, and intimate dining pavilions is very laid back, very Hawaiian.

The old-time Chinese restaurant in the middle of Chinatown is Wo Fat's. My Chinese friends tell me that the food is still excellent but I've only found it excellent when I am with Chinese friends. You need help in ordering and the waiters are not particularly chummy.

Other bistros downtown are Matteo's, Jameson's, and the Croissanterie, all on Merchant Street, and Arthur's on Bishop Street. At noon the area abounds with bean-sprouts-and-avocado sandwich shops.

Downtown, you have to go before 11:30 or after 1:30 to avoid the noontime crowds.

Friday nights, after work, the bars and boites of Merchant Street are favorite watering holes for singles and hopefuls. Once a month the street is cordoned off for a street dance.

Which Brings Us to Action After Dark

Merchant Street is for the young and roving.

The tea dance at the Royal Hawaiian on Mondays at sunset is for the mature and non-roving. Del Courtney's 14-piece orchestra plays the big band tunes of post-war years. If you haven't jitterbugged in twenty years, here is your chance, along with some cheek-by-cheek oldies. Fun. Small cover charge.

For the best information of what is going on in town after dark, consult the entertainment section of the newspapers, read Wayne Harada in the *Honolulu Advertiser*, and scan the calendar of events in *Honolulu Magazine* The give-away publications contain praise for their advertisers only. Thus, you might miss knowing that Jimmy Borges at Trappers in the Hyatt Regency is one of the most popular entertainers in town.

Waikiki features several showrooms. The Monarch Room at the Royal, the Queen Dowager of Waikiki showrooms, still mounts solid dinner shows. You can also go after dinner for a small cover. Through 1986, the Brothers Cazimero are featured. Very popular locally.

The big tourist attractions are Don Ho in the Hilton Hawaiian Village Dome and Al Harrington, a Samoan-born Stanford-graduate, at the Polynesian Palace on Lewers Street.

Danny Kaleikini at the Kahala Hilton Hotel has been presenting excellent Polynesian-Hawaiian shows forever. The reason he goes on forever is that he is a gracious, warm guy whose personality is reflected in everything he does. The fact that the Kahala Hilton named their entrance square after Danny speaks for his enduring and endearing talent.

The big-name shows with dinner are expensive.

Other Polynesian shows are at the Moana Banyan Court, the Bora Bora Showroom in the Waikiki Beachcomber, the Hawaiian Hut in the Ala Moana Americana Hotel, and the Long House at the Hilton Hawaiian Village.

Also at the Village is a Sunday afternoon New Orleans jazz session from 2 to 6 at the Garden Bar. Beery and honky.

Lounge show talent moves around. Locally admired musical groups include the Aliis, the Krush, and the hottest duo, the Cazimero Brothers. Comic Frank de Lima serves up hilarious ethnic humor. Talented female vocalists come in droves. Marlene Sai, Melveen Leed, and Karen Keawehawaii to name but a few. Think Karen's name is difficult? Try Nina Kealiiwahamana. Sweet, sweet voice.

Live dance music is available in the Garden Village bar at the Hilton Hawaiian Village in the evenings.

Popular discos include Annabelle's on top of the Ilikai, the

Fourth Floor in the Hawaiian Regent, Rumours at the Ala Moana Americana, Spats at the Hyatt Regency.

Our daughters, home for Christmas, tested the local disco scene and voted for Spats and against the Fourth Floor. Sophistication won out.

Your best guide to current cultural and entertainment attractions is *Honolulu Magazine's* calendar of events.

On a clear night, when there is a musical attraction at the Waikiki Shell in Kapiolani Park—when the visual is not a primary requirement—it is rare fun to take a blanket or beach mat and a picnic dinner, buy tickets for the grassy section in back and eat and drink, lie back and look at the stars and the palm trees, and listen to the music.

Romping Around the Parks

Waikiki is bracketed by two fine parks.

Flanking the east side of Waikiki's high rise hotels and apartments is a 100-acre expanse of green named Kapiolani Park which was created in 1877 from crown lands by Hawaii's last king, David Kalakaua, in honor of his queen, Kapiolani, who later became the monarch of Hawaii.

It was a futuristic gift to the people.

The park is the scene of a hundred joyful activities.

Starting at dawn the park swings into action. Joggers in large numbers circle the park with the first light. (I wished they smiled more.) They circle Diamond Head in a favorite ten-kilometer run. Around the perimeter of the park are physical exercise stations with equipment and instructions.

A large part of Honolulu's infatuation with jogging rests at the feet of Dr. Jack Scaff, a local heart specialist who has spoken the gospel of running for health. "Black Jack," as he is known, also conducts clinics at 7:30 Sunday mornings at the Kapiolani Park bandstand, and if you listen to this strongly built, black-moustached believer, you too become a believer.

"Go an hour three times a week at whatever pace is comfortable for you. Walk, jog, run. But do it three times a week. Things smell better. Food tastes better. Your sexual life is better."

Oh, he gets to you.

Black Jack helped initiate the Honolulu Marathon which takes place early in December. Almost ten thousand runners gather at Aloha Tower downtown, a dynamic, emotional scene where this mass of laughing, energetic, nervous humanity waits for the cannon to go off and then—*boom*—they are away and two minutes later the place is entirely empty. Go if you get a chance. The runners are routed along Paki Avenue, on the mountain side of Kapiolani Park, on their way out to Hawaii Kai, then finish near the bandstand on the opposite side. I never miss it.

If you are a good photographer, you can get a 3P shot.

The calendar of running events in Honolulu annually numbers about 100. The names and addresses of sponsoring organizations to whom all inquiries and requests for entry forms should be directed are included in the calendar published by the Advisory Board for Jogging and Long Distance Running, Department of Parks and Recreation, City and County of Honolulu, 650 S. King Street, Honolulu, Hawaii 96813.

Kapiolani Park is a great place for flying kites. You left your kite at home? Go across the street to the New Otani Hotel and find Kite Fantasy. Go buy and fly a kite.

You might say that Kapiolani has a history of flying kites because the first airplane in Hawaii, a biplane Jenny from World War I, took off from the park, piloted by Charlie Fern, who later became editor of the Kauai News.

You want to play tennis? Two complexes of courts are available, free of charge. The set nearest the ocean with four courts and night lighting tends to be monopolized by an older crusty crowd by day, but you can muscle in. The better courts, a total of nine, are across Paki Avenue at the far end of the park where you sign on for an hour of court time for doubles or 45 minutes for singles. You are more assured of a game if you bring your own partner or foursome, but you can pick up a match.

Next to these tennis courts is an archery range and, farther along, just before the streets merge into Diamond Head Road, on Sunday mornings about nine o'clock you can see Japanese archers in full samurai regalia at practice with their oversized bows. It is quite a sight.

Along Paki, about mid-park, is a golf driving range, very popular, with a snack bar where you can meet some of the local golfers ... maybe even pick up a game.

The park, always popular, hosts an exceptional amount of action on weekends. There are family picnics and organized group picnics whose banners "home in" guests to the right location. Laughter of children at play and good smells from charcoal-fired hibachis fill the air.

The games field will have a varied menu to offer: softball game, soccer or rugby. No bleachers of course. All open field. Stroll from one to another.

The grassy area next to the Diamond Head tennis courts and archery range is a favorite location for Japanese film companies shooting commercials.

The most popular Kapiolani Park activity is the zoo which attracts over a million visitors annually. It started in 1913 with a few animals staked out in the park gardens. No boundaries. No pens. Very informal. Later it became the Kapiolani Bird Park offering rare tropical birds on display.

Today it is an advanced-design zoo, modest in size but fun for the family.

We like to go in the early hours of the morning—the zoo opens at 8:30 and closes at 4:30—because zoos in the semi-tropics tend to exude rich aromas in the afternoons. The charge is a modest dollar. Kapiolani Zoo is what you might call a nice zoo. It has the usual monkeys and giraffes and tigers and elephants but the main attraction of the zoo is still the tropical bird collection. You'll see the Hawaiian Stilt, Gallinule, and the Nene, Hawaii's state bird.

The baby elephant in the zoo, Mari, is famous because it was a gift to the zoo and presented personally by Indira Ghandi two years before her assassination.

On weekends, alongside the zoo fence on the Diamond Head side, a group of local artists gather to show their work. Visitors may find the perfect souvenir to take home from the Waikiki vacation. The work varies from garish/ghastly to acceptable, but occasionally you'll find a little masterpiece and the price will be right. Worth a peek.

Also note on the north side of the zoo, the little garden plots of vegetables and flowers kept by apartment dwellers who are given a chance to get their hands in the soil under a city program.

Waikiki Aquarium gives you an idea of what is going on in the ocean around you, beneath that calm surface. I particularly like the tanks with the multi-colored reef fish, and the chambered nautilus has to be one of nature's most distinguished pieces of art-and-architecture. A "suggested contribution" is $1.50. Rent one of the headsets which relates what is to be seen in each tank enclosure. The aquarium is located on the ocean side of the park on Kalakaua Avenue.

Also high on most first-time visitors' list of free things to do is the oldest running show in Hawaii, the Kodak Hula Show at the Waikiki Shell. It happens Tuesday, Wednesday and Thursday mornings year round, plus Fridays in summers. The hour show originated in 1939, in pre-flash camera days, under the palm trees near the Natatorium for the benefit of Matson cruise and hotel visitors, so they could take pictures in the sunlight.

Also a venue for free entertainment is the bandstand, where "Black Jack" gives his Sunday go-go pep talk. A scene of frequent concerts on weekend afternoons.

On the west side of Waikiki and across the Yacht Harbor bridge is another long stretch of green grass, ponds, a dozen tennis courts and a mile of nice beach.

Ala Moana Park. Very low-key. Very local. If you want to run away from your husband or wife and rendezvous on the beach, come to Ala Moana because no one you know will see you there.

At the Waikiki end of the park is a peninsula of land called Magic Island, a brain-child of Henry Kaiser who envisioned filling it with hotels and other attractions.

Kaiser was successful in getting the peninsula built but the city fathers snatched it away from him before he could pour any concrete foundations. A rare defeat.

Walter Dillingham fared better.

His Hawaiian Dredging Company created the channel fronting Ala Moana Park, dredging out coral which was then piped to swamp lands which Dillingham owned. He charged the city for storing the coral on his land and then later used the material for fill which became headquarters for the highly successful Ala Moana Center.

One thing you must do in Ala Moana Park is lunch on a 'plate lunch' at one of the two road stands across from the beach. If it is tripe and rice, get a hamburger.

Where We Send People Beyond Waikiki

First you walk to the top of Diamond Head.

The entrance to the crater is from the backside of the crater facing Fort Ruger. If you don't have a car, you take the #8 bus and ask the driver to let you off at the entrance. It is a half-mile walk to the inside of the crater and to the parking area where the trail begins.

We made a party out of it and rendezvoused with a few friends, assembling in the parking lot at the bottom of the trail at 7:30 AM, and then took off on the .7-mile dirt path to the top.

The misnaming of Diamond Head came from British sailors who thought they had found a cache of diamonds at the foot of the extinct volcano, only to find their riches were worthless calcite crystals.

Prior to the British and their erroneous conclusions, the Hawaiians called the volcano Leahi, a place of fire. They believed Pele, the fire goddess, lived there until she moved to the big island. An important heiau was built at the site and prisoners of war were sacrificially thrown into the crater.

The first part of the hike goes along a path through dry scrub and then the ascent starts, not difficult, up the west wall of the crater. Iron guardrails protect you from slipping over the side should you mis-step.

As you approach the rim, concrete fortifications are visible. They date back to wartime when the rugged mountain was turned into a small Gibraltar with gun emplacements and ammunition dumps and miles of tunnels.

Even from the lower level observation and gunnery posts you begin to get sweeping views of the Pacific. Nearer the top you reach a concrete staircase with 99 steps. That's the worst of the climb, although there are a couple of sections of dark tunnel where you are more comfortable with a flashlight.

Finally, a spiral staircase leads to the topmost platform and yields a 360-degree view of the city, ocean and mountains. Spectacular.

On the top we met a 60-year-old hiker who has done the Diamond Head walk almost every day for the past three years.

"Walking under doctor's orders," he said.

"It's better than running around Kapiolani. Here everybody

says hello. In Waikiki, you'd get hit on the head if you tried to start a conversation." (Not true, but it is true that everybody on the narrow path says hello to one another.)

Going down I met a lady going up in a red dress and high heel slippers. "Where are you from?" I asked. "Tahiti," she said. That morning we met Germans, Australians, Kiwis, kids, grandmothers. It is a something-for-everybody hike.

As a reward for our fellow hikers we gathered in the little park at the foot of Diamond Head where we had two chefs and a waitress to serve a barbecued breakfast on red-checkered tablecloths. Delicious end to a fine morning.

(Note: the fortified tomato juice was for health reasons only.—It is illegal to have beer or wine or spirits in a public park or beach which is the reason you will see a lot of people drinking, and pouring, out of brown paper sacks.)

Other Lookouts

The Tantalus/Round Top drive is one we like to do with first-time visitors, which, along with the hike to Diamond Head, is a fine orientation tour with different views of the city and the island from different locations along the route.

Start from Keeaumoku Street, located about mid-section of Ala Moana Center off Kapiolani Blvd., drive towards the mountains, turn right on Nehoa Street and left on Makiki Drive.

You'll wind your way uphill until you are overlooking the campus of the University of Hawaii and the East-West Center. Farther on, the trees now are tall and green, you'll see an HVB marker to the left leading to Puu Ualakaa Park. Marvelous place for a picnic at the point overlooking the entire city, with vistas from Koko Head in the east to Barber's Point in the west.

The Round Top drive crests at the ridgeline of Mt. Tantalus and you can stop your car, walk back to a point where you can look at 3P scenes on each side.

The drive then winds downhill through the expensive homes of Makiki, through the inexpensive homestead houses of Papakolea, and with the help of a few signposts, to Punchbowl, site of the

National Memorial Cemetery of the Pacific where 28,000 deceased members of the military have their final parade-rest.

Punchbowl, another ancient volcanic crater, is beautiful and peaceful and sad.

A lookout at the south side has closer views of the city and is crammed with tour buses.

If you wanted to make a serious visit to Punchbowl, go at 8AM when the cemetery first opens or at dusk when all of the crowds are gone.

Fittingly, the Hawaiian name for the crater is Puowaina, Hill of Sacrifice.

Our next stop is the Bishop Museum.

I am a firm believer in getting to know the territory. If you simply are a hedonistic vacationer, seeking the simple pleasures like getting a deep tan and a meeting a new love of your life, you still will enjoy yourself more if you know about the place where you are playing.

The Bishop Museum is your classroom.

Transportation is easy. It comes with your admission ticket. Bus pickups are made four times a day at the Tapa Tower of the Hawaiian Village, the Sheraton Waikiki and King's Village across from the Princess Kaiulani. For current ticket information and bus times, call 922-1770.

The standard admission is $4.75, the guided tour ticket costs $10. Take the tour.

Much progress has been made in the last few years at the Bishop Museum thanks to a dedicated, underpaid staff, and a group of equally dedicated, unselfish community leaders, exemplified by the new Jabulka Pavilion, a public entrance building containing free exhibits, a gift shop, a cafe and the ticket office. The Pavilion is linked to the planetarium, where two different shows are projected daily, and to the Hall of Discovery, a hands-on exhibit of the wonders of nature and Hawaii.

The planetarium is lesson number one in understanding Hawaii because the stars were the road signs leading to and from islands thousands of miles away.

If we accept that the first migration of Polynesians came from the Marquesas around 500 A.D. and the second wave from the Society Islands arrived around 400 years later and proceeded to explore the Hawaiian archipelago, we have to remember that they had no charts, no formal navigation equipment, not even a written language. Their knowledge was passed on orally, often in the form of ritualistic chants.

One of the most significant areas of knowledge by the sophisticated Polynesians was the understanding of heavenly signposts that led to their successful exploration of the Pacific: the familiarity with stars.

You learn about "Polynesian Skies" at the Bishop Museum at the planetarium.

The principal exhibit halls were built in the 19th century when the Bishop Museum was founded by a successful Honolulu businessman, Charles Reed Bishop, as a memorial to his wife, Princess Bernice Pauahi Bishop who was the last surviving family member of Kamehameha the Great.

Bishop intended that his museum "rank with the museums of the world."

The original black stone building is the entrance to the main museum. Note the handsome koa wood staircase.

To the left of the vestibule is the Kahili Room where a slide show focuses on Hawaii traditions, augmented by an exhibit "Hawaii, the Royal Isles." This exhibit toured seven major United States museums, with the assistance of the National Endowment for the Humanities,

To the right of the vestibule is the entry room to the Hawaiian Hall. Here you'll find a unique display of the various Hawaiian gods carved in wood.

The one little stick god you see was bought at auction in England and brought home to Hawaii at a cost of almost $250,000. The larger fierce looking figure is Kukailimoku, the war god. He rode with the kings into war; he was given to Kamehameha to guard as a sign of Kamehameha's authority; he played a major role in Kamehameha's successful battle for supremacy. (This and much more you will learn about on the Guided Tour.)

The Hawaii Hall rises three floors to a ceiling dominated by a suspended life-sized humpback whale such as you might see at Lahaina during the winter migration period.

The surrounding three stories contain exhibit cases devoted to the history and development of the islands.

On the ground floor are two special exhibits. Take an extra

minute and study the model of the open-air religious structure called a heiau (hey-ee-ow). In your time in Hawaii you may find the remains of many heiaus, but none will be complete. This model shows the oracle tower, the sacred buildings, the carved wooden figures representing various gods of the ruling alii.

The other exhibit is a thatched house (hale) acquired on Kauai and reconstructed in the museum.

A side room off the Main Hall is devoted to the Kalakaua dynasty, the last of the royal line, deposed in 1893. The crown on display hosts 521 diamonds, 20 opals, and 8 rubies.

The second floor is given to monarchs, mariners, missionaries and merchants. I'd love to steal the ship's figurehead of the Hawaiian maiden. On the far side of the balcony is the most complete exhibit of tapa (barkcloth) in the state of Hawaii.

The third floor balcony contains the musical instruments, statues and ethnic clothing of the immigrants to Hawaii. Don't miss the absolutely gorgeous 12-layer kimono dating to the Japanese Heian period (794 to 1185 A.D.).

From the third floor you can walk into the Hall of Hawaiian Natural History. Marvelous exhibits including a quiz on what is indigenous to Hawaii.

Descend one flight to the Polynesian Hall and the "Peoples of the Pacific." Did you know they used red feathers as a form of currency in the Santa Cruz islands? Elaborate coils of red feathers would buy you a bride, a labor force, a batch of pigs.

You could do the same with doughnut-shaped stones in Yap. Some are displayed in the open air Hawaiian courtyard in back.

Next to the main courtyard is the Atherton Halau where a 45-minute show with different themes is staged at 10:15 AM and 2 PM. The show provides a perfect time to rest your feet and is worth every cent of the $4.75. Besides the music and dance performances there are different demonstrations of Hawaiian arts and crafts each day.

Next door to the Atherton Halau, in an historic school dormitory building, is a shell collection where retired navy Commander William Christensen enthralls students with stories of the mollusks of Hawaii and their shell houses. His volunteer performance is booked out months in advance.

He is typical of the devotion to knowledge that makes the Bishop Museum a special attraction to visit.

Put it on top of your list.

The next logical place for you to spend some time is downtown. The core of downtown encompasses a highrise, classy, clean, modern financial district alongside a few restored historic low-slung buildings that headquarter the high and mighty powers of the islands.

At one time it was also the central shopping core of the islands before Ala Moana Center, a unique urban shopping complex, paved the way for other outlying shopping centers.

But instead of deteriorating as many city centers have done, downtown Honolulu has boomed. It is an attractive, exciting area with creative open spaces, thanks to imaginative planning by the Downtown Improvement Association which defines attainable, desirable goals and engages in an active program of sustained education.

Bob Midkiff, a kamaaina financial executive whose roots in Hawaii go back to New England missionary days, who looks like a Phi Beta Kappa from Yale and is, saw a future of deteriorating land values unless a rebuilding plan was put in motion. His vision firmly established the DIA, whose plan, based on experiences in other cities, embraced three concepts: 1. Keep the capitol downtown, 2. Keep the financial community downtown, 3. Get tourists downtown.

Downtown is also unique because it has the only royal palace on United States soil.

Iolani Palace.

Built by King Kalakaua who commissioned, then rejected, a palace built across the street (the Hawaii Judiciary Building), Iolani Palace was constructed at a cost of $360,000 and was occupied by the king in 1882. (The State Legislature spent $6 million on its restoration.) Kalakaua's coronation was held in 1883. Four years later he celebrated his fiftieth birthday. Both occasions called for major festivities which suited the "Merrie Monarch's" style. The palace was geared for formal functions.

Modest in size, measuring 140 by 100 feet overall, half of the first floor was given to the throne room, the other half to a reception area and dining room.

Food was prepared in a basement kitchen and delivered by dumb waiter to the upstairs' pantry. The basement was also used for storerooms and offices for the household staff.

The second floor was used by the royal family as living quarters.

Three errors were made by the three different architects employed in the design of the building. One, the royal pair's bedrooms were not connected. (The first two telephones in Hawaii were installed in the palace and guess where they went? Right. One in the king's bedroom and one in the queen's bedroom.)

The second error was that there was only one staircase. (It is made out of koa wood and it is gorgeous.) The single entry and exit to the second floor meant that staff had to use the same stairway as the king and queen! Horrors.

The third error was even more serious. There was no *en suite* bathroom with the king's bedroom.

You wonder, with three architects, who approved the plans.

The king built still another abode—modest but cozy—on the palace grounds where he could be with his queen.

Anyway, the ongoing restoration is superb.

Over 20,000 of the 50,000 slats in the folding wood shutters required replacing. Everything was repainted.

The hall with the portraits of past kings, the etched glass doors and windows done in San Francisco with their Grecian themes, the original chandelier in the Blue Room, the dining room with 225 pieces of furniture from Davenports in Boston. (The original chairs cost $25. They cost $450 to replace.)

Upstairs, the king's den has been restored just as it was when he used it as his official office. Only the queen's bedroom, last occupied by Kalakaua's sister, Queen Liliuokalani, during the revolution that led to her downfall, has been left bare, symbolic of her having been kept a prisoner in the room.

Because attendance is limited, you must have reservations to tour the palace. You are escorted through by a volunteer docent, and they all do excellent jobs. (Lehua Yim, beautiful of face and melodious of voice, added many dimensions to our last tour.)

Call 536-6185 for reservations. The 1985 admission price was $4 and tickets are picked up at the coral block Royal Barracks adjacent to the palace. Originally, the Royal Barracks building was across the street on the grounds of the present capitol. It was dismantled and reassembled block by block at the new site, where, once, King Kalakaua and his queen had their private living quarters ... in adjoining bedrooms.

On the mauka side (mountain side) of the palace, visit the new capitol. For a state with less than a million people you probably wonder why we have such a grand building ($25 million) and why we have the need of an expensive bicameral legislative system, especially since eight tenths of the population is also governed by the mayor of the City and County of Honolulu.

The only reason I can find is that it increases employment. And public employee pension funds.

The capitol is, however, a grand statement. Note the statue of Liliuokalani on the mall facing the palace. Design architect John Carl Warnecke utilized pillars that look like palm trees, moats to reflect Hawaii's island geography, and a roofless courtyard to symbolize the state's tropical climate. Nice.

The open-to-the-sky design gives a lightness to the massive structure, and if you look closely, you'll see that the ceilings are shades of blue mosaic tiles—which keep falling off—adding yet another dimension to the dramatic architecture.

Look even closer to discern the abstract shapes of twin volcanoes in the construction of the Senate and House chambers. A nod to the origin of the islands.

We like the rugged stone facing of the outer walls and the big windows that allow visual access into the chambers.

Directly beneath the open-to-the-sky roof is a circular tiled mosaic composition called "Aquarius" by Todashi Sato, the winner of an open competition. Its floating colors both restate an island ocean theme and reflect the blue of a Pacific sky. Very appropriate for the setting. Over 600,000 tiles are used in the design.

Before the circular art floor stands the statue of Father Damien, the famous leper priest of Molokai, created by Marisol, a South American sculptress.

Go to the mauka entrance of the lobby. That is an oversized version of the state medallion suspended overhead.

We take overseas visitors to the capitol at night because the night floodlighting gives the building even more dramatic impact.

During the daytime, you can take an elevator to the second floor legislative offices—they are plush—and to the third floor offices of the governor and lieutenant governor—plushier—and enjoy the views of Honolulu from the balconies.

Maybe it was worth $25 million.

On the makai (sea) side of the palace is the golden statue of King Kamehameha. On the eve of Kamehameha Day, a holiday in early June, the statue is draped in 100 elaborate, colorful 12-foot to 18-foot leis. They virtually obscure all but the statue's eyes. It takes a week for 25 lei-makers to string the 75,000 blossoms and ferns together. It is one of the most photogenic events in Honolulu. A 3P-er.

We attended the late afternoon ceremony last year to watch senior citizens dance the hula, followed by a performance of an ancient hula by a halau, a school of traditional hula. We were amused by the gaping-mouthed amazement on the faces of the Elkhart High School Marching Band from Elkhart, Indiana whose 177 members had come to Hawaii to march in the annual Kamehameha parade and participate in the lei-draping pageant.

A city and county cherry picker used to install street lights lifted the drapers on high to ceremoniously position each lei over the head of the great king's statue.

The original Kamehameha statue was cast in Florence, Italy in 1880 and then lost at sea. A second statue was cast and erected in 1883. Later the ship with the original statue was salvaged and the original statue was found on a dump heap in the Falklands, recovered and placed in the former plantation town of Hawi on the Big Island near Kamehameha's birth place.

If you are in Honolulu on the Saturday preceding June 11th, don't miss the Kamehameha Day parade. The women "pa'u" riders dressed in velveteen or satin skirts riding sidesaddle on high stepping horses—both bedecked with leis—are so majestic it brings tears to my eyes.

Behind the statue is the Hawaii Judiciary Building known as Aliiolani Hale, a House of Parliament during Kalakaua's days. Step inside. You'll drink in the atmosphere. One day I was taken up to the tower of the building where the workings of the clock are located with faces on four sides. I thought the name of the clockmaker was familiar. E. Howard Co., Boston.

When I got home I searched my notebooks from research done in Hokkaido for our *How To Get Lost and Found In Japan* travel book.

In Sapporo, capital of the northern Japanese island of Hokkaido, there is a famous building, the Clock Tower, now a museum but originally part of an agricultural school headed by Dr. William S. Clark of Massachusetts State Agricultural School. Completed in 1874, the Clock Tower still has the original clock which, according to my notes, came from E. Howard Co, Boston.

I felt as if I had found an old friend.

The First Days of Change: The Missionaries

A block east of the Kamehameha statue are three modest houses with a rich past. They were the first Western style houses in Hawaii, but more importantly, they were the foothold of the missionary movement in Hawaii.

Throughout the Pacific, one finds a major introduction of the coming Western civilization, for better or for worse, was made by the establishment of missionary outposts.

South of the Equator, the missionaries came primarily from the London Missionary Society, and were, in truth, a grab-bag of journeymen, committed but not necessarily suited to the rigors of their rugged future.

The missionaries who shaped Hawaii into the Western mold came from an American missionary society founded on the zealot fire of conviction—shared with their English counterparts—that the world would be properly served if the word of Christianity was spread to the heathen corners of the world.

At Williamtown near West College in Massachusetts, Samuel J. Mills was holding an outdoor prayer meeting in 1806 with five students when a sudden shower caused them to seek refuge under a haystack. There, they dedicated themselves to spreading the Christian gospel overseas.

From the Haystack Meeting came the inspiration for establishing the American Board of Commissioners for Foreign Missions, the ABCFM.

Recruits for missionary work came from mercantile and farming families and were of a better educated class than their English counterparts, according to Niel Gunson, in *Messengers of Grace*.

Education had its advantages. These intelligent and imaginative messengers successfully converted the high chiefs and then the rest of the native population to Christianity and then later used their commercial and agricultural birthrights to found highly profitable private enterprises in the islands, giving rise to the cliche that the missionaries came to do good—and did damned well.

The missionaries located themselves in 1820 in Kona on the Big Island, Honolulu on Oahu, and Waioli, Kauai. Later, they established a mission at Lahaina, Maui.

In Honolulu the mission was allotted a parcel of land, for a two year trial. And a trial it was. The missionary women were considered oddities. White, pale skin. Small waists. Long dresses. Bonnets on their heads.

By contrast, beauty to the Hawaiian was Queen Kaahumanu, standing a stately six feet, weighing in at an estimated 360 pounds, and sometimes robed. Now, that was a woman.

The Honolulu members received a New England prefabricated cottage in 1821. Today, it is the oldest American house in Hawaii and together with the two coral block houses alongside, constitutes the Mission Houses Museum.

I felt ashamed that after so many years in Honolulu, I had never visited the museum—and I felt worse after finding it so engrossing.

A guided tour is optional but included in the price. The short tour is conducted by one of the missionary descendants, ladies of the Hawaiian Mission Children's Society, more informally referred to locally as the "cousin's society" and consisting of many of the prominent names of the community.

The original frame house is the entry to the grounds and is filled with memorabilia of the times. Next to the 1821 cottage is a coral block annex, originally an extra bedroom which became the printing house. A replica of the original Ramage printing press used to print the Hawaiian language and ten commandments in 1822 is exhibited.

The third house, built from coral blocks cut from the reef, served as a mission supply house, residence for another missionary family, and a mission business office.

This house has a basement whose floor was made from bricks used as ship's ballast.

From this meager handful of dwellings, the Christianity movement fanned out to counteract the wild whalers, convert the ruling royal families and set a standard of Yankee conduct and morals in the fledging community.

Next door to the mission houses is the Kawaiahao Church, completed in 1842 of coral block. It took five years and a thousand workers to complete the church. The coral blocks, for example, were sawn off the reef by divers at ten and twenty foot depths. The church is an excellent place to go Sunday mornings to hear the melodious voices of the Polynesian parishioners and, probably, the only pure Hawaiian you will hear during your visit. The service at 10:30AM is partially in Hawaiian. Beautiful.

Interestingly, it was not the day-long sermons that attracted the Hawaiians to the missionary churches, but the hymns. The Hawaiians had known only monotone native chants. They took to the Christian hymns, (himeni) and the melodic fluctuating diatonic scale of eight major and minor tones, like a baby takes to warm milk. A cappella singing in four-part harmony came as naturally to them as dancing.

Score one for the missionaries.

Take the score away when you learn they put a tabu on dancing, which was not revived until King Kalakaua came to the throne.

The Mission Houses Museum offers a downtown walking tour every day ($5) which takes in the Kawaiahao Church, King Lunalilo's Tomb, Aliiolani Hale, the Kamehameha Statue, Iolani Palace Grounds (but not the palace itself), St. Andrew's Cathedral, founded by Kamehameha IV, the State Capitol Building and Washington Place, the official residence of the Governor and former residence of Queen Liliuokalani, which is across from the capitol. A good buy.

I haven't taken this tour but I'd recommend it highly because the whole area is a pleasant, shady, easy stroll and the Mission guide would be well and accurately informed. In a small group, the tour would be worth the investment. Reservations are suggested. The telephone number is 531-0481.

Note: The important influence of the Boston missionaries was spread throughout the islands during the early 1800s. Several of the mission houses the teachers built survived and have been preserved as private museums. Each gives a different dimension of life of the era. Make time to visit the Lyman House in Hilo, the Baldwin House in Lahaina, and the Waioli House at Hanalei on Kauai.

Chinatown, the Other Cheek of Downtown

I did take the Chinatown Walk-A-Tour which costs only $3, or $7 if you stay for lunch at Wo Fat's. Put that on your list, too. Tuesdays, starting at 9:30, providing the Chinese Chamber of Commerce has enough advance reservations. You convene on the second floor of the Chamber Building, 111 North King Street, at the Hawaii Chinese History Center.

If you are lucky, you'll get Yankee Chang as your tour conductor. Yankee is a famous local character, now well into his seventies, who appears occasionally in shot-on-location TV shows like "Hawaii Five-O" and "Magnum P.I." and TV commercials for the Hawaii Medical Services Association where he totes a surf board and preaches good health. Naturally, he looks fifteen years younger than his true age.

Every resident in Honolulu could learn a whole bunch by taking the tour.

For example, I had never been in a Chinese herb shop. Fascinating. Bought a passel of five-star herbs, excellent in cooking chicken. The proprietor was also the doctor. To watch him fill prescriptions from a maze of small shelf-boxes lining the wall was absorbing. A dash of this, a spoonful of that, a pinch of something else. Many herbs would be combined and mixed for one prescription and then boxed and handed to the patient.

In a fresh noodle shop, I bought a pound of just-made noodles that the Lady Navigator used in a stir-fry dish that evening.

In a bakery-delicatessen, I tasted pastries that I had never seen before—and I know and love Chinese food.

We went down little alleys I never knew existed and into Chinese stores, lei shops, gift shops that were all old in time but new to me.

We toured the produce and fish market on King Street, bought and renovated in 1984 by tenants who had been renting for years, the Chinese Cultural Center a couple of blocks west, now owned by Taiwanese, ending across Vineyard Street at the Kwan Yin Temple to learn the correct way to make an offering.

Great tour.

I loved the names. Bo Wo Co., the oldest Chinese gold shop, the Pantheon Bar, circa 1883, the oldest bar in Honolulu, Wing Coffee Co., McLean Block (1903), Perry Block, (888), the

McCandless Building Square, Lai An Tong Herb Shop (air conditioned), Mendonca Bldg., Shun Fat Cheong Chinese Store (dried squid, dried mushrooms and oyster sauce), Fung Wah Yuk Noodle Factor, Lum Sai Ho Tong building which used to serve 4,000 tong members.

Mind you, Chinatown is now international. Filipinos, Thais, Indonesians are part of the commercial make-up of the community and practically no one lives in the area anymore.

The Chinese were brought to Hawaii in 1852 as plantation workers and houseboys and city laborers under contracts that ran up to three years. They brought over picture brides and intermarried with Hawaiian women. Soon, these few blocks were crammed with joss houses, and opium parlors, tenements and Chinese restaurants. Families lived over the stores.

The great fire of 1886 all but destroyed Chinatown, burning for three days and three nights, reducing to ash 700 buildings.

In 1900, a dreaded bubonic plague sealed the fate of Chinatown. Suspected of being the source of the plague, an area of Chinatown was cordoned off and set on fire. A high wind soon engulfed the whole district, laying it waste. The event caused the Chinese to disperse their residences and today, only one percent of the Chinatown population is Chinese. (Many of them became millionaires and live in the most exclusive parts of Honolulu.)

Streets. One street in Chinatown is Smith Street. Smith? Where did Smith come from? Reverend Lowell Smith, I learned, was the beloved pastor of the nearby Hawaii Church.

Beretania Street was a Hawaiian corruption of Britannia but Vineyard Street. Why Vineyard Street?

Because they used to grow grapes here to make wine, said the guide. What? Who grew grapes and made wine in Hawaii? Research indicated it must have been Don Francisco de Paula Martin, who spoke four languages, including Hawaiian, and served Kamehameha for a time as interpreter and manager of trade. Don Francisco lived well, took minor chiefs' daughters as wives, entertained lavishly at his house near the harbor and poured wine for visitors made from grapes grown in his own vineyard.

Hotel Street was named because it was near the waterfront and was lined with hotels. Later, during World War II, the hotels were brothels and lads from the armed forces formed lines into the street to get in, reading comic books while waiting.

Hotel Street after dark is still not a recommended place to play.

The Chinatown tour takes three hours if you buy the luncheon at Wo Fat's package.

The tours of downtown sponsored by the Mission Houses and the Chinese Chamber of Commerce are ignored by 95 percent of the visitors. A pity. Too many people come to play in Hawaii and miss the best parts.

However, few miss Pearl Harbor. It is the most popular visitor attraction in the state.

Pearl Harbor, Day of Infamy

Pearl Harbor is the most frequented tourist attraction in the state. Hours are 7:45AM to 5PM. Closed Mondays. Go early.

We took a private bus from the Ilikai Hotel which cost us $8 each for a round-trip. Transportation only.

The cheapest way to get to the National Park Service Center is to take a city bus for less than a dollar. Lots of stops but the price is right.

Another way is to take a packaged city tour from a private transportation company like Gray Line that includes a stop at Pearl Harbor, a drive through Chinatown—although a drive through isn't enough—the Hawaiian State Capitol, Kawaiahao Church, Waioli Tea Room, University of Hawaii and East-West Center, and the Diamond Head Lookout, all for $15.50. Not a bad deal.

You can take a Pearl Harbor Cruise from Kewalo Basin but, beware: 1) you don't stop at the Visitor Center so you don't see the documentary movie, and, 2) you don't get off your boat at the Arizona Memorial, two most important parts of the Pearl Harbor experience.

The best way to go is in your own rental car. Not hard to find and lots of parking. Just stay on Kamehameha Highway, past the airport, and you'll pick up the sign to the parking area.

Since the National Park Service has taken over the operation and established a new Visitor Center, the pleasure of visiting Pearl Harbor has doubled. What a fine service the National Park

Service provides. It is one branch of the government which always makes me feel proud.

At the Visitor Center, completed in 1980 at a cost of $5 million, is an information desk which dispenses numbered first come first served tickets. There's no charge for the tickets, but you must have one to get into the theater. When your number is called, you proceed to the theater entrance, all very efficient and orderly, and then begin an immersion of an historical event which will leave you somber, thoughtful and perhaps teary.

The theater goes dark and a 21-minute film takes you back in time.

It is the autumn of 1941 and the war in Europe has been in progress for two years. Allies are urging the United States to become directly involved in the conflict. Japanese/United States relationships are at a new low. I remember the newspaper front-paged the news that the Japanese Ambassador in Washington D.C. was going to call on Cordell Hull, Secretary of State, the next day.

That Sunday morning in San Francisco I went downstairs in my apartment building to meet a close friend and his father who were on their way to play golf.

Pearl Harbor has been bombed, my friend said. Come play golf with us. You never know when you'll be able to do it again.

I couldn't have swung a club.

I went inside and glued myself to the radio.

At 7:55AM Honolulu time, two waves of high level dive bombers attacked the fleet at rest in the Sunday morning sunshine. It was a complete surprise, even though a miniature sub had been sunk at the harbor entrance at 6:40 and a radar warning at Opana Point had picked up and reported incoming airplanes at 7:02.

The U.S. fighting aircraft were destroyed on the ground for the most part and the fleet was ravaged.

At 8:10, a 1,760-pound armor-piercing bomb penetrated the decks of the *U.S.S. Arizona* and exploded, lifting the entire bow of the mammoth vessel clear of the water. In less than nine minutes the ship was underwater. Over 1,000 men trapped in her hull. They are still there.

The *U.S.S.—Oklahoma* suffered a similar fate, but not of the same proportions. She capsized after being hit by several torpedoes and sank at her moorings, as did the *California* and *West Virginia.*

The damage was total. Eight major vessels were sunk or beached, ten more were extensively damaged.

The casualty list totaled 2,403 killed, 1,178 wounded.

Aircraft destroyed, 188; damaged, 159.

The Japanese lost 164 men and 29 aircraft.

However, there was one flaw in the attack. The Pearl Harbor repair facilities, the storage facilities were untouched. The clean up started immediately and all but the *Arizona, Utah* and *Oklahoma* saw action again.

You get all this and more in the film.

When the lights go on, the Ranger fills in the gaps with more information, the side doors open to the dockside ships operated by the Navy and you cruise to the Memorial which spans the sunken battleship *Arizona.*

The Memorial is a gleaming white expanse of semi-open concrete, 184-feet long, divided into three compartments.

The first compartment is the entryway where one of two bells from the *Arizona* is on display. (The other is in the state capitol of Arizona in Phoenix.) It is not polished to protect it against salt air corrosion.

The second hall, open overhead and at the sides, looks down on the remains of the ship. It is a poignant moment when you see the outlines of the deck and think that this is the final resting place for over 1,000 men.

In the hasty action immediately following the December 7 disaster, six of the 14-inch guns were removed to coastal defense positions. The superstructure was cut away and nobody knows what happened to it. One hundred and five bodies were recovered.

"Why weren't the other bodies removed?" you ask.

"It was not a priority," you are told.

"The priority was to repair the damaged ships and get them to sea."

The third room is the shrine chamber and contains 1,177 names of sailors and marines engraved onto a white marble wall.

On March 16, 1914 the keel of the *U.S.S. Arizona* was laid. On December 1, 1942 the ship, contrary to the belief of many, was decommissioned and stricken from the Naval Register but the

Navy Department permits a flag to fly daily from the severed masthead.

In 1983, the first scientific survey was conducted to determine how much was left of the ship.

Among other discoveries, divers found live ammunition on the decks of the vessel, teak decks which had withstood salt water corrosion for over 40 years.

President Dwight Eisenhower approved the construction of the Memorial in his second term and President John Kennedy signed a bill appropriating $150,000 as a contribution for its construction, but the remaining funds came from the private sector.

One of the main contributions came from a concert given in Honolulu by rock star Elvis Presley who donated all of the proceeds to the memorial fund.

In 1962, the monument was dedicated.

If you have good Naval connections, you can visit the Memorial on the Admiral's Barge. It is not really the admiral's barge, but it is a good tour. It departs from Aiea Landing, after previewing a different film from that shown in the Visitor Center, and cruises to the Memorial by way of other waters surrounding Ford Island, the shipyards and the submarine base.

The last time we visited the Memorial, I remember standing in the middle of a platform staring down at the skeleton of the ship. A drop of oil came to the surface and broke, spreading in a rainbow of circles. Three leis dropped by friends or lovers or relatives of men beneath my feet floated on the surface, gradually drifting away.

Silent rings of flowers.

Sacrificial oil.

God bless. Rest in peace.

Next to the Visitor Center is the World War II submarine *U.S.S. Bowfin SS-287*, open to visitors for a small charge. A portable tape recorder to narrate its details comes with the admission price.

To go to sea for months at a time in such cramped, hot, uncomfortable quarters took men with mental strength. A real tin can compared to the roomy nuclear submarines of today.

A Tour To The East, Hanauma Bay

As Waikiki is bracketed by two important parks, Kapiolani Park to the east and Ala Moana Park to the west, so is the city of Honolulu flanked by two important bodies of water: Pearl Harbor to the west and Hanauma Bay to the east.

Pearl Harbor is a national shrine; Hanauma Bay is an underwater park and conservation district.

Just as we insist that visitors go to Pearl Harbor even though it can be a wrenching experience, we always send them to Hanauma Bay.

East of Diamond Head, facing the Molokai Channel, Hanauma Bay was formed by the cave in of the extinct volcano Koko Head. It *is* beautiful.

As part of our Waikiki research, i.e., experiencing one of Hawaii's most photogenic spots the way the average tourist does, we booked a Polynesian Tours' bus for a morning trip to the underwater park.

Besides, we had a small niggle about driving. The park had developed a popularity with members of the car thief union in recent years, unthinkable during our early courtship days when we never even thought about locking the car while we learned how to snorkel there.

That was another thing I checked out with Major Perry of Honolulu's finest.

"The place is patrolled," he assured me. "But that doesn't mean that we still don't have incidents."

The admonition of car rental companies speaks for itself. Don't lock your car. It is useless. That includes the trunk. Never, never leave anything of value in the car, not even for a short inspection of the Blow Hole or a North Shore beach. Professional gangs get their drug money from looting the cars of visitors.

The Polynesian Tours' van was driven by "Cousin Mike" who issued all snorkeling equipment as part of the tour package price. The underwater cameras could be rented.

We arrived before ten o'clock and it was already crowded.

Hanauma Bay, even from the top of the cliff, is one of the all-time beauty spots of Hawaii. A definite 3P. Your first view of it is from two hundred feet above the ocean. You look down at a long curve of white sand beach fringed by classic palm trees practicing the hula. It appears there is little if any surf. You can see the extensive coral reef that divides the cobalt blue of the deep from the aquamarine of the protected swimming and snorkeling area. Pockets of coral heads provide private "bathtubs" for swimmers.

A shuttle bus (50¢ will take you down the long walk to the beach but it is not a difficult stroll on the macadam road.

In 1967, when the bay waters were declared a State Underwater Park, line fishing and spear fishing were forbidden. As a result, the shore waters are alive with small reef fish growing fat on the handouts of tourists.

Hold pieces of bread and they will bunch around your knees. Best of all, offer them frozen green peas and they will eat out of your hand. The Japanese visitors literally squeal with delight.

The shore waters, at depths ranging from one foot to ten feet, are excellent for novice swimmers. An intermediate area beyond the first reef has slightly rougher water from 10 to 30 feet deep. About right for the experienced swimmer/snorkeler.

Near the entrance to the bay, the depths go from 30 to 70 feet and are for experts only. The farther out you go the clearer the water, but there is a current called the Molokai Express at the entrance which, as inferred, will take you to Molokai ... and you don't want that, now do you?

Also be careful about walking along the crater rim rocks that slide into the ocean at either end. Sudden giant-sized wave action can sweep the unaware into churning waters.

Two or three people, usually military, are lost every year.

The beach has a refreshment stand, toilets and fresh water showers.

The ideal time to go, especially in summer and on weekends, according to "Cousin Mike" who has been driving to the beach for ten years, is at 8AM. Stay for three hours, swim, snorkel, sunbathe and leave.

Hanauma Bay is a favorite destination area among the rental scooter bikers. You see dozens of bikers strung out single file, their towels and bathing suits in the wire baskets rolling out to Koko Head every morning, and see the same bikers with frazzled hair and burned-but-happy faces on the way back in the late afternoon.

On our outing at Hanauma, we had been engrossed watching several beginning classes of scuba divers making tentative beach dives. It looked easy.

Then I read an article by Tom Horton, a former Honolulu newspaper columnist and now an excellent freelance writer based in California, about his scuba diving experience at Molokini, a submerged volcano just off the coast of Maui. Scuba diving was the only way to do it, according to Mr. Horton. And, you're never too old to learn.

I decided right then that I had to learn to scuba dive, and I had to dive Molokini.

The girl at the hotel travel desk was cautious about recommending one company over another.

"There are many dive shops," she said. (There are some 27 in the state.) "Some of them are more careful than others. I dive and I know." She finally named Dan's, American Dive, and Aloha Dive at Hawaii Kai.

A doctor friend, Phil McNamee, had just received his certificate at Aloha Dive where the dive boat is berthed alongside the shop and that sounded convenient. I figured that if "Old Pudge" could learn to dive, anybody could do it. We called for information.

The fee for a five-dive certification course was less than $300 and included all instruction, text book, log book, certification card, transportation to and from Waikiki and the use of all equipment except boots to be worn under the flippers, and gloves.

We also found out that our snorkeling flippers, the slip-on kind, would not do for scuba diving. They had to be the type that buckle at the back. More secure. We spent another $150 buying two sets of new flippers, rubber socks and cheap gloves.

Our masks, which allow the diver to expel air and water from the mask by blowing through a nose piece, were fine.

Jackie James, the owner of Aloha Dive, is an unusual diving shop proprietress. Once the singing and dancing star of musical comedies, she toured from London to San Francisco with lead roles in such Broadway musicals as "South Pacific," "Can Can," "Guys and Dolls."

Slightly over her tap-dancing weight, the blond lady with an ebullient, outgoing personality, now runs a unique shop with a staff of professional instructors and takes joy in teaching the handicapped the fun of diving.

"All it takes is a strong will. With the right motivation, you can do anything no matter what your physical problem is," Jackie maintains. She believes, and has proven, that *anyone* can dive. One of her instructors has a wooden leg.

My problem is not physical, it is mental. I am a coward.

Beyond that curtain of water, the world is full of snappies.

"Sharks? Hah! Sharks will never bother you. Moray eels will never bother you. Sharks might be curious, but they are as afraid of you as you are of them," said Jackie.

Where have I heard that before? How do people get such information? Have they interviewed sharks?

The morning of the first dive we met at the shop and were outfitted with rubber jackets and given a mesh sack to put our gear into. Flippers, masks, booties, gloves. Silent time. Nervous time.

A van dropped us in the parking lot overlooking Hanauma Bay where we were strapped into buoyancy jackets and aluminum air tanks, and taught to breathe properly through the regulator attached to the air supply. Then Hugh, our dive instructor, demonstrated how to inflate and deflate the jacket through a hose with two separate valves. A long valve put air into the buoyancy jacket. The short one let the air out slowly. A pull string on the bottom of the jacket expelled all of the air immediately.

A third hose connected to the metal tank holding 2500 pounds of compressed air had at its end two circular dials in a block of rubber. One indicated the existing air pressure in the tank, the second gauged the depth the diver had descended.

"We never stay down with less than 500 pounds of air. Underwater, you tell me how much air you have by holding up one finger for every hundred pounds," said Hugh.

Finally, around each person's middle was strapped a canvas belt with weights attached.

We waddled over to the commuter beach bus, grateful for its existence under the weight of the tank and the diving equipment.

At the water's edge we put on face masks and gloves and rubber booties and slipped into waist deep water and forced the flippers over the booties. The instructor asked us to form a circle around him.

"Now what I want you to learn is buoyancy. Put just enough air in your jacket to float yourself underwater."

I pressed my short valve and sank immediately to the bottom. Pressed the long valve ... went straight to the top. Pressed the short valve, gently, and sank slowly to the middle of the water. Buoyant.

With all parties stabilized underwater, our leader pointed a hand toward the reef and we swam under snorkelers to a clear pool with a sandy bottom, probably about 15-feet deep.

Fun! Breathing slowly, the only sound was that of air being sucked in and the bubbles going out. We looked at reef fish. They looked at us.

The instructor, motioning for us to hang back, swam to a coral patch and tapped it with the butt of his knife. The head of an eel poked out of a hole. Hugh then fed the eel pieces of sliced up squid. It was a pet. He stroked the eel on its teeth-filled smooth head. We were impressed but unwilling to attempt hand feeding personally.

Hugh held up his controls console and asked, through hand signals, "How much air?"

I was already down to 800 pounds! Where had the time gone?

He signaled to head back to shore.

We swam back to the waist deep water and surfaced. The first dive was over.

Lesson number two, the following morning, was our debut dive in an open ocean.

We boarded a dive boat next to the Aloha Dive Shop, roared out of the protected waters into the rolling waters of Maunalua Bay. By the time the boat's captain threw over the anchor, we were in gear.

The initial instruction was to hold the face mask firmly against the face with one hand, breathe through the regulator, sit facing into the boat, then roll off backwards with enough air in the vests to buoy above water.

If that were satisfactorily negotiated, we were to go to the anchor line, release air in the vest and "walk our way slowly" down the anchor line to the ocean floor where we would re-assemble.

If there was too much pressure and the ears hurt, swallow several times and blow gently through a pinched nose, we were told. If the pain continued, rise a few feet to relieve the pressure, and then slowly descend again.

The first time you roll off a boat backwards—holding your breath in spite of all instructions to breathe normally—you wonder if this is your last day on earth, or rather, in the ocean. When you bob to the surface and finally start breathing through your regulator—oh miracle of miracles—it works! What a pleasant surprise.

But, one little victory doesn't get you to the bottom. There is yet the anchor line to "walk down."

Eventually, you get through your ear problems and get to the bottom and start playing follow the leader with the instructor ... and it is all a piece of cake. We saw beautiful fish and even a baby turtle.

It is a magical world.

Forty minutes later we surfaced and I was ecstatic—and then I threw up.

Lesson number two was not yet over. We would do a second dive.

We waited in the bobbing boat for more than a half hour—I was now a nice shade of sea green—and finally got back in for a second dive. I was so grateful to be back in the water again where it was calm and peaceful. The water was much clearer than Hanauma Bay and it seemed we could see forever.

Just lovely—until I surfaced and threw up again.

The Lady Navigator, in the meantime, was having serious trouble with her ears.

That afternoon we spent in class receiving verbal instruction, mostly to do with safety, and then passed a written examination.

The third morning we were back again for another ocean dive, but the Lady Navigator's ears had leaked a bit of blood, and she was forbidden to dive. She pouted.

I followed the same drill as the day before. Dive, play, enjoy immensely, surface ... and throw up. Second dive, lovely experience, excellent instructor, no problem executing the mandated underwater drills. Surface ... throw up.

Nonetheless, at the end of the third dive I was qualified and I received my dive book and the Basic Scuba Diver's card from the Professional Association of Diving Instructors (PADI).

I was now ready for Molokini on Maui.

Driving Around Oahu

Visitors, quite rightly, always ask, What about driving around the island?

Yes, we say, you certainly should.

Oahu is a lovely island. Once free of the boundaries of Waikiki and Honolulu, you are in semi-tropical country where you will see banana groves, sugar cane fields and pineapple plantations.

You'll pass white sand beaches where you can stop off for a swim or a picnic, pretty bays of clear, aqua through blue waters, rugged coastlines of crashing waves.

You'll pass by public golf courses, private golf courses, military golf courses and any number of Hawaii's 249 tennis courts.

Oahu, which means "The Gathering Place," holds 80 percent of Hawaii's million residents. You could get the impression that they all live in Honolulu until you get out into the country and pass through plantation towns and villages where you can meet another type of Hawaiian.

The role of defense expenditures in Hawaii's economy, second only to tourism, becomes clearer as you pass bastions of military strengths: Pearl Harbor, Hickam Air Force Base, Schofield Barracks, Wheeler Field, Kaneohe Marine Corps Air Station.

Oh, yes, do go around the island, we say.

When you look at a highway map it is clear that you can't really 'drive around the island' because no highway goes around Kaena Point, the northwestern tip of the island.

You have a choice of three country drives. One, to the Waianae Coast to the end of the road, almost to Kaena Point. Two, to the northern shore via one route and back another, which is called the Circle Island tour. Three, around Koko Head and Waimanalo and back through Kailua and the Pali Tunnel, which we call the Little Circle tour.

The choices of transportation are by rental car, by tour company in large buses or small vans, or even by public bus. For example, the No. 52 bus will take you from Ala Moana Center to the North Shore by one route and back another. If you don't get off the bus, the cost is 75¢.

If you do get off the bus, say at the Hilton Turtle Bay Hotel and have lunch, it will cost you 75¢ to get back on again.

The Little Circle Tour

The Little Circle is an easy morning or afternoon drive, and, if we are doing the driving, this is the tour we take because it is visually spectacular and soul satisfying.

We recommend going in the counterclockwise direction and going in the morning, even though the sun is in your eyes. Besides, the early morning sun on the eastern coastline is so clean and sparkly that it will make you feel clean and sparkly too.

Also when you drive east on a morning tour, you are going against the Honolulu bound drive-to-work traffic flow but remember that Honolulu is an early morning town. Traffic fills the highways by 7AM, and resumes at 3PM.

For the Little Circle Island tour the directions are easy. Just stay next to the ocean. You go by Kapiolani Park, where all the tennis courts will be in play from dawn, turn right at Diamond Head Road, and go over Diamond Head.

Stop at the top, if you haven't already done so, and look at the view. A 2P stop. The memorial stone is to Amelia Earhart, America's most famous pre-war aviatrix, and beneath the monument is memorabilia saved before she was lost on her last exploratory flight of the Pacific: extra goggles, a flight plan, etc.

The home with the colonnades at the water's edge toward the east was built by Doris Duke, the richest woman in America.

The drive continues through Kahala, home of the wealthy, and along the fringe of Waialae Country Club, home of the Hawaii Golf Open in February, to the Kalanianaole Highway.

Just for the fun of it, pronounce it once.

Kah-la-nee-anna-oh-lee. Equal emphasis on each syllable. Easy, when you break it down. The highway was named after Prince Jonah Kuhio Kalanianaole, an important political figure and Hawaii's delegate to Congress.

The highway takes you past the suburban valleys and hilltops to Hawaii Kai.

When Henry Kaiser grew bored with moving earth at his Hawaiian Village Hotel, he sold it to Conrad Hilton, obtained a long-term lease on an old Hawaiian fishpond at this end of the island, called it Hawaii Kai, and brought in his steam shovels.

Earth flew in all directions. Islands were built, marinas were built, canals were dug. And everything was painted Kaiser pink:

earth moving equipment, catamarans, jeeps.

Today some 30,000 people live in the area and the home and land values top a half a billion dollars. More is to come. Kaiser is gone but the earth is still being moved. He would have liked that.

Koko Head shelters Hanauma Bay to the right of the highway. To the left is Koko Crater. At the top of the crater was formerly a military installation reached by a cable car. The line can still be seen. You probably think that an entrepreneur at one time or another wanted to reinstall a cable car and build a restaurant on top—because Americans like to put restaurants on top of everything. You're right but, no, he couldn't get permission and couldn't understand why not.

Did we say that Hanauma Bay is a 3P stop? It is worth repeating.

So is the rugged coastline beyond it, so dramatically colored. Intense cobalt blue foams to white where thunderous waves from the rugged Molokai Channel waters assault the cliff face. There is lookout parking on the highway where you can stop and watch in wonder.

On a good day you can look across the Molokai Channel—official name is Kaiwi Channel—and see the island of Molokai. During Aloha Week there is an outrigger canoe race from Molokai to Waikiki which draws contestants from California, Tahiti and Australia.

Farther on is the Blow Hole where the waves rush into a lava tube under the rocky promontory, creating a spouting horn of sea water. Kodak has gotten rich off tourists trying to photograph the spray as it shoots out of the hole.

The other people who get rich here are car thieves. It is a local industry. Although there are police staked out, the thefts continue and the caught thieves get slapped on the wrist. The left wrist. The judges wouldn't want to hurt their right wrist because that's the one used to break the door locks.

Beyond the Blow Hole is pretty if windy Sandy Beach which is fine for sunning but tough for swimming. Stay close to shore and stay close to other people in the surf at the south end of the beach.

On the other side of the road is the Hawaii Kai Golf Course. Two courses actually, both open to the public. The executive par-3 was the first course built by Kaiser. Later, an 18-hole championship course was added. A tough course in the wind with challenging holes. Popular with the Japanese tourists who are made to sacrifice a hole if they get one behind. If they repeat the offense, they are taken off the championship course and put on the par-3 course. Try to get a starting time first thing in the morning and beat the crowd. The last time we talked to John Inzer, the head pro, the course was booked solid through the following week.

Up the hill on the other side is a lovely 3P stop. Makapuu Point. The bald island you are see offshore is Manana, or Rabbit Island, and the pretty beach below you with the big waves is Makapuu Beach Park, known in Honolulu as a dandy body surfing bay.

Fun, but be careful.

One day the Lady Navigator turned her back to the ocean and was rolled by a wave that hit her in the back. She got up blinded by sand and was knocked down and bodily rolled again. Got up and would have been flattened the third time if I hadn't reached her in time to drag her out.

Family motto: *never turn your back to a wave.*

Across the street is Sea Life Park. Marine parks are now so common across the southern United States that you might pass it by as just another ho-hum one, but Sea Life Park deserves a stop. A huge glass tank with a spiral walkway around its perimeter contains a man-made reef where you are nose-to-nose with colorful reef fish. Our friends from fish-sophisticated Wood's Hole on Cape Cod found it marvelous.

An open amphitheater features the usual diving, jumping, trick-trained dolphins but, next door, there, in the Whalers' Cove, is a scaled down replica of a whaling ship where a trainer coaxes a dolphin to jump 40 feet out of water to the yardarm to take a fish out of his hand. That's a stopper.

The setting is another stopper. The natural oceanographic background of the ocean, Rabbit Island, and Makapuu Point is superb.

Another visual that frequently occurs on the east shore is hang gliding off the Koolau cliffs. Taking advantage of the topography and the strong updrafts created by the trades, the gliders can literally stay up for hours. Love to try it. But that first step...

Waimanalo is a little community, strongly Hawaiian, with a

good bring-your-own-booze Mexican restaurant on the highway, Bueno Nalo. A bit beyond the stores is the entrance to Bellows Field, an inactive Air Force base converted into a recreational camp for military personnel. The public can use the beach park—good swimming—but watch your car.

Farther along the highway is Waimanalo Beach Park. This is called the windy side of the island, for good reason. The tradewinds blow into your face, strong and refreshing, without any barrier. On a sunny day it is pleasant and cooling.

The highway continues past Olomana Golf Course, a privately owned but public course, and then intersects with Highway 61. Left takes you back to Honolulu. Right takes you into the bedroom community of Kailua.

Go to the right and continue through town to Kalaheo Street which runs parallel to the beach, turn right and proceed to Kailua Beach Park. It's a great place for kids and, if you want to learn how to windsurf, here is the place to learn.

Kailua Sailboard Company, telephone 262-2555, has all-day beginners windsurfing classes. The last price we had was $45 for beginners, including transportation from Waikiki. A good way to spend the day. Kailua has steady wind, a flat ocean being inside the reef, and shallow clean water.

Buzz's Original Steak House is across from the beach pavilion if you stay until dinner time.

Beyond the park is Lanikai. The Mid-Pacific Golf Club is tucked into the hills and has become one of the best kept private clubs on Oahu. Do the little loop drive of Lanikai. Heavenly Sea is what it means . . . and it is from here.

Go back to the road up the Pali Highway (61), past Castle Memorial Hospital, past Castle Junction. To the right you can see the Pali Golf Course, one of Oahu's several municipal courses. The highway swoops up the mountainside, through the tunnels, and a half mile farther on, you'll see a directional sign on the right to the Nuuanu Pali Lookout. A narrow road threads its way through a rain forest. If you watch for it on the mountainside to your left, you may see Upside Down Falls, a stream of water that comes off the Koolaus and is vaporized by the tradewinds.

The Pali Lookout is a 3P stop. The view to the north along the serrated surface of the cliffs—(Pali means cliff)—forever changing color and tone as the sun moves across its face, is one of

Oahu's most enthralling vistas.

Laid out before you is the town of Kailua, a nest of little islands offshore, and to the left, the buildings and runways of Kaneohe Marine Corps Air Station.

Before the tunnels through the Koolaus were finished—the first highway was completed about 1968—those of us who lived in Kailua and commuted to Honolulu drove up a two-lane road that turned the corner around the cliff face just at the lookout point.

On a stronger-than-usual windy day, the wind force would suck open trunks of cars and even tip over a Volkswagen.

Historically, the Pali is famous for the battle in which Kamehameha landed at the beaches of Waialae, caught the enemy in the valley of Nuuanu and forced the opposing warriors up the valley and many of them over the cliff.

When you start your drive back to Honolulu, look for the scenic drive on the left. Take it. You will drive through Oahu's watershed reserve, a green and damp forest. Rain in this upper part of Nuuanu Valley measures well over 100 inches a year. The water quickly seeps through the lava rock to a cap of fresh water beneath the island and is then pumped into reservoirs such as the one you pass on this road.

After the reservoir you reach an area of nice housing which has the climatic advantage of natural air conditioning in the summer and fireplace evenings in the winter, but the disadvantage of constant mold in the clothes closets.

Back on the highway, you'll not be able to see Oahu Country Club—to the right—Honolulu's premier private golf club (1906). On a sunny day, it is a piece of paradise. If you get invited, go!

Opposite the entrance to OCC, watch for the HVB Warrior marker on the left to Queen Emma's Summer Palace built in 1843 and now operated as a museum under the auspices of the Daughters of Hawaii. The gracious, unpretentious mountain retreat is open every day but Sunday and Saturday afternoons.

Below the palace on Nuuanu Highway, the former estates of well-to-do executives now serve as foreign consulates and churches. Near the bottom of the highway is the Royal Mausoleum where the ruling Kamehameha and Kalakaua families are entombed. The grounds are open every day but Sunday.

If you stay on the highway, you'll pass a pullout parking spot overlooking a Shinto temple and cemetery. Farther on to the left is one of the major Buddhist temples of Oahu, Honpa Hongwanji Hawaii Betsuin.

By tradition Hawaii is a strongly religious state. The heritage of the Yankee missionary strong Protestant ethic still runs through the secular fiber of the community. Layered over this is the Japanese Shinto and Chinese/Japanese Buddhist customs observed by 65,000 Buddhist families and 15,000 Shinto believers.

Statistically, Roman Catholics with over 200,000 families, are the single largest religious denomination. All Protestants number over 100,000 families, including 30,000 members of the Church of Latter Day Saints.

The single synagogue has over 400 Jewish families in its temple, most of whom I have lost to in golf or tennis.

To return to Waikiki, drive to the middle of the downtown business district, go to a bar, toss away the keys to the car and call a cab. No, we can't do that. Take the simple route. In Hawaii, when in doubt, drive to the ocean and turn to the left or to the right, and you will find your destination. If you don't know whether to turn left or turn right, then you are in trouble. *Then* you call a cab.

The Circle Island Tour

If we are taking guests around the island, we leave after 9AM to avoid traffic and head west with the sun at our backs on H-1.

The easiest way to reach the freeway from Waikiki is to drive east on Kalakaua to Kapahulu, the street that fronts the zoo, turn left and stay on it beyond the freeway overpass, hang left and follow the signs.

H-1 connects with H-2 to take you to Wahiawa and Schofield Barracks in thirty minutes, a trip which formerly was traffic agonizing, took three days, four lunches and five fights with your wife.

The same freeway takes you to the airport or Aloha Stadium or Bishop Museum. Zip.

After not taking the turn to the airport or Nimitz Highway and the Pearl Harbor Memorial, you'll see Moanalua Garden and its magnificent spreading monkeypod trees on your right. On the hill beyond Moanalua is Tripler Hospital, the major military hospital in the Pacific.

Just beyond Tripler is a road to Moanalua Valley, former estate of the Damons, a prominent missionary family whose members became successful, prosperous civic leaders—a not uncommon pattern.

The Damons' landscape gardener created Hawaii's first golf course inspired by Scottish courses in Moanalua, in 1898. It is also the oldest course this side of the Rockies. Moanalua, eighteen holes, was open to public use but, being out in the country in those days, you had to have your own carriage to reach it. Still open, the course has been reduced to nine holes.

From the freeway you can look across to Aloha Stadium, a comparatively new 50,000-seat affair with a convertible configuration for baseball and football. If you watch football on television, Aloha Stadium is the venue of the nationally televised Hula Bowl, Aloha Bowl and Pro Bowl.

We love to get sunny warm weather during the network bowl games—as well as during the nationally televised Hawaii Golf Open at Waialae Country Club in February—while the rest of America is buried in snow. The airplanes are full with incoming, frost covered visitors after every televised event.

Watch the road signs and keep to the right. After passing the Pearl Harbor Golf Course, non-military and open to the public, follow the overhead signs to H-2. You'll skirt the suburban town of Mililani whose golf course is open to the public, pass Wheeler Field, the military golf course at Leilehua and Schofield Barracks. Incidentally, Schofield has the second golf course built in Hawaii, in 1902, and named for Kalakaua, the last male monarch.

Have you ever seen pineapple growing? At the intersection of Kamehameha Highway (H-99) and the road coming out of Wahiawa (80), Del Monte has planted a species garden, a variety of traditional and experimental pineapple plants. This central plateau of Oahu is surrounded by pineapple plantations. The small garden is a revelation to most visitors who have no idea that the fruit comes from a small, thorny bush, in fact, a bromeliad. It bears no fruit until 18 months after planting, but, after the first harvest, produces a second crop. After three years the fields are replanted.

Farther on is the Dole Pineapple Pavilion where you can taste cold but canned pineapple juice or eat a freshly picked pineapple from the fields. It is beautifully sweet.

James Dole started the first successful pineapple operation around the turn of the century in Hawaii, an agricultural industry that now brings close to $100 million to the state.

You slide down the plateau to sea level and take a detour to the left, on road 930, to Mokuleia. For a while the polo games on Sunday afternoons were suspended because the primary sponsor was detained by federal authorities on charges of improperly diverting investors' funds from bonds to polo ponies and other expensive toys. The case is in the courts at this moment but the polo field for the winter season is again back in action, if modest by former standards.

What is active year round is gliding at Dillingham Field, a former military wartime strip. You can go up in a three passenger glider and take a turn around the field for $30.

We did this many years ago when the cost was $5.

It is a thrill. When you are towed aloft by a truck, you feel the glider pushing against the air as it gains altitude, straining against the rope. When the rope is released with a pop and the glider does a free fall until it gains flying speed, you think about bailing out until you remember that you don't have a parachute.

After that it is all chocolate cake. You don't fly. You soar. You are an angel. The only sound is a slight whistle of wind outside the clear plastic canopy. Taking advantage of the updrafts along the Waianae Mountain ridges, the wide-winged, graceful craft could float forever.

Finally the pilot turns away from the mountain and makes a wide sweep over the ocean and the wind takes the glider swiftly back to the west end of the field where the pilot banks the plane and dives for the runway. Dry mouth time.

At almost ground zero altitude he levels out the glider and, having attained his desired landing speed, he brings the plane over to the edge of the runway. Your seat is on the bottom of the glider and the separation between seat and runway is a piece of canvas. You hunch your buttocks into a tighter and tighter knot as the ground comes closer and closer.

You touch down and roll to an easy stop.

Lots of fun.

If your hands stop shaking on the approach, it is a 3P opportunity.

Reservations are not required. The flights go continually from

10AM to 5:30PM. For more information, call 623-6711 after 5 PM.

Return to the intersection called Weed's Corner, and take Highway-83 into Haleiwa. A long time ago, Oahu Railroad built a resort hotel here and the local gentry came to vacation during summers and play on weekends. Haleiwa is now kind of a funky little village where the old store fronts mask new pottery and gift, flower children dresses and surfboard shops.

If you haven't tried shave ice, a local favorite, then you have to find M. Matsumoto Store. It's like a snow cone—crushed ice with flavored syrup—but different. The flavors are different and, in the bottom of the paper cone, you'll find sweet azuki beans. It is an inherited childhood taste for people raised in Hawaii. Don't say, "Why this just tastes like crushed ice with blueberry syrup on it." They will think you have no taste.

Other places to lunch and munch are Jameson's-By-The-Sea (but across the highway) and Steamers in the shopping center.

Past Haleiwa is Waimea Bay and Beach Park, a nice place to picnic. Dangerous ocean currents in the winter, no reef, and sometimes the waves grow to be monsters. When that happens, the high-tech surfers throng to the shores and the narrow, two lane highway is clogged with spectators.

Across from the beach is the entrance to Waimea Falls, a privately created and operated nature park. A good job in Hawaiian plant life with a tram that takes you to the 50-foot waterfall, a fast-food restaurant and gift shop. Not bad, but not earthshaking.

The next community is Pupukea. The huge house and gardens on the hillside belong to Maurice J. Sullivan, an Irish born A&P trouble shooter on the East Coast who came to Hawaii in the military, married the Chinese daughter of a Kailua grocery store owner and went on to found Foodland, Hawaii's first chain of supermarkets, and made a fortune. A generous donator to local causes.

Beyond Pupukea is Sunset Beach and the awesome Banzai Pipeline where waves so big and so powerful that they can snap a surfboard as if it were a toothpick are common in the winter months. If you are really macho—and all surfers are macho—here is where you come to test your courage and your skill.

Sunset Beach is the surfing grounds of the championship heats, along with Makaha on the western coast.

You can get some pretty frightening pictures from the beach with a telescopic lens when the surf is up but, of course, the best shots are taken from the ocean with a float and a waterproof camera—and a whole bunch of experience.

At the time of this writing a daring young man challenging the world's tallest wave was taken by helicopter out to where the first surf breaks—a mile and a half offshore—and dropped in the water. A picture in the newspaper the other day showed him sliding down a 25-foot wall of water. That's a 5P picture.

He even wore an emergency three-minute oxygen tank in case he was driven so far underwater that he couldn't otherwise breathe.

At the northern tip of the island, past Kawela Bay, you will find Turtle Bay and the Turtle Bay Hilton Hotel with golf course and tennis courts and swimming pool.

The property was developed by the Del Webb organization of Phoenix and Las Vegas with large infusions of Prudential Insurance money. People in Honolulu shook their heads. What would they do about the wind? People in Honolulu are still shaking their heads. The property went from Del Webb to Hyatt under the name Kuilima, and now Hilton has poured millions into refurbishing it as the Turtle Bay Hilton and it is nicer now than when it opened. The rooms are extra spacious, with twin double beds, large lanais, all facing the ocean.

We went back and stayed there one weekend while attending the King Kamehameha Hula Festival at nearby Brigham Young University campus adjacent to the Polynesian Cultural Center.

We enjoyed the dining facilities, as do many Honolulu people getting away for a drive-out weekend.

But the wind still blows.

The amazing thing to the people shaking their heads in Honolulu is that Prudential has announced plans to build two more hotel properties at Turtle Bay and another golf course.

The Arnold Palmer Golf Management Company has assumed administrative control of the 18-hole golf course and is upgrading facilities and planning the second course under a 20-year master plan.

The north shore beaches feature the only dune buggy rides on Oahu. One such operation is located on the Hilton grounds ($18 plus tax, my notes say).

For an hour's worth of roaring fun, you get into a Japanese-made, loud vehicle with oversized tires and a smelly motor in the back and take off for the beach where you are allowed to follow a track through white sand and go round and around playing daredevil driver. (About twenty minutes of that is all you need.)

Actually it takes you fifteen minutes to get to the beach area and the funniest scene was passing the 11th green and the 12th tee of the golf course on the way out. As you know, it is considered profane to even breathe heavily while a golfer is putting or teeing off, and here comes this incredibly weird procession of buggies belching black fumes and blasting loud va-rooms past tees and greens. Putters and drivers teeing off just stood there with wide eyes and open mouths. Funny sight.

A side note: between Turtle Bay and the Kahuku Mill, opposite three power poles marked by broad red stripes, is the entrance to the North Shore Naturalist Park. Clothes are *not* optional. You take them off.

Basic and simple and secluded, says the park's brochure, and with safe potable fresh water, hot showers, and modern toilet facilities.

You can camp or rent vacation cabins or go for the day with a picnic hamper and coolers.

Dune buggies and gliders, okay. Volleyball in the buff. Sorry, I have a previous engagement.

The North Shore Naturalist Park, P.O. Box K, Laie, Hawaii 96762. Telephone (808) 521-4235.

The Polynesian Cultural Center in Laie is a destination unto itself and has been a successful tourist attraction since it opened over twenty years ago.

In 1984, it drew an audience of over a million people and rivals Pearl Harbor in numbers of visitors.

Laie is the location of the Church of Latter Day Saints and an important Mormon Temple, built in 1919. The Brigham Young University Hawaii was added after the war. Students come from throughout the Pacific.

The students form an integral part of the Polynesian Cultural Center where, amid 42 acres of gardens and trees, waterfalls, lagoons and a canal system linking each of the seven villages, they present authentic songs and dances of their cultures and demonstrate crafts of each.

Samoan, Maori, Fijian, Hawaiian, Tahitian, Marquesan and

Tongan huts, true to the architectural heritage of the islands they represent, are the centers for many activities.

Your admission ticket entitles you to roam freely about the compound as long as you like, ride the trams and trolleys or cruise the waterways by canoe.

It's a good idea to go first to the Orientation Center for an introduction to what is available in the complex. Trams leave from here for cruising tours of the villages every few minutes. Replicas of vintage Honolulu trolleys also depart for 45-minute tours of the university and the Mormon Temple grounds. (Propaganda time.)

Our first stop was at the Samoan fale where a guide was literally up a coconut tree, mostly assuming comic poses for cameras.

On the ground, he reported previous audience suggestions before demonstrating the technique of opening a coconut.

"An English lady said she would use a lawn mower.

"A lady from Los Angeles said she would use a microwave oven.

"A Texan said he would shoot it between the eyes with a .45, providing his wife was holding it at the time.

"There are eyes in the coconut. See," he held the coconut aloft and pointed to two dark spots on one end.

"A ridge goes from a spot between the eyes to the back of the coconut. What you do to open the hard shell is to give the middle of that ridge a sharp blow crosswise with a heavy instrument ... " He popped the ridgeline with the handle of a machete and the coconut split in half ... "—And there you are."

He poured a watery fluid from the cracked nut into a paper cup and gave it to a nearby lady to drink. She indicated that it was delicious.

"That's good," he said, "because it is a laxative. Works every two minutes.

The audience laughed.

"Don't believe me. Follow her."

The "guide" was Lokeni V. Lokeni, a student, like most of the guides and entertainers, from across the equator. Lokeni was from West Samoa and, with such natural timing and comic delivery, could have been a professional entertainer.

When we told Mike Foley, the public relations head of the Center, about Lokeni later he said, "Oh, yes. All Samoans are natural comics.''

We ambled leisurely through the other villages. The New Zealand Maori village, called Aotearoa, is a compound of intricately carved whares (houses) whose carved panels denote an advanced artistic culture. A Maori girl was twirling balls on the ends of string while dancing, and another Maori miss was teaching children to play a stick game, tititorea.

Lots of audience participation. In the Hawaii village, pale skinned and freshly scrubbed adolescents were learning the hula and how to make ti leaf skirts.

The visitors come and go at their leisure, taking in as much or as little as they please.

In every village, except the Marquesan tohua, there was a scheduled fashion show of native garb, a ceremonial canoe visit from another village, demonstrations of local crafts, a show of the cultural national dance, and some form of hands-on participation by the visitors.

The Marquesan village is left empty as an example of what can happen to the delicate structure of Polynesian culture. Once vigorous, now almost dead, it is unable to cope with the Western world.

Between 2PM and 5PM, villagers board double-hulled canoes to glide along the Center's waterways, singing and dancing as they cruise from one village to another. But you don't have to be in a village to see and hear; you can sit by the waterways and watch the colorful groups float by.

You can take a canoe tour of the microcosmic Polynesia from landings near the Tonga and Tahiti villages.

Along the paths are several booths where you can buy a cooling soft drink—no alcoholic beverages are sold in the Mormon-sponsored Center—or an ice cream. Snack bars offer sandwiches. A gift shop provides a get-something-to-take-home diversion.

Our favorite spot was a tucked away corner behind the Marquesan village. You take a little path that follows a descending waterway and leads up a knoll to a tiny pool of water surrounded by Norfolk pines. Benches overlook the BYU campus, providing a peaceful spot to rest or re-group.

We also liked the Village Plantation where many Pacific agricultural products are grown and displayed at a kiosk: three kinds of bananas—apple, williams, Chinese—star fruit, sour sop, breadfruit, sugar cane, kukui nut, pineapple, wood rose, tapioca, etc.

In essence, I think the Polynesian Cultural Center is successful because of its authenticity. In the last ten years we have traveled and written about most countries of the Pacific, including a series of seven travel experience books entitled *How To Get Lost And Found In ...* And the costumes and dances, the crafts and architecture, and the customs exhibited at the Center—although Fiji is not in Polynesia—have great integrity.

Mind you, it is all professionally staged, a Mormon tradition, but it is not Disneyland. It is real.

What is copied from Disneyland, and by every other successful theme park, is attention to immaculate grounds, plenty of drinking fountains and clean restrooms.

At 5PM there is a final parade of canoes, and at sunset a touch of Disneyland with a parade of a brass band. As it swings through the villages and through the middle of the entry complex, by the Hale Aloha, by the Gateway Center where people are queuing for dinner, the band sets the mood for a musical evening, drawing visitors into the parade amid much clapping of hands and laughter.

The Gateway Center serves an ample buffet dinner: salads, chicken, curries, homemade biscuits, fruit, an assortment of desserts, and soft drinks. No alcohol. No coffee.

Meanwhile, the brass band has ended its parade at a turn- of-the-century gazebo-styled bandstand (a 2P shot) to continue playing for the throngs awaiting the opening of the Pacific Pavilion where the show, "This Is Polynesia" is elaborately staged.

The extravagant show leans more to Hollywood than to the strum-an-ukulele and watch-the-hands authenticity of the Pacific, but the audience loves it.

Despite written and spoken requests not to use flashbulbs during the performance, the theater twinkles with a continual popping of camera lights. Do you think that line-up of Tahitian dancers is not going to get photographed to show the friends back in Osaka and Des Moines what the visitor was seeing in Hawaii? Not for a minute of it.

We do advise our friends *not* to drive home from the Polynesian Cultural Center after the show because the road down the east side of Oahu is along the coast, winding and narrow. To the first-time visitor especially, the route near Kaneohe is confusing, especially at night.

It is a trip that should be made and enjoyed in daylight.

We advise our friends to skip the dinner buffet and evening show, if they are driving. The option is to go by a tour bus, devote an entire afternoon—the Center does not open now until 12:30—and evening to the Center. Letting someone else do the driving back to the hotel after dark makes the trip easier and more enjoyable.

The present packaged price for admission, dinner and show is $36 plus $7 each for a round-trip bus fare. The individual prices are: admission $14, dinner $13, show $15.

Take your time driving down the east coast of Oahu. Pass through Punaluu, pretty name that means dived for coral, where many Honolulu people have second homes. "I am going to the country this weekend" means that the person is going to Punaluu or another of the nearby beaches.

The road sweeps around picturesque Kahana Bay, a photographic stop, maybe 2P for a good cameraman, and reminds us of beach scenes on Tahiti, only the sand is better here. Good picnic, fishing spot.

Farther down the highway, the Crouching Lion has been there forever. It used to be the only restaurant on the highway and was patronized by the locals in the country for the weekend but now it is a luncheon tour bus stop. Ideal setting, however, overlooking the shore and reef.

You pass several more picnic-inviting beaches—Kahana, Kaaawa, Swanzy—and many roadside stands. Much of the same junk you find in Waikiki is here, but you might want to pick up fresh fruit to take back to the hotel with you.

The lonely chimney stack is the remains of a former sugar mill and then you'll see offshore a small island shaped like a coolie's bonnet and aptly named Chinaman's Hat. It marks the entrance to Kaneohe Bay.

In the same area is the entrance to Kualoa Ranch where horseback riding in a rustic setting is available.

At the Hygienic Store, bear right on Highway-83, watch for the sign at the Valley of the Temples Memorial Park, and drive through the cemetery to the back to the Byodo-in Temple. This exact replica of a famous temple in Kyoto is made out of concrete to resist the water and termites of the area but it looks like timbered construction.

With the foreground of bridges and lily ponds filled with koi, gigantic, colored and costly carp, and the dramatic background of the Koolau Mountains, you have, on the right day, a 3P shot.

Small admission fee, but you get to bong the 3-ton bronze temple bell.

You might even encounter the "Birdman" of the Byodo-in, a sparrow of a man who talks to the birds. He calls the birds by name and they come and flutter around his head and perch on his shoulders. He also "calls" and feeds the fish.

This outgoing man's name is Hisa (meaning long), Yoshi (good). His interpretation of his oriental name is "Long live a good man."

Highway-83 connects with Highway-63, more commonly known as Likelike (pronounced "leaky-leaky") Highway, which takes you through the Wilson (named for a former mayor) Tunnel to H-1 and back to Waikiki.

The Waianae Coast Tour

The temptation for a local travel writer is to ignore the Waianae Coast because there have been several ugly incidents involving tourists in the area.

Yet, many of the beaches at Nanakuli and Maili and Makaha are as lovely as anything in Hawaii, and the winter surf at Makaha is famous. It is the place of surfing championship tournaments.

We used to go to Makaha and park a white convertible Thunderbird next to the beach, play cribbage and drink rum punch and swim and sun all day. We wouldn't dare do that anymore. What a shame. Too many tough locals, unemployed, frustrated, are apt to get into a joint of marijuana and a case of beer and—look-out. Still, there are many wonderful people in Waianae who would give you anything they had in the house. True Hawaiian spirit.

Certainly you can go to Makaha when there is a surfing contest.

But don't ever go at night.

What we still do and recommend to golfing friends is to spend a weekend at the Makaha Inn which is not on the coast but in a secluded, secure, beautifully landscaped valley a mile behind the village. Now managed by Sheraton, the hotel chain is bringing a level of operational standards to the Makaha property that had been missing.

Fine, big swimming pool. Two golf courses. The West Course, managed by the hotel, is the better of the two. The back nine is a humbler.

Tennis courts and horseback riding.

Our own drives for pleasure on a Sunday afternoon late usually take us up into the residential hills to see what is being built—particularly Waialae Iki because it is so new.

Watching the undulating ocean and the vistas of Oahu from Koko Head to Barber's Point change in the golden light as the sun starts to settle down for the night, enjoying the fresh air, it is a heavenly place.

It give substance to the local saying "Lucky you come Hawaii."

2. Molokai—
Friendly People,
Sometimes Friendly Mules

Shadow was not a real close acquaintance.

Although I was putting my life on his back, we never struck up what you could call a blood-brother friendship.

When I first mounted his back at the Molokai Mule Ride stables preparatory to taking a 3-mile ride down a cliff face with 26 hairpin turns to the isolated peninsula of the Kalaupapa leper settlement, I knew it was imperative to establish a position of immediate authority.

I started to take him on a turn around the corral. A firm circle to the right. A firm circle to the left. That sort of thing.

Shadow ignored all commands of reins, heels and voice and went resolutely to the lineup of other mules at the fence, and stood there. No circles.

The line of authority had been established.

We were at Kualapuu on the island of Molokai, about 50 miles from Honolulu, above the principal city of the island, Kaunakakai, which has a population of 2,231.

Our purpose was to enjoy the pleasures and pains of the famous Molokai Mule Ride.

Prior to meeting Shadow, we talked with Gena Sasada, the manager of the stables, a pleasant, articulate, part-Hawaiian lady, born into the Meyers family, long-time residents of this upper level of Molokai and owners of a cattle ranch, originally a sugar plantation.

"Our company took over the mule ride operation in 1983 and gave it more organization and a stronger marketing effort," she told us.

"We are licensed to take 34 riders down into Kalaupapa. Today we have 28 riders. The experience is becoming more and more popular and we are getting increases every month, so it is important that people make reservations.

"The rides go every day even if there is a light rain. We supply rainproof ponchos. The mule skinners decide if a ride should be canceled.

"We have 42 mules. They are still solid working animals after 20 years. It costs $500 and up to replace a good mule. We buy them at Bishop, California which is the mule capital of the world."

(I had delved into the library to update myself on muleology before leaving home. A male donkey or ass is a jackass. Crossing a jackass with a mare, a female horse, produces a mule. Crossing a stallion, a male horse, with a female ass produces a hinny, somewhat rare. The resultant mules and hinnies are seldom fertile and don't reproduce. Among the gift items in the stable shop is a green visor bearing the legend: "A Good Ass Is Hard To Find", a legend not found in my encyclopedia.)

Each rider signs a liability release form which doubled as his "boarding pass" and is handed over, upon selection by weight and riding experience, to a mule skinner who helps him mount the mule.

The head mule skinner, bald and bow-legged, gives instructions before the departure.

"These mules are like little children. You can't let them do everything they want to do." (He didn't know Shadow.)

"They will want to feed all of the time and put their heads down to graze and if you don't have hold of the reins, the reins will fall over the animal's head and you are in trouble.

"Put the reins around the horn on the saddle, that way they can't drop their heads. Don't pass. Stay in a single file. These animals are not very smart, but they know what they are doing. Trust them. The only accidents we have had on the trail is when the intelligence of the rider is lower than that of the mule." (Shadow gave me a long look.)

We left in single file with a lead mule skinner, another riding in the middle of the pack, and a sweep at the back.

The ride started along the road and then cut into a dirt trail which led to the edge of cliff. We started down.

Fortunately at that juncture, we couldn't see over the cliff face.

At the first hairpin turn, we could. Down below—way, way down—was the peninsula of Kalaupapa shoving out into the sea. Beyond the hairpin turn there was a void. An empty void, as the redundant cliche states for emphasis. Like my stomach, at the time.

Actually the turn, like many of the subsequent turns, was highly

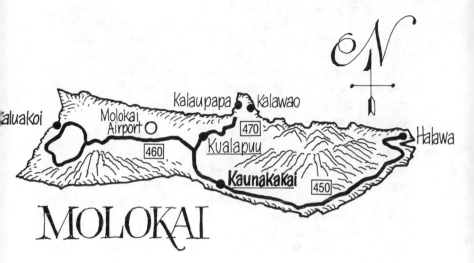

banked with earth and deeply rutted. The hairpin turns were not
the problem. The trail, from a hundred years of usage, was too
well used and was worn down to loose, large rocks on the straight-
aways, much like a toboggan slide. The mules had to pick their
way cautiously and carefully over every rock and boulder down
the path.

The incline was often severe and the riding technique, according
to the mule skinners, was to hold onto the rear part of the saddle
to keep your weight off of the mule's forequarters as much as
possible.

My confidence increased with Shadow's evident experience and,
as the tension eased, I began to appreciate the scenery. The sight
of the surf below. The blue ocean beyond. It was nicely cool
because we were always in the shadow of the cliff, out of the sun.

Half way down, the caravan stopped for a rest. We couldn't
dismount but we could take pictures. The steeple of the village of
Kalaupapa could now be seen clearly, as could the airstrip where
daily flights bring in supplies to the colony, as well as medics,

tourists, residents and relatives.

The lepers still residing at Kalaupapa number a mere hundred, and all of them are well over 50 years old. When they are gone, the peninsula will be maintained by the National Park Service.

The former patients of what is now called Hansen's disease are free to come and go, their infliction arrested by sulfone drugs, but most chose to stay because of the embarrassment of disfigurement and the feeling that Kalaupapa is home.

Slowly, the string of mules and riders descended the cliff, riders of all configurations and in all kinds of outfits and almost of all ages. Riders less than 16 years of age are not allowed, due to health regulations enacted by the government. Riders weighing more than 225 pounds are not allowed, due to health regulations enacted by the mules.

We were surrounded by brush, vines and scrub kiawe trees with wild flowers growing out of the cliff face. Now we could hear the sound of surf.

In a little over an hour's time we were at sea level and riding along the beachfront another mile to a rendezvous point where we dismounted, stiffly, and waddled over to two waiting vans.

I had been so concerned about the mule ride that I hadn't focused on the more important part of the day: a three-hour tour of Kalaupapa, including lunch, and an exposure to one of the cruelest slices of history in Hawaii's annals.

In the middle of the 19th century a horrible disease began to appear among the Hawaiians who had been cursed by being so pure that they couldn't withstand any of the white man's afflictions: measles, typhoid, venereal diseases. Their numbers dropped from a population in the hundreds of thousands to around 50,000 within a hundred years after Captain Cook landed.

The new disease was called *Mai Pake*, or the Chinese disease, because it was well known in China. Trade with China was frequent and Chinese laborers were coming to Hawaii in large numbers. Mai Pake was leprosy. The disease mutilated the body. Fingers would drop off. Faces would be horribly disfigured and scarred. Early death was predictable.

The disease reached such large proportions that, in 1885, an Act to Prevent the Spread of Leprosy was passed by the legislature and approved by the king. In January of the following year, the first group of lepers was put ashore in the most isolated piece of land imaginable, a peninsula imprisoned by towering, wind-blown seas, and cut off from the rest of Molokai by an almost insurmountable cliff.

Fear of the disease surpassed all reason. Lepers were literally thrown into the sea to swim to safety or drown. The wooden cages in which they had been confined on the crossing, now "unclean," were thrown overboard after them.

Little help, if any, was offered to the patients. No medical supervision. The meagerest of rations.

Children were separated from their parents, wives from husbands, lovers from lovers. Bounty hunters were hired to bring in suspected lepers who were clinging to their families.

Drunkenness, orgies, anarchy followed on the Peninsula of Little Hope. Into this caldron of hell stepped a barrel-shaped Belgian peasant, Joseph de Veuster, a Catholic brother in the order of St. Mary's, who volunteered to come to the Hawaii mission in place of his real brother, also a clergyman, who had fallen ill. In Honolulu he was ordained into the priesthood as Father Damien.

He was assigned to Molokai where, at first, he built churches for flocks of the faithful. His principal work, however, was at Kalaupapa where, at the age of 33, he became the shepherd of the leper colony. Father Damien was the organizer, the comforter, the adviser, and eventually, the martyr. He shared everything he had with the lepers and, disregarding any steps of caution, finally fell victim to the disease ten years after he stepped ashore at Kalaupapa. He was dead five years later.

Father Damien's name has been put forward for sainthood. (He wasn't a saint to the Board of Health which he constantly badgered, or to the superintendents in the colony whose authority he constantly usurped, or to the private donors whose contributions he dictatorially diverted.)

What the Belgian peasant priest represented was self-sacrifice, bravery in the face of community fear, sensitivity to the cause of the helpless. For these reasons, his statue stands in the courtyard of Hawaii's state capitol and a duplicate in the national capitol at Washington D.C.

The vans took us into the center of Kalaupapa for refreshments after the two-hour mule train. A sign in Rea's Store and Bar stated that the Bud was out until the arrival of the next barge.

The village of Kalaupapa today has a hospital, stores, churches, library, museum, and a fire station with a fire truck donated by a visitor from Chicago, a memorial hall donated by the Paschoal family. It is a complete community. At one time there was a girls' school in the middle of the village and a boys' school at a safe distance in the "country" but today's aging population has removed the necessity for schools.

The original leper colony was located across the peninsula, at Kalawao, where, when Father Damien died, there were neat clapboard houses, churches and a hospital. (You can see the colony as it existed then at the Damien Museum next door to St. Patrick's Church in Honolulu, Waialae Avenue at 7th Street. There are photographs of the colony and memorabilia of Father Damien.)

Today, nothing remains at Kalawao except the well kept renovated church of St. Philomena which was built by Damien. Alongside the church are his grave and black headstone, although the body was removed in 1936 and returned to Belgium with full military honors, on orders from President Franklin D. Roosevelt.

We sat in the church and listened to Issac K. Keao, a leper and owner of Ike's Scenic Tours. He also owns the town's garage and service station.

He had contacted leprosy in Honolulu at age 11, had spent three years in a Honolulu hospital, and then was shipped to Kalaupapa at 14—to die.

"You can't imagine what it was like for a 14-year-old boy. People were dying every day. They didn't die of leprosy. You never die of leprosy. You die because the body is so weakened by the disease that you die of a cold, pneumonia, or TB. Any slight infection can kill you. You have no resistance. In the hospital we were used as guinea pigs. Try anything. They didn't have any idea how to help us. Finally the war led to the use of sulfone drugs and one of them labeled DDS proved to be completely effective in arresting leprosy.

"Today, I'd rather be a leper in Kalaupapa than have herpes or AIDS in Los Angeles. I'm safer.

"Only I don't know my relatives any more. I know this couple here sitting on this bench better than I know any of my relatives. My relatives don't want me to see or touch their children. That's the hardest part."

Jack London, in his time the most popular writer in America, loved Hawaii and stopped off in the islands during a tour of the South Pacific in his yacht, the *Snark*, in 1907. A determined adventurer, he obtained permission from the Board of Health to visit the colony although he had earlier described it to Charmian from their passing yacht as "the pit of hell, the most cursed place on earth."

He returned with his wife in July on a steamer to spend a week, and found Kalaupapa a charming village. They were serenaded by patients, witnessed a Fourth of July parade, participated in an organized shoot at the Kalaupapa Rifle Club and served as judges at a horse race where the present airstrip is located.

Although warned of the danger, he was determined to leave Kalaupapa via the cliff trail which the couple negotiated safely on mules, although London had to dismount several times to allow his mule to make the tight hairpin turns.

Since that time the cliff route has been known as the Jack London Trail.

We returned to the Jack London Trail after a box lunch at a seaside pavilion and a last drive through the village.

The ride back seemed much shorter and surer. In less than an hour we were inside the corral.

Once Shadow was divested of me and my saddle he rushed into the barn for evening oats without so much as a goodbye.

Riders are asked to fill out a questionnaire afterwards and I asked Gena to let me see a collection of answers. The majority of them went along this vein:

"The best tour investment I have ever made."

"An incredible day with a great mule."

"It was the best pain I've ever experienced."

"Just great. The most interesting day I've spent in Hawaii."

One commentator missed the point of the trip entirely: "Would like to take the trip again but to stay on the beach and skinny dip and sun bathe."

Riders are given a certificate from the Order of Alii Mule Skinners of Molokai, having "faced the obstacles, precipices and hazards of this treacherous trail and endured the vicissitudes of the narrow passage between rim and destination."

Each rider also receives a bumper sticker: "I'D RATHER BE RIDING A MULE ON MOLOKAI."

Molokai Mule Ride, P.O. Box 200, Kualapuu, Molokai, Hawaii 96757. Telephone: (808) 567-6088. Toll free from Oahu: 537-1845.

Tell Shadow I sent you.

If you go beyond the stables on the highway, you come to Palaau State Park and the lookout over Kalaupapa. Inside the forest reserve is a 3P oddity. The phallic stone. A very large phallic stone. There is no mistaking this for anything but a phallic stone.

The legend goes that a childless woman who spends the night beneath this monument to manhood will soon find herself pregnant. Others say that all a woman has to do is to rub her hands over the giant rock. I know women who won't even look at it for fear of a late crop.

A pleasant pavilion inside the park makes an ideal picnic stop. It's okay to pick lilikoi from the vines and eat the yellow guava that has fallen from the trees.

Molokai is relatively small. Ten miles wide and 36 miles long. When you are in Palaau State Park on the north side in the middle of the island, surrounded by paperbark trees, the tradewinds talking to themselves through cool branches, you might think you were on an Oregon mountain.

But go to the west end of the island, within sight of Oahu, and the country is mountainless and arid. You would think that you were in an African veldt.

The east end, however, rises to the sky again and you can drive to the edge of Halawa Valley and look down on a carpet of greenery, once the home of prosperous taro farmers who abandoned the valley after the 1946 tidal wave. At the head of the valley are two magnificent waterfalls. If you are rugged, you can descend to the valley floor over a narrow but paved road with many blind curves and hike into the waterfalls. The beach is a public park and popular with campers and local picnickers. For most visitors, including ourselves, the picture from the top is enough.

At one time the lush valley was the center of Molokai's population and remnants of giant heiaus can still be found.

The flavor of Molokai is low key, country quiet, non pushy, non touristy, non commercial. You don't go to Molokai to find action—unless you like to hunt. It is an island where you have time to relax, where you set your own pace, where you let the island come to you.

Kaunakakai, the main village, sets the pace. (Kaunakakai is another pretty name on the tongue. Try it. "Cow-na-ka-kigh") It is a one-street town with touches of modern architecture accenting the older "down country" store fronts. The townsfolk still go to the post office to get their mail and socialize with friends while, incidentally, doing the marketing.

The Molokai Bakery is well known for its bread—you can buy it at the airport—and the Midnight Cafe where a neighbor, Shirley Carter, said she had the best fresh fish dinner in her life.

At one time, the economy of the island was healthy, even prosperous, from the major pineapple plantations operated by Libby and Del Monte. The demise of the plantations has meant the flight of the island's young labor force to work elsewhere, and the island population has decreased from 10,000 to about 6,000.

Diversified farming and tourism will shape the new future of Molokai.

Two moderately priced accommodations are on the fringe of Kaunakakai, the Pau Hana Inn and the Hotel Molokai, but don't expect the familiar amenities of a full scale resort complex such as those at Sheraton Molokai on the west end of the island.

Molokai Ranch is the largest landowner on the island with about 46,500 acres. In addition to grazing some 6,000 head of cattle, the ranching company has formed a joint venture with Louisiana Land and Exploration Company to develop a planned resort called Kaluakoi.

The first increment includes the Sheraton Molokai Hotel, an 18-hole golf course (signs warn golf cart drivers that turkey and deer have right-away path crossings on the fairways) and four night lighted tennis courts. Kepuhi Beach, in front of the hotel, is a family beach, a place to build sand castles and cast for surf fish. People from Honolulu like the resort as a take-a-break weekend spot. The Ohia Lodge, the principal restaurant in the hotel, is a relaxed, pleasant room which had a good chef the last time we were there. (He didn't overcook the vegetables.) Rattan furniture bar. Evening music. Nice place.

Molokai Ranch also has a wildlife park with a 400-animal population of giraffe, Barbary sheep, Indian black buck, eland, sable antelope, oryx, ibex, greater kudu, sika, mouflon, ostrich, rhea and axis deer.

This is not a drive-yourself-through park. You go in an escorted touring van. Three departures in the morning. Three departures in the afternoon. We booked for the last tour one afternoon, but that was canceled because the driver had to report for his early evening shift as a waiter in the Ohia Room.

Laid back Molokai.

The highway from Kaunakakai to the arid west end is not particularly scenic except in a rugged sort of way.

Beyond Kaunakakai, going towards Halawa Valley, there are interesting spots along Highway-45 that fringe the southern coastline.

Ancient Hawaiian fishponds once dominated the shoreline (history recorded as many as 54). The remains of many can still be seen from the road; a few are still in commercial use.

Farther along is the Our Lady of Sorrows Church, one of the churches built by Father Damien when he was still physically able to leave Kalaupapa and minister to the rest of his Molokai parish.

Also, there might still be an HVB marker at the spot where, in July 1927, aviators Ernie Smith and Emory Bronte finished the first civilian Mainland-to-Hawaii flight upside down in the kiawe trees after crash landing, out of gas, following a 25-hour/2-minute crossing from Oakland, California.

It was a time when headlines were focusing on Hawaii.

In 1927, Lindbergh had made his historic crossing to Paris in the single-engine *Spirit of St. Louis* The flight inspired James Dole, president of Hawaiian Pineapple Company, to offer a $25,000 prize to the winner and a $10,000 second prize in the Dole Derby, the first similiar flight from California to Hawaii.

Honor and glory were greater than cash and two military flyers made the flight successfully prior to the start of the race, as did the two civilians, Smith and Bronte.

The Derby itself was a calamity. Disabled airplanes and dead bodies were scattered from Oakland to Honolulu. Planes crashed on take-off, planes disappeared into the ocean, rescue planes met with disaster looking for contestants' planes that had already met with disaster.

I used to see Emory Bronte frequently in the building where we both worked. I saw him as a living legend. An easy thing to do because he had the face of a hero: calm, handsome, far younger than his true years.

3. Maui—
Two Islands
For the Price of One

From the top of Haleakala National Park the vistas on a clear day are staggering.

The problem is that there is seldom a clear day from the summit. If the 10,000-foot mountain is not under siege by a rain storm or, at the least, a mountain mist then the lower levels will be surrounded by a halo of clouds, like a white brim on a green-brown hat, cutting off all views below 6,000 feet.

If you should luck into a rare phenomenon of clear weather, you would quickly appreciate that Maui is, essentially, two islands. There is a West Maui in the distance while you are standing on East Maui.

In between the two islands there is an isthmus of land covered with sugar cane that used to be ocean.

The body of water you see to the south of the isthmus is Maalaea Bay, famous as the breeding and calving site of the humpback whales in the winter months, December to April. The body of water beyond the bay, between Maui and the islands of Lanai and Kahoolawe, is Lahaina Roads, once filled with whaling ships and now bordered by resort developments equally famous to travel agents: Kihei, Wailea, Kaanapali, Napili, Kapalua.

To the north of the isthmus are Maui's principal towns of Kahului and the capital of Maui, Wailuku. Kahului Bay forms the harbor for the island and the airport is not far away.

East Maui is another planet. Still agriculturally oriented, it is a land of cowboys and Hawaiians and old traditions. On the back side of East Maui is the peaceful community of Hana where time just ticks along.

Haleakala is a fitting mountain for East Maui because it appears indomitable, a broad, towering mass of earth and rock that protects a dormant volcanic crater larger than the island of Manhattan.

Maui residents and veteran visitors have all notched their belts with a pre-dawn drive up the 38-mile road to the observatory on top to witness the sun come up and fill the darkness of the crater with pink shadows and then touches of gold and then a flood of blazing yellow light. Put it on your list.

75

Besides the dawn experience, there is another rare adventure available on Haleakala: cruising to the bottom on a guided bicycle tour.

One October day, the Lady Navigator and I signed on with "Cruiser Bob" for the tour in a shaky spirit of research.

At 10,000 feet, at nine o'clock in the morning, it is cool even in Hawaii, especially at the crest of Haleakala where swirling winds were creeping up my seldom-worn, mothball-scented sweater.

Apprehension had been creeping up my backbone too since the moment the van deposited the other riders and the battery of bikes on the mountain top preparatory for the winding, curving, 38-mile ride down the macadam road to the sea-level village of Paia.

"A drop of 10,000 feet in 38 miles. There is nothing else like it in the world." It is a bit too long to include on a tombstone but would ring nicely in an obit column.

My rationed equipment consisted of a plastic racing helmet, a windbreaker bearing the logo "Cruiser Bob," garden gloves, and a chocolate bar for an energy crisis.

What I needed instead was a stirrup cup of cognac.

I remembered with anxiety the liability release we had signed at 7AM over hot coffee and sweet pastries at the assembly office in Lahaina.

> "Life is full of risks, each person makes choices to take action in life by weighing the benefits versus the risks ... the Haleakala mountain roadways contain steep grades, sharp turns, and occasional wet slippery pavement. Rain and windy weather conditions are a risk and motor vehicles, tour vans, and buses can also be a risk."

Yeah.

The realization comes to you that you could go out of control on a turn, put your body into the windshield of an oncoming Gray Line bus, thereby ruining the driver's vision and spoiling everybody's day. Especially yours.

It never happens. The whole three-hour adventure is a piece of coasting cake.

The bicycle is a rebuilt Schwinn cruiser with balloon tires, raised handlebars with an English nanny's wire basket between the

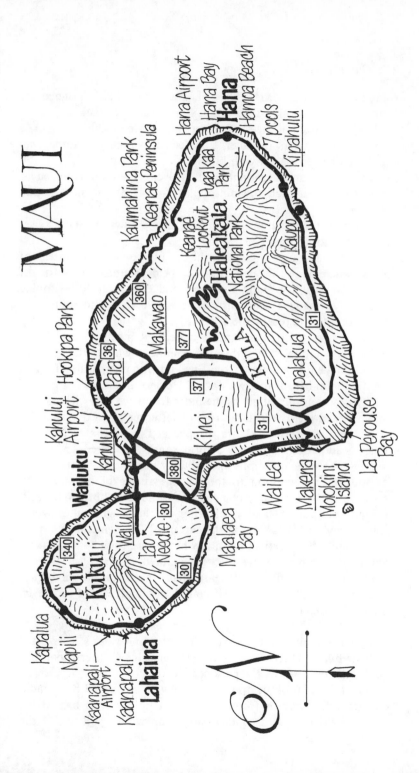

handles complete with tinkle bell, and megabrakes designed for motorcycles ... brakes that would stop a Sherman tank.

We had started at the the Cruiser Bob office in Lahaina, picked up two more riders in Kihei, transferred in Paia to another van pulling a trailer loaded with bikes.

On the way up the mountain the driver talked about the sugar cane fields and then the pineapple growing at the next higher elevation.

"Here is the Veterans' Cemetery, also known as the Cruiser Bob's Memorial Park." Ho, ho, ho.

We drove through Makawao, the cowboy town in the district of Kula, where Hawaii's best rodeo is held around the Fourth of July, past Seabury Hall, a school, and the Oscar Rice Roping Arena. We made a right turn off the side road and joined the main road to the top of the crater.

"You have to look around you here. Remember some landmarks. If you don't make this turn coming down, you'll end up in Kahului. We had a couple from England who missed the turn and we didn't find them for two days." Ho, ho, ho.

"They weren't as funny as the older fellow we had who sneezed and his false teeth fell out and went clattering down the road."

At the 7,000-foot level, we stopped at the Haleakala National Park headquarters where a helpful ranger answered—most patiently—the same questions undoubtedly put to him by thousands of tourists. In addition to the usual maps, exhibits and clean restrooms, there is a pen of nene birds, the state bird of Hawaii, behind the station, and a planting of the fragile silversword, found only on Haleakala, at the entrance. The nene, at one time, was thought to be extinct but a few birds were found at Haleakala and they have been successfully regenerated.

Through the exhibits you learn that Haleakala National Park has over 27,000 acres in its boundaries and is one of seven national parks in Hawaii.

At the summit, the bikes were unloaded and rider's seats fitted to their bikes. There were fourteen riders plus Cruiser Mike, our guide, the limit set by the park service.

The van that took us up would follow us down and be in radio contact with Mike in front. In case traffic piled up behind the van, the driver would contact Mike who would pull us off the road to let the traffic move by.

The company is very careful to be a good neighbor—not an irritant—to other people on the highway.

"Keep your eyes on the road and stay in a single line formation. Never pass another bike. Lean into the curves and keep your hands on the handlebars at all time. When you use the hand-brakes, use them gently but firmly, applying equal pressure with each hand so that you have equal pressure on each wheel. We'll take a short run-down to the next observation station just below us. Let's go."

At 10,000 feet your breath comes laboriously as you try to force the thin air into your lungs. Fright doesn't help you breathe easier either.

We peeled off in jet fighter formation and made a steep descent in swooping curves to an observatory not more than a mile away where we parked the bikes and went to the rim of the crater for still another view of the ever changing vistas.

Haleakala ("House of the Sun") is an impressive canyon. Encompassing 19 square miles, Haleakala is the world's largest dormant volcano. It last erupted in 1790. Within the crater are cinder cones which catch the light and cast shadows. The walls are sheer lava and the bottom of the crater is a blanket of black cinders. You can understand why astronauts trained for the moon surface venture in Haleakala.

A long time ago, I had taken two subteen daughters on a three-day, two-night horseback ride into the crater where we stayed at two of the three cabins maintained by the park service. It was a unique experience and one which the three of us most remember because of the nearness and the clearness of the rim-to-rim roof of stars at night.

You can hike through Haleakala, staying at the cabins if you win out in a lottery for reservations. Or, you can take a helicopter and fly through, but not land in, the crater.

You can go luxury all the way on a three-day horseback trek into the crater, accompanied by a chef whose menus designed to please your predetermined palate are enhanced with Dom Perignon champagne. Cost $1,500 for two, sleeping, not in cabins, but in the most ultra camping facilities.

Another outfitter offers morning or full day or overnight rides into the crater.

"On your bikes!" came the call. Thirty-seven miles to go.

Soon we were slaloming downhill again, not speeding but not losing any time either. The pleasure increased as the miles sped by. I learned how to sit up when I wanted to slow down without using the hand brake, letting the air against my body act as a wind brake. Leaning low over the handles cut the wind resistance and increased my speed.

I liked staying at the end of the line watching the riders ahead and below me fly through the curves single file like a well-trained flock of helmeted birds.

In no time we were back at the ranger station. The back of the van opened to offer cold drinks or hot coffee. Time for the chocolate bar.

The stretch of highway after the ranger station was one of the best because the paved road was wide and the curves broad and gentle as we glided down through a mist of clouds and reached the tree line of eucalyptus, their aroma even more pungent in the moist air. It was delicious.

We were out of the park now and in cattle country. During World War II, ammunition was stored in the surrounding hills and concrete bunkers can still be found.

Ranch land dissolved into truck farms and commercial flower nurseries and the air was tinged with fragrances of blossoms.

At Sunshine Market, a fruit and vegetable stand, we stopped for a picnic lunch, peeled off layers of sweaters and jackets, and sprawled on the grass munching sandwiches and sipping soft drinks. It was warm now and, having been up since six, a tempting time to doze on the lawn.

The stand did a booming business in coconuts and Maui onions to mail home and to friends, and to a lesser degree, in protea, Hawaii's newest exotic flower, an immigrant from South America that thrives in the cool Kula air. Protea is a strange, other-world flower, its unusual blossom looking like an artichoke dressed in a ballet tutu. It is becoming increasingly popular as an export blossom and has the potential of becoming as profitable as Hawaii's orchids and anthuriums.

Feeling a bit logy, we remounted after snapping photographs of each other, and started the last leg.

Before making the jog off the main highway to the secondary

roadway where the English couple had gone straight ahead, we encountered the only patch of rough in the entire downhill thrill. Rough is too strong a word. Energetic, perhaps. The road dipped and rose again and, while it did not look too difficult a stretch, our bikes were equipped for cruising not pedaling, and we had to dismount finally and walk a few hundred yards to the top of the hillock. That was the only pedaling and walking we did in 38 miles.

Descending a steep grade into Makawao, Cruiser Mike had us cautiously ride our brakes to the stop sign at the intersection. He didn't want anybody barreling through the stop sign, nor did he want us strung out in too long a line interrupting traffic.

He gave us 15 minutes to browse Makawao's shops. We rushed to Komoda's Store and Bakery for freshly made macadamia nut cookies—they are also famous for buns. Once, a manager of an elegant Maui hotel took us to Makawao to eat at a funky, two-scoops-of-rice cafe, Kitada's on Baldwin Street, where we had chopped steak and onions and cold beer out of the can. "The experience of a basic eatatorium," he said, "is good for one's perspective."

After Makawao, the fleet of bikes dropped down past the historic Makawao Union Church, the cemetery, past the upper level pineapple fields, the lower level sugar cane fields and into little Paia. Safe and sound.

The most common remark was that everyone expected to be seat-sore and nobody was.

Enough time before going back to the hotel was allotted for poking around Paia or going next door to Dillon's and having a "Downhill Cruiser" which is dark rum, Seven-Up, and Rose's lime juice. Terrible.

We took the break to talk to Bob Kiger who introduced downhill biking on Haleakala with phenomenal success, escorting 5,000 riders in his first year of operation at about $75 per head.

Kiger, 38, is a medium sized man with a medium head of hair, intense, wholly involved in his enterprise. He was born on Manhattan and raised in LA. His background in television and his distaste for traveling the same road twice were factors contributing to the embryo idea. He could see the optical pleasure that Haleakala would give downhill bike riders, yet the return trip would be an entirely different experience coasting down on a bicycle as opposed to driving up in a van.

"Part of the secret of the success lies in the bike. We have taken the basic frame of a Schwinn cruiser and redesigned it, starting with the drumbrakes. You'd wear out a coaster brake in one trip. We have never had a brake failure.

"Saving weight was not a factor. The bikes weigh about 55 pounds each. What we wanted was durability and dependability so we have stainless steel parts throughout the bikes. One will last about 30,000 miles.

"What the ride provides is an experience that a grandfather and a grandson can share equally together. Older people actually do better on the ride because they have better concentration. Young people tend to be careless.

"Women in the 35 to 55 age bracket are wonderful. They come in afraid, scared, unsure. When they come down off the mountain, they are blooming. They become our biggest boosters and many come back again and again."

The idea continues to grow. When we last talked to Kiger, he had 75 bikes and expected to do a volume of 30,000 riders for the year by offering a variety of different times and options for the downhill ride.

An unmatched experience.

Cruiser Bob's Rent-A-Bike, 505 Front Street, Lahaina, Maui, Hawaii 96751 (808) 677-7717.

Adventures on Horseback is the contact for the $1,500 ride for three days into Haleakala operated by Frank Levinson whose bread-and-butter ride is not into Haleakala but to the Haiku waterfall, a four-hour ride through fern forests, timber stands of eucalyptus trees, along clear running streams, ending at the isolated waterfall for a refreshing swim. Cost is $95. Take your own picnic, swimming suit and towel. (I know his ride is popular because when I tried to reach him by telephone, (242-7445) his answering service lady said he was the busiest tour operator on her roster.)

Another Maui stable offering half-day and full-day rides into Haleakala is Pony Express Tours, P.O. Box 507, Makawao, Maui, Hawaii 96768. (808) 667-2202.

A third option is overnight camping trips from Kaupo Ranch, departing from the south end of the crater and riding through the Kaupo Gap. Write Charles Aki, Jr. c/o Kaupo Store, Kaupo,

Maui, Hawaii 96713. 248-8209.

The Center of Maui

The attraction of Maui's beaches, golf courses and weather is evident in the number of hotels and condominiums—and the airport.

The airport at Kahului is a mess.

It was built as the Neighbor Islands' first modern airport and was a symbol of progress and pride. At the time, the new airport—concrete-clean, sweeping lines, extraordinarily spacious—was used only by the inter-island carriers, Aloha Airlines and Hawaiian Airlines,

Today, there are several other interisland carriers in addition to daily jumbo jet flights to and from the Mainland. The result is a cobweb of airplanes, baggage, frustrated people, shuttles, rental car vans, buses and lost children—a mess.

Once clear of the airport, Maui becomes easy.

The single road out of the airport forks into a three-way intersection. The road continuing straight ahead goes to Kihei and Wailea and branches off to Lahaina and West Maui. The road to the left goes to Hana. The road to the right goes into Kahului, the urban core of the island and a major shopping district.

On the way into Kahului look for the Aloha Restaurant, reported to us as having the best Hawaiian food on the island, which we tried. A concrete block charmless building, it nonetheless has good laulau and poi, and fantastic chicken long-rice.

Up the hill from Kahului is Wailuku, the capital city of the islands of Maui, Molokai and Lanai. Formerly the commercial center of an agricultural community, it is now only the political center of an increasingly visitor-oriented community.

On the way to Iao Needle on Highway-32, just after the intersection in Wailuku, stop if you have the time, at the Hale Hoikeike of the Maui Historical Society.

At one time the building was the seminary for young royal Hawaiian ladies and then the home of Edward Bailey, the former schoolmaster, who bought the schoolhouse and became a sugar planter and an amateur painter. His paintings are exhibited in an attached wing gallery.

In addition to the historical items found in the museum there is a three-dimensional map of the nearby, controversial island of

Kahoolawe. Once upon a long, long time ago, the 13-by-5-mile island supported a thriving Hawaiian community but now is uninhabited except for wild goats and is used for bombing practice by the U.S. Navy. Landing on Kahoolawe is forbidden, a sore point with segments of the Hawaiian society which claim the bombing is destroying sacred artifacts.

Surrounding the topographical map in the middle of a room are cases displaying artifacts found on the island, their locations keyed to the map. The artifacts were donated by the U.S. Navy. (Typical miscellany found while writing books: the ancient name of Kahoolawe was Kohemalamalama, meaning bright vagina.)

The valley of the Iao Needle is the caldera of the Puu Kukui volcano which formed West Maui, and is second only to Mt. Waialeale on Kauai in annual rainfall. You should take the time to drive into Kepaniwai Park, a curious melange of ethnic sub-parks including pavilions of Portuguese, Chinese, Hawaiian and Japanese architecture.

A curiosity near the bend in the road approaching the Iao Needle parking lot is a rocky profile on a cliff face that resembles John F. Kennedy. You look through the iron tube fixed on a stanchion in the ground to find it.

The Needle itself is a basalt rock covered with green moss, dwarfed by the surrounding cliffs of the former volcano although the needle itself is over 1200 feet high. You reach an observation point from the large parking lot on a path that looks down on a pleasant stream and then climbs to an area affording a 1P possibility across the valley towards Wailuku and Kahului. That is, weather permitting.

The state park is so narrow that it lies in a near perpetual shadow. A somber moody place, befitting its historic and bloody battle in which Kamehameha ravaged the Maui forces so badly that the river ran red, thus giving Wailuku its name: water of destruction.

The highway from Wailuku towards Lahaina goes through the tiny village of Waikapu, immortalized in a favorite Hawaiian tune: "I Love a Pretty Maui Girl. She comes from Waikapu."

It is immortalized in my mind by a word picture painted by an oldtimer who told me that when he was young, Waikapu was a plantation village with plantation housing. At the end of the work day, pau hana time, the children, scrubbed and bathed and dressed in neat bathrobes and nightgowns, walked down to the open air theater, sat on wooden benches and watched a motion picture.

The name of Waikapu will be more easily remembered in the future because it is the location of a brilliantly assembled, $6 million, 60-acre, agricultural showcase with free admission, the Hawaiian Tropical Plantation.

When we were in Queensland researching that country for our fifth travel book, *How to Get Lost and Found in Australia*, we came across Sunshine Plantation, a most colorful attraction with a collection of agricultural products, both raw and processed, to buy, to see growing in a microcosmic environment, and to sample in the cafeteria. I remember we skipped lunch and had gigantic fruit sundaes with whipped cream and nuts on top, products grown at the Sunshine Plantation and viewed from an open-air sugar cane train.

The Taylor family, creators of the Australian plantation, in partnership with C. Brewer, one of the major sugar growers of Hawaii, developed a similar attraction in Waikapu. Maui Plantation opened in the summer of 1984 to immediate success. As it should have.

At no expense to the visitor, the Plantation gives an overview of the agricultural and aquacultural products of Hawaii. You have the experience of learning about and seeing how the products grow, of touching and tasting and, optionally, of buying the state's produce.

The first building is the "Tropical Market" featuring the fresh Hawaiian fruits and vegetables and flowers, plus their processed items, to take back to your hotel room for feasting or to send home to the relatives. (There is a mailing service by the door.) Glamorous fruits made into glamorous jams, jellies, syrups; pineapple wine and other exotic alcoholic beverages made from roots and stalks; macadamia nuts, roasted or glazed or chocolate coated; taro and banana chips or sun-dried pineapple chunks; the famous Maui potato chips. It's all here, including exotic plants.

Fifty yards away is a circle of pavilions called the Plantation Village where industry exhibits are mounted, each giving the background on the care and feeding of Hawaii's prime export items: sugar cane, Kona coffee, the root plants such as taro and ginger, fruits such as papaya, avocado, guava and lilikoi, the macadamia nut, flowers such as orchids, anthurium and protea. Aquaculture, too, is featured in a series of cascading ponds in the center core of Plantation Village. Here you see how wet taro, a staple from which poi is made, is grown and how commercial farming of prawns, shrimp, mullet and oysters is carried out.

The Village is as informative to local people as it is to visitors. I had no concept of the diversity and the importance of Hawaii's aquaculture industry, for example.

The only major industry missing is pineapple, if you can believe it. Industry leaders declined the free space saying they didn't need the exposure. (Dumb. The Plantation will draw nearly a million visitors a year.)

Having inspected the Village exhibits, the next logical activity to engage in was the Plantation's 30-minute tour on the "Tropical Express," a canopied caravan of trolleys pulled by a tractor. A $5 charge.

Our tour, conducted by a giggling Auntie Kahiki, took us through planted sections of all of the produce featured in the Village, *plus* pineapple. Although recently planted, many of the crops appeared mature. The papaya trees looked as if they were developed by and for giraffes. The lilikoi (passion fruit) vines had been staked like grape vineyards. We stopped in a banana patch (apple bananas, William bananas) for photos and a sampling of pieces of iced fresh fruit.

The tour and the giggling continued on through an avocado grove, mango trees (we can't export mangoes to the Mainland because of the fruit fly), past guava trees, a macadamia nut farm and, finally, through the tropical nursery.

The Tropical Express stopped at the Lagoon, which also serves as a water reservoir, in front of the Tropical Restaurant.

The restaurant, a big, cool, Polynesian-styled building in a neo-plantation motif, is a place to try fresh Hawaiian fruit in parfaits or salads. Have a buffet breakfast or lunch.

A first class attraction which is memorable.

If you luck out and find Leihuanani Bissen, the on-site public relations beauty and a former Miss Hawaii, you won't forget her either.

Pretty Resorts vs Pretty Bad Condos of East Maui

The highway from Wailuku to the Maui Plantation is High-

way-30 and its official name is Honoapiilani. South of the plantation, turn left on Kihei Road and head southeast along the waters
of Maalaea Bay to Kihei and Wailea.

Witness a classic case history of unplanned versus planned
development.

Kihei was an open market to every condominium operator who
came down the pike. The result along Kihei Road is a jumble of
apartment buildings of every size and style, a visual mishmash of
diverse and sometimes questionable taste.

Beyond Kihei, on the other hand, you can see what taste and
money can buy. You can travel the Clutter Condo Route along
the coast or take Highway-31 directly to Wailea, sparing yourself
the sight of Kihei until you feel stronger.

Wailea, a development by Alexander & Baldwin, another of
Hawaii's Big Five, represents tons of money and years of patient
study and planning and a library of coordinated blueprints.

The result at Wailea is an eye-pleasing, peaceful, beautiful
oasis.

There are two first class hotels, the Intercontinental and the
Stouffer's Wailea Beach Resort, two excellent 18-hole golf
courses, the Blue and the Orange, 14 tennis courts, three of which
are grass courts, the only grass resort courts in Hawaii, and three
night-lighted courts. (I must do a survey some day on the extent
of usage of night-lighted resort courts. Very little, I suspect.)

A handsome two-story clubhouse with bar and restaurant strad-
dles the Blue and Orange courses. The Blue was the first course
built and it is a sensible resort course. Broad, forgiving fairways,
honest greens, enough variation in topography, and seascape
views to be interesting.

The Orange course, however, is a golf architect's monument.
The golfer is challenged to place each shot for a favorable
following shot. Old lava walls and heiaus were left largely intact
to become integral parts—and obstacles—of the course which is
carved through wiliwili trees, a favorite timber in old Hawaii for
making outrigger canoes.

The 4-par 18th hole, a dogleg left, is a good example of this
architect's satanic design. An easy second shot to the green is
from an elevated fairway, but the back of the green is decorated
with a natural rock garden. It does get your attention, particularly
if you overhit a ball.

One of the most challenging golf courses in Hawaii.

About 600 low-rise townhouses and apartments are clustered discreetly and landscaped lavishly throughout the complex. Many of them are for rent.

A small convenience shopping village is adjacent to the Intercontinental Hotel with a restaurant, a grocery, and ice cream, liquor, jewelry and boutique shops, and a sports activity center.

South of Wailea is another development, at Makena Beach, slowly being brought on line by Seibu, the giant Japanese conglomerate. The leisure/recreational division of Seibu employs about 50,000 people and is involved in everything from operating ski resorts in Alaska to bowling lanes in Okinawa. The company has one golf complex outside of Tokyo with six golf courses back-to-back where it costs $150 to play one round on a weekend. The company is not new to the vacation industry and is willing to make major investments and wait for the payoff down the line.

For example, play at the Makena golf course was very limited when it opened. It was protected like a first child. It adds another first-rate golf course to the Maui collection.

Makena Beach has always been known for its fine setting and good surf. When it was difficult to reach, it was the habitat of flower children and indiscriminate campers, but that is all gone now. A condominium has already been completed and a new hotel will soon be under construction, bringing the number of integrated resorts on Maui to four with a combined seven golf courses and, literally, acres of tennis courts.

My first reason for getting a scuba diving certificate was to dive Molokini, a remnant of a tiny volcanic cinder cone shaped like a new moon that lies off the coast of Wailea.

Ocean Activities Center, with a shop in the Wailea Shopping Village and desks at both the Intercontinental and Stouffer hotels, owns two boats, including the 65-foot catamaran *Wailea Kai*, which makes daily trips to Molokini with snorkelers and scuba divers, returning at midday before the tradewinds brisk up.

At one time, the catamaran picked up passengers at Wailea Beach but the unpredictable ocean surge made it necessary to leave and return from Maalaea Harbor, fifteen minutes away by car. Bus transportation to the harbor is included in the picnic/snorkel/scuba package.

We left Stouffer's in our own car at 7AM with plenty of time to be on the "cat" before the published 7:30 departure—she left at 8—and were able to park almost directly in front of the ship which was awash with divers, grandmothers and grandchildren and everything in between.

Passengers were separated immediately into interest groups; snorkelers or divers. Snorkelers aft; divers, fore.

Face masks and fins were issued to snorkelers who did not bring their own, and divers were outfitted with vests, tanks and respirators, and fins. (I will never leave for another diving trip without my own mask. A vow.)

There were two of us for scuba diving. An 18-year-old girl from New Jersey who had never dived in the ocean and me, holding a diving certificate that had been issued two days earlier, facing my first non-instructed dive, and scared to death of throwing up again. We were not what you would call a deeply experienced team of divers.

However, our guide, Frank O'Brien, was the ultimate professional diver: calm, assured, relaxed but meticulously precise in his pre-dive instructions. He also looked like he had been manufactured by the Professional Diver Factory. Number 643: blond, lean, bronzed. Next.

He took us through a review of underwater hand signals and then rehearsed the coming dive.

"We'll jump off the aft end of the ship where the water will only be about 12 feet deep. Swim to the anchor line up front, let the air out of your vest, and go to the bottom. We'll assemble there.

"The bottom slopes gradually away from the island and we will follow it down to about 50 feet, make a large sweeping circle and return to the ship. Don't go wandering off by yourself and let me know when your air pressure is down to 1,000 pounds."

He traced the coming dive on a map.

The sail out to the island took less than an hour on a happy morning, full of bright sunbeams that faceted the ocean into patterns resembling a well cut sapphire. The bantering crew went through their routine of cruise jokes and an "aloha" yelling contest and, it seemed in no time, we were approaching Molokini.

Two other boats were already at anchor. The Lady Navigator and 74 other snorkelers in standard issue orange flotation jackets slipped into the swim from the *Wailea Kai's* broad aluminum steps that lowered beneath the surface.

A large area was marked off by yellow nylon lines cornered by buoys. Snorkelers were asked to confine their swimming to the marked area. The ocean surface was soon covered with a blanket of orange jackets dotted by black rubber breathing tubes.

My diving companion and I waddled in our giant fins, penguin fashion, to the gunwale, pushed our masks firmly against our faces, and jumped finned-feet first into the ocean.

When you are a novitiate at diving, there is a large cloud of doubt in your mind whether this breathing apparatus is going to work. The cloud of doubt is matched by the great sense of relief when the air comes through the respirator just as it did on deck.

I went to the anchor line, released the air from my vest and sank down the short line to the sandy bottom. Above me were the hordes of snorkelers crowding each other, paddling around in what looked like great disorder.

Beneath the surface, all was spacious and quiet.

Frank was soon with us holding up a circle of thumb and and forefinger. "Okay?" he was asking. The same signal returned says "A-Okay."

He turned and pointed ahead with a vertical flat hand, signaling "Follow me in this direction."

Away we went, kicking slowly and evenly from the hips which sent us smoothly along the ocean bottom, over white sand, over pieces of colored coral. Fish were everywhere. The yellow tangs, the graceful Moorish idols, the bright butterfly fish, wrasse, goatfish, parrot fish.

I got a strong feeling of swimming around in my own private exclusive aquarium. Once, a scuba diver from another boat joined us for a minute and then left us to our solitary pleasure.

We descended along the sloping bottom as effortlessly as the fish around us, leaving a trail of air bubbles. The depth didn't seem to make any difference in the visibility; the water remained as clear at 50 feet as it had been at 12 feet, and always warm.

Although I felt confident and almost relaxed in the dive, I had the bad snorkeling habit of pulling myself forward with my arms. Frank, by contrast, kept his hands clasped together under his chest. My unnecessary arm action used up extra oxygen and three quarters through the circle I had to tap Frank and point to my air-pressure indicator. I was down to 800 pounds.

He directed us toward the island and we were soon under the shadow of the catamaran. He pointed up, meaning "go aboard" and he and the girl went off in another direction. She hadn't used as much air as I had.

I inflated my vest, surfaced and swam to the ladder. No one was there to help me. Still burdened with tank and flippers, I floundered up the ladder, awkwardly swinging one flipper-clad foot out to sea and then bringing it up to the next step on the ladder.

A kind gentlemen came over and pulled me up by the shoulders and I flopped on the deck like a landed fish.

The Lady Navigator swam in to help me off with the heavy tank and sloshy vest and flippers.

"I did it," I told her. "I made the dive at Molokini. I did it."

It was a victory sail back to the harbor. A cold buffet was spread out in the cabin: salads, cold meats, buns, Maui potato chips, cold beer and wine.

The wind was up fresh now and the cat raced towards home while I inhaled the beer as if it were Indianapolis champagne.

"I did it," I repeated at intervals until she gently placed a hand over my mouth.

"Yes, you did it. Now you don't have to say it anymore. You wouldn't want people to think you were showing off, would you?"

"Oh, no," I told her. And under my breath I said, "I did it." And silently: "And I didn't throw up."

Lahaina, a Place of Royalty and Whales

The capital of West Maui, and once the capital of all of Hawaii, is Lahaina.

As a matter of fact, once upon a time it was also the capital of the whaling industry with as many as 400 ships anchored in Lahaina Roads, the straits between Maui on the east and Lanai and Kahoolawe on the west.

The humpback whales make the 10,000-mile roundtrip from the Bering Sea every winter, the longest migration of any animal on earth, to assemble around Lahaina, their winter bedroom, where they breed and give birth. Mating takes place one year and birth the following year.

Where once the schools totaled over 25,000 annually, today they have dwindled to less than a 1,000.

The sight of these sea giants, as big as railroad freight cars, gives you a never-ending sense of wonderment. You can spot them at sea by their spouting stream of air and water as they breathe at the surface. You can see their dark shadowy backs as they roll through the ocean.

Occasionally, a whale will jump clear out of the water and fall back with a gigantic splash. It's like watching a falling redwood.

Once, driving from Lahaina, we spotted a family of whales next to the shore and from the cliff we could look straight down on two immense leviathans and a baby calf. It would have made a 5P picture and still remains sharply in my mind.

In the December to April season, Lahaina tour boats feature whale-watching cruises. This has become a winter industry. Some 75,000 passengers paid $18 each last year to catch sight of the 40-ton mammals breaching, blowing, fluking (diving), and mating.

Over 30 boats are now taking passengers out into Lahaina Roads including the *Spirit of Windjammer* which is chartered on weekends by the Pacific Whale Foundation, a non-profit organization whose objectives are to increase the scientific knowledge of whales and to educate the public about the humpbacks' ever slimming chances of survival. If you can't go with the Foundation but book your tour through them, the boat they book for you will make a donation to the Foundation. The numbers to call in Lahaina are 879-4253 or 879-6530.

A curious fact from the ongoing study of the noises whales make under water: they have a "theme melody" which all members of the school repeat exactly. Every year, when the whales return to Lahaina, there is a new variation of the theme, and all of the whales know and "sing" it.

My favorite photograph of Lahaina is shot from the air off-shore framed by the fringe of surf in front of town and includes the small boat harbor with its nifty and tacky yachts, the early American flavor of the Pioneer Inn, the old wood waterfront buildings on Front Street, the Pioneer Sugar Company mill's smoke tower, and—best of all—the undulating rise of variegated greens as the sugar cane fields reach and surround the school of Lahainaluna and the big white "L" on the mountain side.

The Pioneer Inn reflects the mood and motif of Lahaina. Built in 1901 by a former member of the Royal Canadian Mounted

Police on the personal taro patch of Kamehameha the Great, the green, two-story wooden building with white curlicues is really the capitol of Lahaina. The floor has original planks still in place underfoot. Genuine whaling utensils are nailed to the walls.

The bar is honestly raunchy and has a deep, rummy odor from many generations of spilled drinks.

Every tourist guide book duplicates the rules for house guests still hanging in the lobby, and so must I. It is too good to resist:

"You must pay you rent in advance.

"You must not let you room go one day back.

"Women is not allow in your room.

"If you wet or burn you bed you going out.

"You are not allow to give you bed to you freand.

"If you freand stay overnight you must see the mgr.

"You must leave you room at 11 am so the women can clean you room.

"Only on Sunday you can sleep all day.

"You are not allow in the down stears in the seating room or in the dinering room or in the kitchen when you are drunk.

"You are not allow to drink on the front porch.

"You must use a shirt when you come to the seating room.

"If you cant keep this rules please dont take the room."

When we stay at Kaanapali we always make a ritual visit, at least once, to the Pioneer Inn for breakfast, sitting on the verandah facing the park that is filled—literally—by one huge banyan tree planted in 1873. With the small boat harbor in the background, the place has unbeatable ambiance. A good breakfast, too, and strong coffee served in big white mugs.

If we're just passing through Lahaina, beyond breakfast time, we go to the corner ice cream parlor in the Pioneer Building facing Front Street for a cone to be eaten slowly in and around the park. Frequently, there is art exhibited beneath the banyan arbor. The Courthouse on the far side of the park and facing the harbor now fulfills the unusual combined functions of police station and art gallery.

At the corner is a jumble of coral blocks called the Waterfront Fort but it is really symbolic only, because the original fort was dismantled to build a prison. At one time the whalers, wild for rum and women, were raising hell in the town and the missionaries were saying that rum and women were forbidden. It led to a virtual war which in turn led to a fort being built at the direction of the queen in 1831.

A touch more of history that cannot be seen. Two blocks farther east of the fort site, you will come to a baseball diamond and a park at Front and Shaw streets.

At one time a sizable pond, some 40 acres, occupied the area and within the pond was a small island called Mokuula, or "Sacred Island." The island was the residence of King Kamehameha II and later his brother, Kamehameha III. Two neat grass shacks were incongruously fitted with glass windows. An on-site mausoleum held the remains of Princess Nahienaena, their sister and Kamehameha III's lover.

A small sentry-guarded gate provided entry to the island.

When Pioneer Mill irrigated its cane fields by redirecting the flow of water, the pond shrunk and eventually, together with the island, disappeared.

Across the street, a formal palace was built with windows and an iron roof but it was never completed and the building materials went into the structure of the new courthouse facing the harbor in 1859.

Coming back along Front Street to town, opposite the "banyan tree park", is the Banyan Tree Inn, a traditional place in Lahaina to have Portuguese bean soup. Hearty. Spicy. Bean-y.

Let's continue our history walk along Front Street. The Baldwin House Museum is on the corner. Rev. Dwight Baldwin was a medical missionary who came to Lahaina in 1835 and he built and lived in the two-story stucco house until 1868. A smallpox epidemic swept the islands in 1853 and the doctor/minister tried single-handedly to save his community through vaccinations. He only partially succeeded.

The restored Baldwin House contains wardrobe, furniture, and medical instruments of the 19th century. Under the old grape arbor in the rear, Mrs. Baldwin's pride, she taught school and sought relief from the heat of Lahaina, literally "cruel sun."

Lahaina Restoration Foundation has offices in the missionary complex. A good place to step back 150 years into another time zone.

The Baldwin name is still most prominent in today's Hawaii,

being half of the Alexander & Baldwin, known simply as A&B.

A curiosity is the old prison on Prison Street, Hale Paahao, or "Stuck-In-Irons-House" because criminals were shackled to walls or put in balls and chains. No longer to be seen is a catwalk around the coral block walls manned by rifle carrying guards to prevent the prisoners from climbing out.

The necessity of the prison was prompted by the report of the sheriff in 1850 to the marshal of the Sandwich Islands:

"The amount of crimes and misdemeanors for the last year has been steadily on the increase, which is attributed to the vast influx of foreigners from California. The gold brought by these has been the cause and means of a general laxity of morals, and prostitution has been carried out to an almost unparalleled extent."

Prisoners had slept on the ground in the original prison without cover which led to sicknesses. The present building was constructed from the coral blocks of the old fort.

Front Street is a favorite place for strolling and shopping with such places as High As A Kite, a kite shop not a bar, and Apparels of Pauline, a boutique for women not a silent movie for little boys.

Eateries abound. Fast food, French food, fish food, Italian pizza, Japanese sushi, Chinese noodles, Hawaiian stew and rice, croissants and coffee. It is all there.

A justifiably favorite with residents and visitors for breakfast, lunch or dinner is Longhi's, a half open-air room with lots of charm, looking to the ocean, much greenery. A long, long menu with many daily specialties.

En route from East Maui, approaching Lahaina, is another restaurant which we have patronized for many years. Chez Paul, located in a tree-covered patch of the highway six miles south of Lahaina, looks like a dump but its quasi-French food is quite good.

Before we leave Lahaina, we must mention the island of Lanai, directly opposite the harbor, which is easiest reached aboard cruisers from Lahaina.

Ocean Activities Center took over the Lanai Lodge in late 1984, the only commercial accommodation on the island, and renamed it the Hotel Lanai. They have converted the tiny, 10-room establishment into a diving center—a strange diving center since its location is in the middle of the island—but it will make reaching the prime diving spots on the coast of Lanai much easier and smoother than crossing the Kealaikahiki ("The Way to Tahiti") Channel.

The prime diving spots are near Manele Bay at the south end of the island. The Cathedrals are two volcanic spires of rock created by lava runoffs into the sea that hardened into pinnacles. Over a period of time sea action eroded the pinnacles, boring holes into and through them. They are perfectly wonderful and eerie habitats for different kinds of lobsters, coral and reef fish ... and for the divers who pursue them.

The company also has a cruiser, *No Ka Oi, IV*, which takes divers on 2-tank dives anywhere the diving is good, including Lanai.

A most popular Lahaina-to-Lanai ship is the trimaran, *Trilogy*, operated by the Coon family for many years. It leaves at 7AM and returns at 4PM for snorkeling and scuba diving at Hulopoe Bay on the south end of Lanai where the family has private beach property. Included in the cruise is an air-conditioned van tour of Lanai. (The Coons also own the bus company and the only gas station on the island.)

Ocean Activities Center: 879-4485. Coon's *Trilogy*: 661-4743.

The reason for Lahaina's bustling shops, shopping centers, cruise boats and restaurants is very simple: Kaanapali.

Kaanapali, four miles north of the former whaling capital, was Hawaii's first planned development. It started in 1962 with an agriculturally unproductive tract of land covered with thorny kiawe trees (mesquite) but adjacent to three miles of perfectly gorgeous beach. Today, those 500 acres hold six major hotels, seven condominiums, a single-family residential community, two 18-hole championship golf courses, 40 tennis courts, its own airstrip and a shopping center built around a whalers museum.

The writer who came up with the headline "WOWEE MAUI" had to be thinking of Kaanapali.

I can remember standing on Black Rock, now the site of the Sheraton Maui Hotel, when there was nothing there but a battered concrete pier from which small oil tankers off-loaded fuel, and barges docked to pick up cattle fattened on pineapple tops at holding pens behind the tiny harbor.

Local families would brave the kiawe thorns weekends to get to the beach to picnic, swim and camp.

In 1959, momentous events happened in Hawaii. The state achieved statehood. The first commercial jet, a Qantas Airways' Boeing 707, landed at the Honolulu International Airport. Ground was broken for the infrastructure of Kaanapali's roads and utilities.

In 1959, the visitor count in Hawaii touched an unprecedented 250,000. Who would have dreamed that the attractions of the state would draw five million annual visitors by the mid-80s?

The success of Kaanapali with the facilities to entertain more than a half a million visitors annually on its own was the model project for other resort developers, regionally and internationally.

In December 1962, the first hotel cottages of the Royal Lahaina Hotel opened in conjunction with the first 18-hole course designed by Robert Trent Jones. The next month Sheraton Maui opened with an award winning hotel design that cascaded down the Black Rock cliff.

Over the years other hotels followed: Kaanapali Beach, Maui Surf, Marriot and the Hyatt Regency.

Private residences and expensive condominiums were constantly added along the way. The airstrip was opened to small plane commercial traffic with direct flights to Honolulu, and an executive golf course was added.

It is a first-class place to spend a vacation.

I like the atmosphere in the Discovery Room on top of the Sheraton Maui for breakfast. The air is so clear, clean, fresh and the views of the sugar cane uplands of Maui and across to Lanai are superb in the morning light. You can also see the wind line on the ocean's surface ... the tradewinds playfully ruffling the open channel, undeterred by land barriers.

A highlight at dusk is to watch the loin-clothed beachboy gingerly "run" down the ridgeline of Black Rock to its end, light the last torch (thank you, Grace Buscher), and, as a conch shell blows, lift a lei in a salute to the setting sun, toss the lei into the ocean and then—cameras ready?—swan dive into the ocean behind the garland of flowers.

Another highlight is to go to the south end of the beach, to the Hyatt Regency and sin.

Every evening one of the hotel's restaurants, the Lahaina Provision Company, features a Chocolate Bar, a do-your-own-chocolate-on-chocolate sundae, calories on top of calories. The Lady Navigator goes faint whenever the restaurant is mentioned. (They feature a Yogurt Bar at noon. Probably to get you into training for the big gun in the evening.)

We also went on an evening sail aboard Hyatt's teak-decked catamaran, *Kiele V*, easily the most luxuriously appointed cat in Hawaii, where, in addition to the open bar, we were served "dipping" fruit for a silver bowl of hot fudge fondue. And we almost had to remove the Lady Navigator from the ship with a giant claw hammer.

The Hyatt is spectacular. Over 800 rooms, a gigantic swimming pool-cum-lake with a curving slide, waterfalls and swing bridges, all of which looks like it was copied out of a book on fantasies but was really copied from the Princess Hotel in Acapulco, and a lobby filled with a million dollars of antiques and Oriental art.

Busy, busy, busy but still beautiful. The whole mirage of the Hyatt is another dream-come-true of Chris Hemmeter whose ultimate you-haven't-seen-anything-yet fantasy is to take shape at Waikoloa on the Big Island. The Hyatt Regency Maui, incidentally, is immensely successful.

The area between Kaanapali and Kapalua will remind you of the overdeveloped area of Kihei. Junky condominiums, too many condominiums, too big condominiums.

Again, as in the case of Kihei and Wailea, a new by-pass highway has been built above the beach road so you don't have to drive through this disaster zone unless you want to.

At Napili Bay on the beach road, however, is a fine swimming beach and an old favorite of long-time visitors. The Napili Kai Beach Club apartments have kitchens and guests have access to swimming pools, tennis, a putting green and the complimentary use of all sporting equipment.

Above Napili is the new resort development of Kapalua whose logo is the butterfly. (Papillon, the Kauai helicopter company with the butterfly name in French and the butterfly logo, also flies out of Kapalua and one wonders if the Kapalua butterflies and the Papillon butterflies get together and make little butterflies.)

At one time the area was known for Fleming's Beach, a small but idyllic curve of sand with gentle surf; the run-away-and-kiss-on-the-beach kind of hideaway.

Now there is a hotel, resort developer built condominiums, tennis courts galore, restaurants and two 18-hole golf courses.

The dreamer who could afford to create this heavenly corner of Maui is the Prince of Pineapple, Colin C. Cameron, the head of Maui Land & Pineapple Company who devoted 750 acres of his fiefdom to the realization of Kapalua.

Relatively small, less than 200 rooms, the Kapalua Bay Hotel was designed by the same architects who did the magnificent job with the Kahala Hilton. At Kapalua, it would appear they used the same great taste in designing the expansive lobby—and then went home.

The combined registration-cashier's desk area is slightly larger than a telephone booth. The rooms are nice but not luxurious. Strangest of all, the design of the hotel seems to turn its back to the ocean. With one of Maui's nicest beaches at its doorstep, the hotel disassociates itself from the sand and sea.

The changing management of Kapalua was always a subject of local gossip. Round One: The first management of the hotel was under the professional care of RockResorts, Laurance Rockefeller's hotel company. Round Two: Regent International Hotels, a sophisticated management company headed by Bob Burns and Georg Rafael, whose roster of properties include such known-for-elegance establishments as the Dorchester in London, the Mayfair Regent in New York, and the Regent in Hong Kong, had a go at it. Round Three: At last report, the hotel was being managed by the development company ... and rumors of its impending sale were floating about.

If the hotel is less than a smashing success, the development and sales of the condominium units was equaled only by the Yukon gold rush. The Kapalua properties came on line at the top of the market. People queued to pay cash for apartments that *started* at $250,000—apartments that hadn't even been built yet. The developers had to hold lotteries to determine those lucky buyers who couldn't wait to plunk down small fortunes.

Today you can rent apartments in the Kapalua Villas or The Ironwoods, perhaps even have Carol Burnett as a neighbor. She is, or has been, in frequent residence in the condominium she bought.

Arnold Palmer was involved in the design of the two golf courses: the Bay Course was finished prior to the Village Course.

As the name implies, the Bay Course includes a couple of holes that head for the ocean, then cross an inlet. (It is mandatory in building an oceanside golf course in Hawaii to have a hole that shoots over the water, a precedent set by Mauna Kea Beach Hotel's now famous third hole.)

The real shame at Kapalua is that only golfers get to enjoy the views from the 6th and 7th holes of the Village Course. Just awesome. The two holes are built on the ridgeline of a mountain. At the 6th tee you are beside a lake and you can look off to the left for one magnificent panorama of sky and ocean and greenery and then look to the right over the hilltop lake to another spread of pineapple fields and distant mountains and ocean.

The 4-par 6th hole is a dogleg left. The 7th hole tees off from the highest point on the course—more splendid views—and shoots down to a green beside the lake. Two of the most dramatic holes in Hawaii. Papillon should run helicopter-champagne-picnic trips to the area with skinny-dipping in the lake.

Each autumn, the two courses are the scene of an international invitational golf tournament, the first prize of which is over $100,000. It brings out the biggest stars on the tour. Hale Irwin is the club's touring pro. To enter the pro-am costs around $5,000 but that includes a week's stay with almost everything but underwear thrown in.

You don't have to stay at Kapalua to enjoy dining at the Bay Club, a handsome, expensive, public restaurant that looks as if it belongs to a polo club. Quietly posh, with a menu to match the elegant ambiance. It's one of those restaurants that makes you feel good the minute you walk into the room. Lunch or dinner.

The restaurant at the golf course clubhouse is not run by the developers but operated by Kimo's from Lahaina. The Kapalua Grill & Bar is probably the best golf course restaurant in the state. Super hamburgers recommended for lunch—and I never order hamburgers—with fat country-style French fries. Or try the Kapalua Salad. Evenings, the restaurant will have as many as three different fresh fish entrees. Good bar and wine list, too.

Above the beach on Pineapple Hill is a former plantation manager's home that found a new career as a restaurant. The long drive up is still guarded by noble pine tree sentinels, and it is fine for sunsets but little else, although at one time they had a pineapple and chicken dish which was delicious.

Fleming's Beach is now better known as Kapalua Beach and, together with Napili Bay, is one of the best walk-in snorkeling spots on the island, according to a map available at Hawaiian Reef Divers in Lahaina. Another of the map's "five best" recommendations is at Honolua Bay beyond Kapalua.

You can drive a bad road from Kapalua around the north end of the island back to Wailuku and Kahului but the drive has nothing unusual to offer except that it does bring you into a good municipal golf course, Waiehu, the only "muni" on Maui, which is kept a secret from visitors and is only a five minute drive from Wailuku.

Everybody Loves Hana

The drive you should take is to Hana at the east end of the island.

Heavenly Hana.

Our strongest recommendation is to go to Hana but to give yourself lots of time. To try and make the drive around and back in a day, or less, on the winding, narrow, but scenic road would be straining and, in the end, joyless.

To drive all the way around the east end of the island—and you need a four-wheel drive vehicle to do it—is madness. But there are a lot of mad people in the world, we among them.

We planned to complete the circle drive from Kahului to Hana around the back side of Haleakala because it was the only road we hadn't driven in Hawaii.

The road is so rough that car insurance is not valid on a standard rental car.

We turned in our National Car rental and picked up a new, red, four-wheel jeep with roll bars but no top from Sunshine Rent-a-Car on Dairy Road in Kahului (871-6222).

Oh, yes, we also had two books with us, *Hana Road Highlights* and *On the Hana Coast*.

The first book is optional. The second book is mandatory if you are going to spend any time in Hana. Much good information from a team of excellent local writers and a nostalgic collection of old photographs never before published.

Plan to stay overnight at Hana. Or, better, stay a week and let the peace of living flow back into your veins.

If you are going to do it in a day, leave early in the morning, go into Paia where the Cruiser Bob bicycle rides to Haleakala take off. Go to Picnics, a store a half a block off the highway and order sandwiches and beer or soft drinks, or kiawe broiled chicken and rent an ice chest and take off.

This should be a morning of unhurried frequent stops.

The first stop should be two miles out of Paia at Hookipa Beach Park. (If you are making a roundtrip to Hana, note Mama's Fish House on the Paia side of the park. A fine place to stop off for dinner on the way back.)

Hookipa is boosted as the best windsurfing beach in Hawaii and is the scene of nationally televised windsurfing competitions. To get down into the park, you have to drive past it and enter from the east end on a one-way road.

One November day, under a cloudless sky, we stopped by Hookipa to watch the windsurfers. The wind was blowing strongly and the surf was gigantic. There were no sails in those waves.

Two young men in a car which had windsurfing equipment lashed to its roof were staring resignedly at the towering surf.

"It starts happening at this time of year," said the driver.

"There won't be any action today. That's just too tough out there."

We asked him how long he had been a windsurfer.

"Oh, I've been on surfboards all of my life but I just started windsurfing a year ago. I thought I'd pick it up overnight but it took me about three months. If I'd known then what I know now, I'd have taken lessons.

"If you were a sailor and knew how the wind worked, you'd get the hang of windsurfing faster than if you were a surfboarder like me."

Hookipa means hospitality in Hawaiian but it wasn't very hospitable that day. Where there are often 100 windsurfers in the ocean at the same time, the surf remained empty.

From Hookipa we set off for Hana on Highway-36 cutting through sugar and forest lands away from the sea in the area of Haiku, down through a gulch, up the other side, wind in the hair, flying free but driving slow—it is not a highway in the broad sense of the word.

From Kahului to Hana is only 52 miles but Maui residents will tell you to plan on three hours to negotiate the 600 curves and the 56 narrow, often one-way, bridges. And to enjoy the beauty of the place.

The first 3P stop is at Kaumahina State Park where you'll find flush toilets and picnic tables and a lookout from which you can see a shoreline of pretty bays below you, and, farther on ahead, the attractive green Keanae Peninsula, a valley greener because it is surrounded by a turquoise sea.

The second 3P stop is on the road above Keanae Peninsula, looking down on the peaceful plot of agricultural green pregnant with taro farms, banana groves and coconut trees, fed by the watershed from Keanae Valley behind you. At one time the peninsula was filled with rice paddies installed by Chinese immigrants who had worked off their contracts at sugar plantations, married Hawaiian women and become independent farmers. The church you can see is the Congregationalist Church, built in 1856.

The next place to pull over is at Wailua Lookout, site of St. Gabriel's, a Roman Catholic church. The churches in this rugged rural area were serviced by ministers and priests who traveled a religious circuit going from community to community.

After Wailua is the Puaa Kaa ("Rolling Pig") State Park, a traditional resting place with waterfalls and freshwater pools where you can swim. Depending upon the time of year, the whole length of the road to Hana is marked with picture-taking waterfalls.

I learned from *On the Hana Coast* that the village of Nahiku, beyond Puaa Kaa State Park, once was the center of a thriving rubber company. Some 25,000 rubber trees of various species planted at the turn-of-the-century gave rise to a small town, but the experiment proved too costly. The plantation and its rubber processing shed were closed down in 1912.

Various other crops also failed and the people moved away. It is said, however, that Nahiku is back in business ... but with the illegal crop of pakalolo, marijuana.

When you come down the hill from Nahiku into the flat of Hana, you will understand why so many celebrities have picked this corner of Hawaii as a hideaway. Hana breathes tranquility.

In the distance you can see the small Hana airstrip used by charter and private aircraft.

On the Nahiku side of the airport is the largest ancient place of Hawaiian worship in Hawaii, Piilanihale Heiau, a temple dating back to the 15th century. Its setback terracing is unlike anything else in Hawaii. As big as two football fields, the stone platform is enclosed by 10-foot thick walls that rise on the north end to a height of 50 feet and slope on the south to 10 feet. The platform is paved with slabs of lava and small rocks.

Hana is a haven for heiaus of different sizes, built by different chiefs supplicating help from the gods before going into battle, then building another heiau in gratitude when their battles were won.

The first buildings you see as you enter the village of Hana are the Hana Medical Center and the Police Station. You stay on the highway and you go by the Hotel Hana Maui and the Hana Ranch complex, the village churches and the Hasegawa General Store.

That's it. You go any farther and you are out of town.

Take the left fork in the road at the police station, Uakea Road, and you go by Heavenly Hana Inn—very small—Hana Kai Resort Apartment—bigger and with a number of oceanfront house-keeping apartments—and then take the road down to Hana Bay.

On the right hand side of the bay is Kauiki Head, a small mountain, which became an almost impregnable fort in times of wars. You can hike to the top on a path behind Hana School, if you are fit, to look across the Alenuihaha Channel to the Big Island of Hawaii.

The pavilion at the bay is the favorite community gathering place for Hawaiian luaus. Everybody comes. Tutu's, the local version of a fast-food stand, sells saimin, mango bread, plate lunch specials (usually stew and rice), hamburgers, soft drinks.

Why Hana?

We frequently receive requests like this: "I want to come to Hawaii where it is quiet, where there is a good beach, where I can stay a week and not do anything. I don't want to play golf. I don't want to go bar crawling or dancing at night. I want to swim, sun, relax and find out again why I am on this earth."

Hana is on top of the list.

Some friends want a place where they can cook their own meals. Others say they don't want to lift anything heavier than a menu—certainly not a skillet.

For the folk in the latter group, Hotel Hana Maui is perfect. For the others, we used to tell them about a place called Hana Kai Resort Apartments, a small two-story condominium complex on the bay. We had never stayed there but a friend we trusted had been one of the developers. We called and booked ourselves in for two nights. A one bedroom apartment with a kitchen, fully equipped, a generous lanai with an ocean view was $63 a night. No telephone, no radio, no TV.

The furniture was adequate. Not done with any great expenditure or taste, but adequate.

A different amenity was a small free-form swimming pool fed by a fresh water spring that put goose bumps on our bodies and a bounce in our steps. Very fresh.

If you flew into Hana on a scheduled Royal Hawaiian plane, you could rent a car at the Hana Kai for about $25 a day.

Another alternative for seeing Hana is to sign on for a local day tour with Tiny Malaikini (248-8685) who takes visitors places they would never find on their own and "talks story," telling them tales they would never hear anywhere else. And some of them are true!

A two-day food supply was our first chore, shopping before closing time at the Hasegawa General Store. Hasegawa's is famous with travel writers and song writers for its got-anything-you-want line of merchandise that runs from plumbers helpers to fresh papaya. If you can't find it, ask Harry Hasegawa who will know where it is. He also delivers to the Hawaii Kai three days a week.

One item the Hasegawa Store does not have is fresh meat. Frozen, yes; fresh, no. For steaks and chops, you drive around to the Hana Ranch Store, a small grocery store with a bit of liquor and wine, run by the ranch.

Hana Ranch, with 15,000 acres of land running 9,000 head of Herefords, is the closest thing there is to a local industry. At one time sugar plantations at Hana employed some 6,000 people but that has been long gone.

A San Francisco financier, Paul Fagan, married Helene Irwin, daughter of a prominent Honolulu gentleman—Irwin Park at the bottom of the Aloha Tower is named after him—and acquired a sugar plantation from the Hana Sugar Company in the 1930's. C. Brewer owned the adjacent Kaeleku Plantation and mill.

After the war, C. Brewer discontinued its marginal sugar operation at Hana for fear it would endanger future relations with the growing union powers. The shutdown put hundreds of Hana people out of work. Fagan started the Hotel Hana Maui in an effort to create a new industry. The new hotel had ten units with views oriented, not to the ocean, but to the ranchlands behind the hotel. Shades of Kapalua! Fagan preferred to look at the hind end of his prize herd of Black Angus over a surf and sea scene.

In 1984, a most dramatic happening occurred in Hana. Rosewood Hotels of Dallas bought the Hotel Hana Maui and the ranch. Hotels are bought and sold almost daily in Hawaii without fanfare, but when the heiress of the late oil tycoon, H.L. Hunt who created one of the largest oil fortunes in the United States, buys a remote inn, that's exceptional.

Exceptional also is what Caroline Hunt has done with the other hotels she has acquired in pursuit of her new hobby: The Bel Air in Beverly Hills, the Mansion on Turtle Creek, Dallas, the Remington in Houston. Wonderful little toys.

The new owners appointed Carl Lindquist, a long-time Hanaphile and Honolulu publisher, as the new general manager of the hotel and set forth on a $10 million upgrading plan for the existing 82 units in the single story cottage complex.

Lindquist hopes to make the hotel a cultural center for the entire Hana community with lectures, visiting artists and musicians and other activities.

The future of Hotel Hana Maui is in good hands and should prove to be exciting. The new Texas owners are not strangers to the cattle business and are also planning to introduce new breeds into the ranch's herds.

Visitors can eat breakfast, lunch, and, with reservations, dinner at the hotel. At the Hana Ranch headquarters there is also a coffee shop along with the town post office and bank.

Back at the apartment we found a "treasure map" of Hana and a list of activities and suggested excursions.

The first suggestion was to try the water in Hana Bay which is generally calm and good for swimming and snorkeling.

Another suggestion was to go along the cliff path beyond the pier to a point of land where Kaahumanu, the favorite wife of Kamehameha the Great, was born, the daughter of a defeated Molokai chief. She was destined to become the wife of a great chief, the prophets said. At 17—and a beauty, according to George Vancouver, the famous British explorer—she became the third wife of Kamehameha, left him for a lover but was reunited and later became the queen regent, in effect the ruler of Hawaii. She was responsible for the breaking of the religious tabus before the arrival of the missionaries.

The water can be so clear at the base of the rocks. Wonderful swimming but only if the water is calm.

On the other side of the bay is Nanualele Point where the surf never touches the shore. The legend is told of a young and handsome Tahitian prince who came to the bay to surf. Two maidens saw the striking young prince and, vying for his attention, dropped their pa'u, and stood naked on the beach. The young prince was so surprised and shocked that he never came to shore—and, of course, neither did the waves. And that is why the waves at Hana only come so far and then stop, never coming all the way into the beach.

Waianapanapa State Park, two miles back towards the airport, was another mandated stop.

Oceanside of the highway we saw the sign to—lovely name—Waianapanapa. The road through the densely forested countryside looked like a backroad in Tahiti. Some of the houses, and "near" houses, also recalled scenes of other South Pacific islands. Tents, seemingly permanently installed, stood beside cultivated gardens, a horse munched on nearby vegetation.

A dozen vacation cabins are available at the park, cabins with bunk beds for six people, completely furnished including bedding, towels, cooking and eating utensils, electricity, hot water, an electric range and refrigerator.

The maximum stay is five nights and the rental is an inexpensive $14 per couple per night. Reservations (hard to get) and information are available from the Department of Land and Natural Resources, Division of State Parks, P.O. Box 1049, Wailuku, Maui, Hawaii 96793.

As you come into the park, the caretaker's cabin is straight ahead, the vacation cabins are to the right in a cul-de-sac, camping grounds are to the left and beyond is a parking area near the Waianapanapa Caves. Thread your way through a jungle of ferns to a fresh body of water not more than 15 feet in circumference and surrounded by lava walls. The water connects with other freshwater pools through a lava tunnel.

The legend of Waianapanapa goes that a beautiful young princess was abused by her husband who accused her of infidelity. She ran away and hid in the caves of Waianapanapa accompanied by her retainer. Secreted from view, the retainer was fanning her princess with a kahili, a feathered symbol of royalty, when the pursuing husband spotted the reflection of the feathers in the water and killed the young princess in a most brutal fashion. In the spring, the time of the murder, red shrimp gather like droplets of blood and turn the bottom stones to red.

En route back to Hana, we saw a sign to Helani Gardens, a nursery where for a small fee you can tour the grounds. It's nothing to get excited about but the sweet Hawaiian girl at the admission booth gave me a ginger lei and a kiss that made it worthwhile. It went along with the sign that said: "Don't hurry. Don't worry. Don't forget to smell the flowers."

In Hana we found some old friends who invited us over to for a sunset drink and we not only stayed for dinner but returned for breakfast. That's Hana style.

In turn, we prepared a pile of chicken and salad, took a bit of wine and that afternoon we all went on a picnic.

Our hostess said that if I wrote about her private picnic spot, she would kill me. Later I found her secret picnic spot on the Hana Kai's map given to every guest but, keeping the pledge, I can only tell you that we followed a path down to the ocean, hiked along a cliff trail until we dropped down into a sheltered cove protected on three sides by high lava walls. The opening to the sea was also protected by a line of lava, making an ideal calm pool for swimming. We took diving masks but the snorkeling was not unusual.

Pleasant spot. Our leader said that the beach was also known as a nude beach. Not while we were there.

Guests of the Hotel Hana Maui are taken to swim at Hamoa Beach where there are private facilities and where an al fresco lunch is prepared. The first Hana airfield, a grass strip, was located here. Paul Fagan's original idea was to build his hotel near the beach and the airstrip but his wife talked him out of it.

Behind the village, on Lyon's Hill, is a tall lava stone memorial to Paul Fagan. You can drive up to it or walk. The good chance for a 3P shot of Hana.

We left Hana on a rainy morning and gassed at Hasegawa's filling station. The Lady Navigator went inside and bought large plastic garbage bags in which we cut out corners for arm holes, the middle for our heads. It was a workable raincoat. Our small bit of luggage and our picnic lunches were tucked into other bags.

Off in the rain we went. Our first designated stop was at the Seven Pools, ten miles away.

The Seven Pools, and indeed the entire Kipahulu Valley down to the ocean, was made part of the Haleakala National Park in 1969 when a group of private citizens, including Laurance Rockefeller, fearing that the natural beauty of the area was going to become the private domain of estates and, therefore, off limit to the public, donated the land to the government.

We crossed over the Oheo Bridge, looking down on the lower four pools in the cascading wonderland, and continued on to a rudimentary parking area. A path leads down to the first pool at oceanside. Nearby was a nice flat area, grass covered, which was a camping area. A National Park ranger was there to answer questions.

On Saturdays at 9AM the ranger meets those interested at the bridge and takes them on a four-hour hike up Pipiwai Valley, through old taro farm land, to the Waimoku Falls, 200 feet high. (That sounds like a good adventure.)

The pools are fun, too. By this time, the rain had lifted and I had worn a bathing suit as rain gear, and also expecting to take a dip into at least one of the seven pools. At one of the natural stone-lined basins full of very chilly water I slipped into—what? Pool three? There I floated on my back and had my picture taken a thousand times by a bus load of Japanese tourists.

Later we walked up a path alongside the bubbling, falling stream of water, all very pictorial. The path leads up to the bridge where we connected with another trail through the woods to return to the parking area. Three more falls are above the bridge but we pressed on reluctantly, fearful we might lose the clearing skies. You could spend a happy day at Seven Pools, swimming, sunning, picnicking.

Not far beyond Seven Pools, Highway-31 (Piilani Highway) goes to dirt and is a place where the insurance on standard cars is invalid. Turn back.

The grave of Charles Lindbergh is also a couple of miles farther on.

This is the district of Kipahulu and the get-away-from-the-crowds homesite for many famous people who had the option to hide out any place on earth and chose this quiet, hidden, southeast corner of Maui. Probably Sam Pryor, one of aviation's most valuable pioneers, was the Pied Piper who discovered Kipahulu. He converted a hundred acres into an Eden of the Pacific where he entertained a coterie of powerful visitors, some of whom, like Lindbergh, stayed to build a home.

I hope they keep the road tough. Some places should remain unpaved and free from tour buses. Those who came to find peace and privacy should be allowed their sanctuary.

Lindbergh's grave is an ironic case in point. Here is the Lone Eagle, an inaccessible hero who zealously guarded his privacy during his lifetime, and now, dead, defenseless. Available to everyone.

His last resting place is in the small seaside cemetery of the Hoomau Congregational Church in Kipahulu, in the shade of a small natal plum.

Lindbergh planned every detail of his death including the instructions that he was to be buried the day he died, that he be buried barefoot and friends attending should wear their work clothes. He even supervised the construction of the grave, sketching the tombstone, picking out the passage from the Bible to be engraved underneath his name:

Charles A. Lindbergh

Born Michigan 1902

Died Maui 1974

If I take the wings of the morning and

dwell in the uttermost parts of the sea—

C.A.L.

The wind blows gently across the green plateau of the cemetery high above the sea, shaded by plums and palms, mangoes and plumeria.

The unobtrusive square plot is marked off by a foot high chain and surrounded by privet and river rocks, in the center of which is a block of gray Vermont granite.

When we were there, someone had put a spray of white bougainvillea on the tombstone.

And when we were there an insensitive tourist stepped over the chain onto the grave to get into position to take a straight on picture of the engraved epitaph.

He's there, the Lone Eagle. Vulnerable.

Too many of the curious will step over the chain or drop cigarette butts or track mud into the church.

You and I can't stop them. But if you go, go in reverence and say your own prayer for the peace of a man who had such difficulty finding solitude when he was alive and now almost impossible when he is dead.

The touch of humor on the Piilani Highway is a sign that reads: Caution: Baby Pigs Crossing.

After that the tortuous, twisting highway is nothing to laugh at. We passed dry streams beneath craggy walls that would have been pretty with waterfalls were it not for a lingering drought.

The road went from heavy vegetation to dry and dusty country in a matter of a few miles.

Occasionally, there would be nice glimpses of the sea from the elevated highway. At Huialoha, a church still remains although the coastline is empty of people.

When the French explorer, La Perouse, sailed along the coast in 1786, with his two-ship fleet, the *Boussole* and the *Astrolab*, he recorded in his journal that the water cascaded off of Haleakala and irrigated a solid line of coastal villages that extended for three or four leagues. A bay at the south end of the island is named after the Frenchman who was later lost on the reefs of Fiji.

We stopped off at the only village still extant on the coast, Kaupo, where there is only one store and a few homes and little water. Hikers stop at the store who have tramped through the Haleakala crater and have come out the Kaupo Gap. From this point you can also take the overnight horseback ride into the crater.

Kaupo is a tour vans' stop for beer or soft drinks, the occupants looking as if they have been put through a concrete mixing machine.

It is hard to imagine, but Kaupo once was green, its soil irrigated by large, abundant springs. Limes and oranges grew in profusion until the springs were covered by landslides caused by earthquakes.

After Kaupo, the dirt highway becomes the barest of paved roads interspersed every few miles with cattleguards as you slowly climb into the grazing country of Ulupalakua Ranch. Another pretty name. Ooo-lou-pah-lah-koo-ah.

The ranch is a 22,000-acre spread and, like most cattle raising operations, turns and twists in every direction trying to stay alive. C. Pardee Erdman, the present owner, bought the property for $3.5 million in 1963 and, much later, sold a 1,000-acre parcel to Japan's Seibu for its golf resort development at Makena. Price tag: $7.5 million.

Erdman experimented with sheep grazing, explored the possibilities of geothermal energy from the most recent lava flows, and now is involved in Hawaii's only wine producing vineyard.

He went into partnership with Emil Tedeschi of Napa Valley growing different varieties of grapes while first producing a wine called "Maui blanc" which is made from a pineapple base.

You can stop off at the winery in the first welcome shade you find on the highway driving east to west. The sign is difficult to read but there is ample parking and you can go into the former one-room jail—now the sampling room—and sip the pleasant wine. Buy a bottle or two and also buy a bottle of the new champagne, "Blanc de Noirs," produced by the winery and aged four years in the bottle before it is brought to market.

We were shown through the grounds at the winery by Judith Tedeschi, the attractive blond wife of the winemaster. She told us that the harvesting of the 20 acres now under cultivation produces 20,000 pounds of Carnelian grapes, all of which are picked by six local ladies.

In the spring there is a ten-kilometer run to the winery which ends up with a picnic on the grounds. It costs $15 to enter and is now drawing hundreds of thirsty jocks.

The newest wrinkle at the Ulupalakua Ranch is a hot air balloon ride. When I first heard about a hot air balloon ride at the winery, I couldn't believe it, although we had found such a tour over the Napa Valley a first-rate experience. But in Hawaii? If you put up a balloon at the mercy of our strong tradewinds, you'd end up in the Marshall Islands.

I immediately got on the telephone to the number of Skyrovers of Lahaina, operators of the project.

"Oh, no, no," said the voice at the other end of the telephone.

"We are tethered to the ground at all times."

For $65, last price quoted, you can go up in the air about a 100 feet, take a nervous photograph of the scenic surrounding cattleland and vineyards, come down and have a celebration.

One wonders what James Makee would have thought of today's ranch. He would have enjoyed the partying. Makee was a former whaling captain who survived a hatchet attack by a steward, left the sea to become the owner of Rose Ranch, forerunner of Ulupalakua, and ran a successful sugar plantation and mill from 1865 to 1883 when the sugar operation was closed down permanently by drought conditions.

Makee was a party man and entertained royalty royally. His three-day bash for King Kalakaua included an escort of 150 horsemen and a five-mile torchlight parade.

Another party story still being told at Ulupalakua occurred when the ranch was owned by the polo-playing Baldwins, offspring of the missionary doctor from Lahaina. After leading an army polo team to defeat on Maui, a young officer named George Patton filled a glass with a mixture of hard liquors and then stood on his head in a doorway, feet braced on either side, and consumed the contents of the glass in his upside down position.

We left the winery and the ranch on the last lap back through Kula to the Kahului airport but had to stop at the top of a shady knoll where a sign proclaimed: Leis and Lemonade. The proprietresses were two subteen girls.

Did you ever sell—or buy—lemonade that mother made for 1¢ a glass or 5¢ a glass? These little darlings were selling theirs for 75¢ which tells you that inflation has reached Upcountry Kula.

Upcountry has a special flavor to it. New, expensive, retirement estates are starting to proliferate the countryside, estates and homes built by wealthy people attracted by the sweet, fresh, unpolluted air, the ambiance of the weather, the see-forever views.

The rolling ranch lands and the pungent eucalyptus trees and the commercial flower farms are all part of the environment. Not too shabby. Not shabby at all. All part of the wow that goes into the MAUI WOWEE.

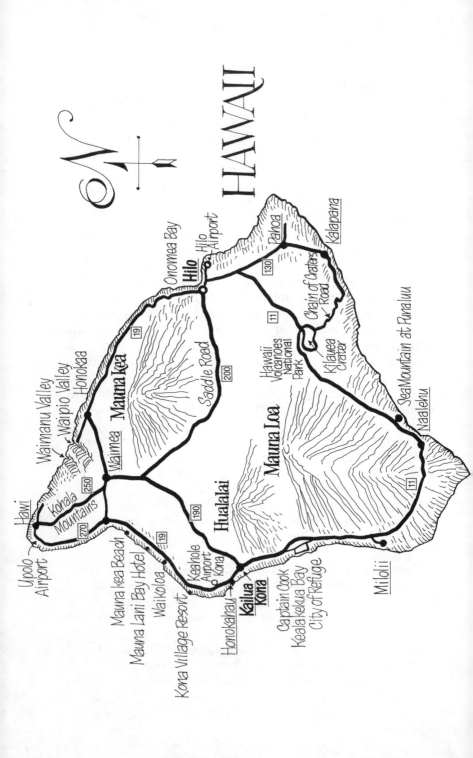

4. The Big, Big Island Where Big is Better

The island of Hawaii is twice as big as all the rest of the Hawaiian islands combined.

Big in size and big in variety.

The Big Island has huge, often active but tame volcanoes. Kilauea is known as the "Drive-In Volcano" because when a volcano erupts in the crater, it is possible to drive to the rim and watch the red lava spout and bubble in the cauldron below.

Two volcanic mountains are higher than 13,000 feet and in the winter can be topped with skiable snow.

The lava flows, rich in nutrients, created a prosperous agricultural island which still lives off of a diminishing sugar cane industry, but is optimistic about the tremendous growth potential of macadamia nut and commercial flower production. (Hilo is the largest commercial orchid and anthurium growing area in the world.)

From volcanoes and mountain tops, you can go to deserts, rain forests, white sand beaches, black sand beaches, even green sand beaches, through miles of orchards and cattle ranches ... all within a matter of a few hours.

Several years ago the Society of American Travel Writers held an annual convention on the Big Island and the Lady Navigator was the convention chairman.

Convention delegates convened in Hilo, separated to go on different story-gathering tours for three days, then reconvened in Kona on the opposite side of the island.

To provide the maximum variety of source material, she put together 14 tours which still serve as a benchmark of Big Island interests. The tours included an islandwide historical tour, camping in state parks, a Wagon Train of recreational vehicles, a survival-wilderness tour into the remote valleys on the west coast, a "second-time-around" tour for writers who thought they had done everything Hawaii had to offer, scuba diving, snorkeling around the coastline, and deep-sea fishing, tennis, golf, hunting, botanical, and scientific tours.

The last tour was a do-it-yourself tour and Frances Kay Harris of the Galveston Daily News, a sparkly lady, wrote not just one story but a delightful series of articles called "I Did Nothing in Hawaii." She stressed the luxury of and need for pampering yourself ... just wiggling a toe in warm sand and cool water.

(Her husband, Lewis, is just retired and told me that when he wakes up in the morning, he has nothing to do and when he goes to bed at night, he's only half done. Funny couple.)

The population of the Big Island is around 107,000. The Japanese total about 25 percent, the Caucasians 28 percent, the Filipinos 7 percent, the Hawaiians and part Hawaiians 27 percent, and a scattering of Koreans, Thais and others filling in the balance.

Because of its size, the island offers ethnic enclaves where racial customs are still observed. A plantation town dominated by Filipinos, an Hawaiian fishing village, a Caucasian retirement/second-home community, a cowboy-Hawaiian-Portuguese center, a Japanese coffee-growing town. The food, the religions, the annual celebrations reflect their different cultures. Yet, the people are all very much American. An added attraction is the graciousness and an inherent aloha spirit that comes with the Big Island.

You could call it the land of the Big Heart.

Nowhere is the diversification of the Big Island more pronounced than it is in Hilo, capital of the island and the state's second largest city.

Hilo is a most distinctive city.

With a population of 45,000 and a rainfall of over 140 inches a year, I tell my friends in Hilo that there is so much moisture in the air that it gets in their middle ears and makes them different from anybody else. They think this is amusing.

I cite a small diversion to illustrate. At one time there was a nine hole Hilo Country Club on the lower slopes of Mauna Kea—now a subdivision—where members who could get off work would meet Wednesday afternoons to play a round.

Usually only about 12 golfers showed up, so they would all play—and bet—together. Using gasoline powered golf carts and hitting when ready, the twelvesome looked and sounded like a tank corps charging an enemy with iron sticks and white bullets.

Everybody bet against everybody else and the impossible combinations were somehow kept straight by the Chinese postmaster.

At the end of the eighteen—playing the nine holes twice from different tees—money from the bets lost was placed in the middle of a table and the twelvesome drank until nothing was left and nobody was rational. Bodies were scattered all over town every Wednesday night.

That, to my mind, is still Hilo.

So is Richard Henderson, at present a state senator, who was one of the twelvesome. Richard, a taciturn Scot, a graduate of Wharton School of Economics, is also the protege of the late "Doc" Hill. "Doc" Hill *was* Hilo. He started as an itinerant door-to-door salesman of reading glasses and grew to be the town's leading investor and a most influential state senator. He was a short man with a halo of white hair, a pair of glasses—the kind you would buy from an itinerant salesman—perched on his nose and, always, on his shoulder was perched his parrot. No wonder he was constantly re-elected. Hilo wouldn't want anything less.

In the 1984 elections, a hotelier, Bob Herkes, was voted onto the County Council after he had carried a stuffed but quacking white goose to all campaign functions.

Hilo doesn't change fast.

More than any other city in the state, Hilo has taken a battering.

In 1946, a tsunami (tidal wave) generated in the Aleutian Islands swept into many Big Island valleys with a wall of water over 50 feet high. In Hilo, the height of the wave was over 30 feet, causing 83 deaths.

Again in 1960, another wave generated in Chile was just as high. It lashed across Hilo Bay, broke against the northern cliff of the bay and bounced back into the city, killing 61 people and destroying the southern part of the downtown area.

I remember a newspaper picture that showed a line of flattened parking meters. Gone was the line of weatherboard stores from behind them. Swept away. The area is now a large public park.

When the airlines were vying for permission to establish routes to Honolulu, part of the persuasive arguments was based, politically inspired to be sure, on providing flight service to Hilo.

Rights were given, a new airport complex was built, many new hotels were constructed—and nobody came.

United Airlines and Continental landed in Hilo, and then Continental withdrew and United cut back.

Hilo was too damp for the tourist trade, travel agents said.

Hotels closed down and converted their units to condominiums.

There was a bright side: the remaining hotels increased their occupancy to more profitable levels.

Then there was the matter of sugar becoming less profitable than in times past, production being reduced, mills being closed. All of the support facilities and services and personnel in Hilo suffering accordingly.

So it would be reasonable to assume that Hilo, between tidal waves, tourism frustration and sugar woes, would fold up and fade away.

Not Hilo.

New shopping centers continue to crop up everywhere. New cars are being sold. New homes are being built.

Hilo is still the center for the island's commerce and the island as a whole is doing very well economically.

Papayas grow commercially in Puna, macadamia nut production worth $27 million (1982 figure) is being expanded islandwide, half of all of the state's beef is grazed on its ranches, sugar cane still contributes over $150 million to the County coffers, and a flourishing flower industry continues to grow. It all flows into Hilo.

The prosperity of the tourist industry in Kona and Kohala brings smiles to the cheeks of Hilo merchants.

What is not discussed is pakalolo (marijuana), although it is a major economic factor. In 1982, the authorities destroyed marijuana plants valued at $31 million. The tip of the iceberg by most indications. How much of the illegal drug is going undetected? There are no official figures, of course.

An undisclosed source said that the county's statistical department includes the figures from marijuana sales under the category "four-wheel drives and trucks!"

The Naniloa Surf is the town's principal hotel and faces the waterfront on a visitor-oriented peninsula. In the morning, when the skies are usually clear and you can look from the hotel's breakfast room across Hilo Bay to the top of Mauna Kea, it is so serene you wonder why you would go anywhere else.

Hilo can be lovely.

A turn around the horseshoe shaped Banyan Drive whose trees have been planted by celebrities will bring you to one of the largest formal oriental gardens outside Japan, Liliuokalani Park, named for Hawaii's last reigning monarch. Its 30 acres are dotted with pagodas and other ornamental stone structures, gifts from Japan. Both the park and the sumo wrestling pavilion in this area are symbols of Hilo's large Japanese population.

The tiny island opposite the park is Coconut Island and it can be reached by the arched Japanese bridge from the parking area. In Hawaiian history, the tiny, palm-covered island was a sanctuary with birthing and healing stones.

A touch of color you shouldn't miss at 8AM or before is the Suisan Fish Market at the junction of Banyan Drive and Kamehameha Avenue. There is a fascination in watching the giant tuna, the mahimahi and the smaller ocean fish being marked, auctioned and trucked away.

Next to the wholesale market is a store. Fish store? No, not in Hilo. It is an ice cream parlor.

At the corner is the electric power plant. I remember seeing this not-so-secure structure after the tidal wave when it was knocked cock-eyed and wondered when they would tear it down. They never did. Not in Hilo.

The airport with its smashing all-weather terminal is practically in downtown Hilo. Writing about it recalls the memory of landing in the first 707 jet airplane to arrive on the Big Island.

It was a Pan Am plane taking a group of Honolulu businessmen on a demonstration flight. The captain of the plane didn't get the huge ship down until we were in the middle of the cross runway and the new 707 ended up at the very end of the strip facing the kiawe trees. The welcoming committee and the people lining the fence thought it very exciting.

Two suggestions to help you catch the flavor of Hilo.

The first is to go to the Paramount Grill.

At one time in the old part of town facing the bay, the Hilo Drugstore with its counter stools was where the local businessmen gathered for morning coffee. It is gone, but the Paramount Grill at 37 Haili Street across from the old Palace Theater still remains. Twelve stools, five booths and a dining room upstairs. Calendars on the walls, fresh flower on shelves, sprigs of orchids. We ate spam'n'eggs, fried rice and homemade biscuits. A wall sign read: "Today's Specials: crab foo yung, fresh corned beef and cabbage, Italian spaghetti, cold fried chicken and fries." Good food at reasonable prices. Old Hilo.

While we are at it, let's mention other Old Hilo favorites: K K Tei for Japanese food, Sun Sun Lau Chop Sui House for Chinese food, the Hukilau Hotel for breakfast, and Rosey's Boathouse near the civic auditorium for anything else (but not for lunch).

The other starting suggestion for the taste of Hilo is to visit the Lyman Mission House & Museum farther up Haili Street (276 Haili).

The Lyman Mission House, built in 1839, reflects the life and times of early missionaries. Like the Mission Houses in Honolulu, the Baldwin House at Lahaina, Maui, and the Waioli Mission House at Hanalei on Kauai, it is a part of that historical time when the cultural axis of the islands changed from a simple but highly structured tribal society led by a hierarchy of chiefs to a democracy, with all the mores, strengths and weaknesses of the Western world.

Next door, the descendants of Rev. and Mrs. David Lyman built the Lyman Museum. Although small, it has mounted the most effective exhibit of the migratory procession of races to Hawaii of any museum in the state. You stroll through history in a single room, one ethnic presentation flowing into the next as, in fact, one racial group melded with another in history.

It is an interesting progression to review because the unique mix of races is the foundation for Hawaii's prime asset—her lovely people.

The Polynesians came in two principal echelons, first about 600 A.D. from the Marquesas and, again, about 400 years later from what is now known as the Society Islands of French Polynesian, 2,700 miles away.

The Polynesians developed their own lifestyles and agricultural and fishing communities, undisturbed until the arrival of Captain Cook in 1778.

The missionaries came in 1820 from the East Coast of the United States, setting sail in the *Thaddeus* on October 23, 1819. It took 164 days to come around Cape Horn to their new home.

Missionaries and their offspring established a prosperous sugar industry, and, looking for labor to work the plantation fields, they negotiated an arrangement with the Emperor of China to import Chinese nationals in 1852. The flow of cheap labor was cut off by the Chinese Exclusion Act 30 years later.

In 1878, Portuguese were brought from the Azores and Madeira whose volcanic islands had climatic and geographic similarities to the Hawaiian islands. Unlike the other laborers who came as single men, the Portuguese came with large families.

A famine in Japan was a primary consideration for the Emperor to allow Japanese citizens to accept labor contracts in Hawaii in 1885. They came principally from the Hiroshima and Yamaguchi Prefectures.

The Russian-Japanese War of 1904-1905 shut off the Japanese labor flow, but Koreans, under the protection of Japan, were allowed to emigrate because of a severe drought. The emigration ban went back into force in 1905.

The last major wave of labor immigrants came from the Philippines in 1906.

During all of this time, Caucasians were arriving as missionaries from all denominations, as whalers and sailors, businessmen and confidence men, engineers and agriculturalists, etc.

My regret is that no museum in Hawaii has done a comprehensive presentation of the Polynesians' exploration of the Pacific with dates—or time frames—and places of the occupation on all the islands in the Hawaiian archipelago. Visitors to Hawaii have little understanding of the heroic exploration of the "Eastern Polynesian Triangle"—one of the most astounding feats of discovery in the history of mankind.

The Polynesians, without compass or charts, emigrated as far south as New Zealand, as far east as Easter Island, and as far north as Hawaii. They traversed these thousands and thousands of miles of empty ocean with only an understanding of the stars, the shapes, the colors and even the sounds of waves and currents, the moon, the sun, the birds, the clouds. A superb story.

Upstairs in the Lyman museum is probably the state's most comprehensive exhibit of rocks. Geologists and mineralogists conceivably could find Orlando Lyman among his rocks, cataloguing his beloved collection.

Also on Haili Street is the Haili Church built in 1824. The wood for the church came from a forest known as "haili" or in English "loving memory."

Hilo in April is the scene of the Merrie Monarch Festival, an event created to draw tourists to the Big Island but which has proven so popular with the hula dance studios (halaus) on all the islands that it is almost impossible for a tourist to get a ticket. (See your travel agent.)

We were able to get tickets only because the Lady Navigator's hairdresser dances with a Honolulu halau and he promoted a pair for us. In turn, the Lady Navigator worried like a little mother whether Dennis would perform well. He did.

The festival is a marathon of the hula, a three-night event featuring the ancient (kahiko) hula, and modern (auwana) hula, and the chant (mele). Participating troupes of dancers, male and female, train rigorously all year long. It is a very local, cousin-kissing event, overflowing with the aloha spirit.

The competition of dances and chants goes until midnight and when the winners are announced at the Saturday finale, it is a time of cheering and weeping—very emotional.

Interestingly, there has been a renaissance of Hawaiian culture in the islands, and the music and dancing of Polynesia are finding a larger and larger audience of appreciative people.

Put it down in your book if you are going to be in the islands the week after Easter: The Merrie Monarch Festival in Hilo. Even if you never get to the festival, you'll reap its rewards at any Polynesian performance you attend in the Islands—so strong has been its influence in regenerating pride in the ancient Hawaiian performing arts.

Another annual Hawaiian event, the Kamehameha Song Festival, which has contributed to this resurgence of Hawaiiana is also in early spring ... and televised. An acappella battle of the classes of the Kamehameha High School, (only part-Hawaiians can be students) it is an emotional, highly charged event. We promise you, you will cry, whether you attend the performance, or watch it on video.

Orchids and Gardens

In Hilo, you should visit one of the many orchid or anthurium nurseries, like Orchids of Hawaii near the airport. Neither the orchid nor the anthurium is native to Hawaii, but both grow so well that the Big Island is referred to by the floral industry as the biggest greenhouse in the world. (You can buy and send inspected seeds, plants and cuttings back home.)

Another botanical experience we recommend to friends is the Hawaii Tropical Botanical Garden five miles north of Hilo on Highway-19. Take the blue "Scenic Drive" sign to the right. Drive a short distance to the Old Yellow Church on the left, where you find parking. A van takes you down the gate-locked, one-way road to Onomea Bay.

Oh, yes, you should make reservations because visitors are limited to 50 a day in order to protect the environment and to allow visitors enjoyment of the garden's natural beauty without the bustle of crowds. Very smart.

A few years ago the bay was visited by a West Coast lumberman who appreciated the natural beauty of the surroundings and, fearing that lands of this sort might disappear in the future, he bought 17 acres on the coast and set about enhancing the Eden-like setting with exotic plantings and garden paths.

To locals, the area is known as Onomea Arch because the sea carved a natural lava bridge at land's end. In 1958, the bridge collapsed, but the name still remains.

The van leaves visitors off at a circular drive area flanked by a lily pond. What you do first is go to the nearby rain shelter and spray yourself with mosquito repellent that is thoughtfully provided. If the day so dictates, borrow a Japanese umbrella. Besides umbrellas and repellent, there is jug of water, paper cups and benches for resting. No gift shop with T-shirts, no food stand with hot dogs and no picnicking but—another nice touch—you can sample the mango, passion fruit and guava that have fallen from their trees. All are edible but you are asked not to pick any fruit or touch any of the plants, some of which are poisonous.

A map in a brochure tells the visitor what is found where and path signs point to different gardens.

The number one path on the map takes you out to a vista point overlooking the bay. It is a peaceful, scenic spot where you can watch the waves sweep into the cove, the former landing area for immigrant laborers, and imagine the arch that once connected the now isolated island to the mainland.

Nearby is a tiny cemetery with unmarked grave stones.

The path goes along the coastline for a hundred yards to Turtle Point overlooking the outlet of the Alakahi Stream. Ocean waves that seem to accelerate as they near land explode white spray against the lava rocks. On a calm day, you can still see giant turtles.

You walk back to the starting point, the rain shelter, through a natural jungle along the stream.

From the lily pond, path signs point to the Bromeliad Hill—remember, bromeliad is the family name of the pineapple plant—on to a banyan grove and down to the Onomea Stream where a platform permits you to look down on the clear waters and into the banyan canyon. Pretty place. You immediately wish you were in a bathing suit and could jump into one of the pools.

The path goes upstream, through a fern forest, a banana grove, a palm jungle to the Onomea Waterfalls.

You won't see a more perfect waterfall in Hawaii. Larger waterfalls, yes. More spectacular waterfalls, yes. But the Onomea Waterfalls are ideally sculpted, falling first one direction to swirl briefly in a pool, rushing to the opposite direction, then reversing itself once again ... spilling poetically down the craggy cliff. We called them the "Hula Waterfalls." On a sunny day, a 3P picture.

Plots of exotic plants have been created throughout the garden: heliconias, colorful bird of paradise, torch ginger, all sorts of plants of medicinal value, and ornamentals.

The lily pond is filled with colorful Japanese koi (carp) and the jungle areas are aflutter with birds of many feathers, including peacocks and Chinese thrushes.

Time is a factor of your own making; take as much or little time as you want to browse the pathways, a total of only a mile. The van comes and goes at frequent intervals.

When you are returned to the Old Yellow Church, you are given a red anthurium and a brochure from Kuaola Farms, just outside of Hilo, which also offers nursery tours.

For a small additional charge, visitors to the Hawaii Tropical Botanical Garden can be picked up at hotels.

Note: wear flat-heel shoes for easier walking and take a hat.

The Noble Nut

While we are in this botanical/agricultural mood, let us urge you to tour the Mauna Loa Macadamia Nut plantation and processing plant two miles south of Hilo on the highway to the volcano. (Hours are 7:30AM to 3:30PM.)

The macadamia nut story in Hawaii is a Horatio Alger success story in its own right. Its prosperity has replaced, to a large extent, the loss of sugar cane income to the County.

Starting as an experiment in 1956 with a small grove on trees in the same area as the present Mauna Loa operation, C. Brewer saw macadamia nuts as a long range gamble. First there was no market for the nuts. The trees had been brought to the islands from Australia during the time of the whalers and were used as ornamentals because it is a pretty tree, full and deep green.

Commercially, the macadamia tree was discouraging because it took so long to bear fruit. First modest yields occur at the fifth year and full crops are more likely to take seven years.

An added deterrent was that the nickel-sized nuts were almost impossible to crack. Old timers tell of putting nuts under boards and then driving a car over the boards to crack the shells. (The name of the nut should have come from *macadam*, that highway paving material, it is so hard. It came, however, from Dr. John Macadam, an Australian chemist, he being the first man to discover their delectability.)

To crack the shell without shattering the kernel was a major Hawaii-pioneered achievement. So was the roasting process. Because the nut is 74 percent oil, it goes rancid without the proper roasting.

If you drive from Hilo to Kona along the southwestern route, you will be amazed at the miles of acreage devoted to the rich trees. Islandwide, there are 15,000 acres planted on 460 macadamia nut farms, and 5,000 of those acres haven't yet reached the bearing state. We find the sight of the unending orchards magnificent and awesome.

Today's production in weight exceeds 36 million pounds and $27 million in value.

Many of the present producers plus major companies not presently into macadamia nuts are planning to devote thousands of acres to future plantings, making it a fair certainty that macadamia nuts will be twice as valuable to the economic future of Hawaii within the next ten years.

Which is the reason we recommend to friends a visit to Mauna Loa, the world's largest grower, processor and marketer of the macadamia. It is another dimension in understanding Hawaii. (And it doesn't take very long.)

You drive from the highway through a major grove of mature trees where the nuts are scooped up from the ground by mechanical harvesters.

A stroll along a second floor glass-paneled walkway permits you to view all of the Mauna Loa plant operations—the cracking, weighing, sorting, cooking, salting, candy-making, and packaging. Taped commentaries tell you what's happening at different stations.

Across a driveway is a shop where you can buy the variety of products manufactured, or they will mail for you. Also an ice cream stand. Macadamia nut ice cream is delicious. We insist that out-of-town guests taste macadamia nut ice cream, preferably served in a fresh papaya.

Chocolate covered macadamia nuts are one of the most popular sellers—calories on top of calories—which Mauna Loa started producing in 1985.

Half of the producing trees in Hawaii are owned or managed by Mauna Loa which is expanding its acreage by 100,000 seedlings a year.

Waterfalls And Volcanoes

Hilo is wet.

One scenic advantage of rain, lots of rain, is the waterfall. You can't miss the 3P waterfalls in and around Hilo.

Just above the city is Rainbow Falls.

North of Hilo, on Highway-19, is Akaka State Park and two more spectacular cascades of water: Kapuna Falls and Akaka Falls.

All are spectacular. So is the foliage surrounding them. Look carefully at some of the "trees" of Philodendron and monstera, and remember they are the same plants you grow in small pots back home. Go see what a lot of water can do and shoot all three.

The beauty of the Hilo waterfalls is a good warm-up for the rarity of the Big Island's most popular attraction: the Volcanoes National Park where the earth is still alive, hissing, bubbling, sometimes blowing hot rocks to God.

There are two ways to go to the park. (See map.) The easiest way is straight up Highway-11, a 30 mile 45-minute drive.

The longer way, the more scenic way, is via Puna (Highway-130) along the coast, then up the Chain of Craters Road. This circuitous route rewards you with vistas of papaya orchards, orchid and anthurium nurseries, the chance to shop in small village stores and "talk story" with residents, but best of all, the opportunity to witness some of the fascinating phenomena of past volcanic eruptions such as jet-black sand beaches, "lava trees", the spring-fed lava basin that served as a queen's bath, even a field of petroglyphs.

Near Kalapana, watch for the sign to the Queen's Bath, just off the highway and take a dip in the open fresh-water pool.

As you drive up the Chain of Craters Road, you are following the active rift line of the present volcanic action.

Note: in the past Madame Pele has shown her displeasure with this road and covered it with lava. Be sure to check if it is open before you make the drive.

In any case, we strongly advise obtaining a rental tape recorder and the Apple Tour Tapes before leaving Hilo. The recorder permits all occupants of a car to hear the commentary clearly and provides you with the flexibility to keep your own pace yet learn a lot about that you are seeing.

One tape is devoted to the trip between Hilo and the Volcano on Highway-11, with different information about the return trip on the opposite side of the tape. Another tape describes the drive along the Chain of Craters road.

A third tape takes you on a drive around the rim of the Kilauea Crater starting at the park's Visitor Center, and programs stops and comments at the most interesting spots.

Russ Apple, a Ph.D. Historian of the Pacific and a National Park Service ranger for 35 years (now retired) created and narrates the tapes. Perfectly.

We have been to the volcano countless times, but using the Apple Tour of the Crater Rim with Russ Apple as a personal, portable guide was a delight, and a new learning experience.

We never knew, for example, that Hawaii had "acid rain," that controversial issue of the Vietnam war we have read so much about.

South of the crater is an area known as the Kau Desert, a wasteland unusual for Hawaii. What we learned from Russ was that when the fumes from the volcano become airborne, tons of toxic material are blown south by the prevailing tradewinds, and in the constant moisture of the volcano area, that material is converted into acid rain, killing almost every plant striving to live.

When you use the tapes outside of the car, expect people to sidle up to you and listen in. Makes you feel like an authority.

The Apple tapes can be rented in Hilo at the Hilo Hawaiian Hotel and the Lyman House Museum, at the Volcano in the Volcano Art Center, and, in Kona, at the Kona Activities Center in the lobby of the King Kamehameha Hotel.

If you rent a tape in Hilo, you can leave it off in Kona and vice versa.

The Volcanoes National Park is a most unusual place.

It is filled with scenic contradictions. Ashen, undernourished and gnarled ohia trees aflame with red lehua blossoms somehow remind the Lady Navigator of the Hunchback of Notre Dame. How's that? His incredible gentleness, she says, is like the delicate flower of the suffering tree, a comparison which could only be created out of a squirrelly Texas mind.

Smoldering firepits are rimmed with gigantic ferns and 'ohelo bushes. Even on a stark lava field, as barren as a lunar landscape, life can be witnessed in a tuft of grass or a skinny sapling.

Frequently, the park seems to be in the eye of an enwrapping cloud, mysterious and haunting. At 4,000 feet above sea level, the weather moves easily, and instantly, between bright sun and mountain mists. The air is crisp and clear. A sweater and raingear are de rigueur.

Madame Pele, the fire goddess, dwells here and stories of a beautiful lady in a red dress accompanied by her dog are often told: she is beautiful ... she is seen alongside the road ... she appears out of a crater ... she inexplicably disappears.

After you have heard enough of these stories and you find yourself on a road after dark in the volcano area and the mist settles around your car, you begin to feel things that are not natural. Your eyes widen. You sense that *she* might be around the next turn ... and *she* might be.

The ultimate aspect of the Volcanoes National Park is to see a volcano in action.

It does not happen all of the time.

Twenty years ago it seemed to happen infrequently and when news broke that the volcano had erupted, the local airlines were filled with Honolulu people rushing to Hilo to rent a car and drive to the volcano.

I remember in October of 1959 we were at a dinner party in a suburb of Honolulu when the radio news announced that the small crater next to Kilauea, Kilauea Iki, was erupting.

We immediately voted to go and chartered an airplane, drove to the airport and took off in full moonlight in a twin-engine Beechcraft.

It was cold-on-cold and we huddled and shivered on the flight until, half way to the Big Island, the glow of the volcano was visible. From then until we were on the way back home, we forgot the temperature.

As we approached closer and closer, the sight became more and more awesome.

A shaft of fire spurted skyward, a fountain of red-white lava over 1,000 feet high spewing out of the corner of the crater. In addition to the fountain, one entire lip of the crater looked as if it had been ripped open by a giant can opener and a sheet of red lava from the crater wall was cascading down to form a red river that poured into the bottom of the caldera.

It had the sound of the roar of a blast furnace, only cranked up to unbelievable decibels, almost drowning out the airplane engines.

In spite of the roar, we could still hear tiny strings of lava, called Pele's hair, tinkling as they hit the plane's wings and body as we circled 2,000 feet above the fountaining.

It was so terrifying and so beautiful.

Recently, there has been almost continuous activity in the area. Even Mauna Loa erupted in 1984 for the first time in ten years.

Often, eruptions are visible only from airplanes—weather permitting—because they break out in inaccessible locations.

Even if you don't find visible action at the park, there is enough to occupy a full day or at least a half day.

You should go first to the Volcano House, a modest lodge at the edge of the Kilauea caldera and look across its vast, circular, two-mile expanse of canyon with the smaller fire pit, Halemaumau, at the bottom. Fissured openings vent ominous wisps of steam periodically.

The Volcano House is a great place to spend the night if you can get a reservation. The restaurant is too packed at lunch with tour groups to enjoy, but breakfast and dinner at the venerable inn are most enjoyable. There is always a big fire stoked in the stone fireplace, the rooms are comfortable and the volcano in the first morning light and at dusk are irreplaceable experiences.

The hotel dates back to the middle of the 19th century, to grass shack roots when guests slept on lauhala mats on the earthen floor. It gradually evolved into a respectable hotel, hosting every celebrity who ever visited Hawaii.

In 1895, the hostelry was sold to "Uncle George" Lycurgus, a legend during his lifetime, and still, for his bond of friendship with Madame Pele. He supplied her with gin wrapped in ti leaves tossed ceremonially into the caldera; she invoked volcanic action to supply him with full houses of customers.

One hospitality room in the Volcano House is wallpapered with pictures of the famous people who signed autographs for "Uncle George."

After visiting the Volcano House, go to the Visitor Center for an orientation film and a small museum run by the National Park Service. A ranger will be on duty at an Information Booth to answer your questions.

You can learn about cabins and camping in the park but reservations are handled by the Volcano House. (The Center has clean restrooms.)

Within a hundred yards of the Visitor Center is the Volcano Art Center housed in the original frame Volcano House, circa 1877. It was the first Western-style building in the region and was known as "a thirteen pillow" establishment. In 1921, it was moved to its present site to make room for a larger, grander lodge.

The art center has an extensive collection of paintings, posters, cards, handicrafts, jewelry, etc. It is also the venue for local dance concerts, art shows, poetry readings.

Past the sulfur pits is a military recreation camp and on the other side of the camp is the Volcano Golf Club, the most unusual club in Hawaii because it is the only golf course in Hawaii where you can't see the ocean and where at places steam vents from the hot lava beneath the course distract the delicately balanced golfer who has never played the course before.

(Can you imagine the stories a visiting golfer might tell his regular foursome back home after playing golf on Maui where he saw whales breaching at Kaanapali and then, on the Big Island, where he witnessed volcanic action at the Volcano Golf Club?)

The golf course is private but open to public play. You should reserve tee times to ensure that you aren't running across a tournament or a time restricted to membership play. It is a challenging 18-hole par-72 course with an added attraction that wild bird life can frequently be seen in the surrounding forests.

I have played there in the late afternoon when the mists have rolled in and the weather could have been that of Scotland. It is also the only course in Hawaii where you will need a sweater.

From the Volcano to Kona: Cane and Nuts and Coffee

The drive from the Volcanoes National Park to the town of Kailua-Kona is 96 miles. You can take two and a half hours through varied, interesting country or you can stop and dally and take a full day.

Let's dally. First stop before leaving the park is the Hawaii Visitors Bureau marker to Footprints Trail. About a mile in from the roadside are the footprints left in 1790 by members of a retreating Hawaiian army who were trapped in the ashes of an erupting Kilauea and buried alive. It happened.

When you leave the park, you are almost immediately in a different environment.

It becomes agricultural land, miles of sugar cane, followed by miles of macadamia nut groves.

This is land controlled by C. Brewer, the Big Five company that is a major sugar factor on all islands, and the owner of the Mauna Loa macadamia nut operation.

At Punaluu, the company made a strong effort to convert coastal land into a resort complex. They built an attractive 18-hole golf complex called SeaMountain with condominiums and a nearby restaurant at the black sand beach of Punaluu. At one time the resort was having a problem because every visitor wanted to take a scoop of black sand back home, and the beach was disappearing. Good place to take a swim if the surf is not too high.

An HVB marker on the left directs you to the resort. If you are looking for a peaceful, undisturbed golfing vacation within driving distance of the southernmost spot in America—that's right!—and adjacent to two non touristy rural Hawaiian communities, try SeaMountain.

Have you ever been in the southernmost city in the United States? It's not Laredo, Texas or Key West Florida, but Naalehu, Hawaii, a couple of miles beyond Punaluu. Stop and mail a postcard.

Naalehu holds a Fourth of July annual rodeo that is an exotic down-home hoot. A local hospice is the Shirakawa Motel, built 25 years ago, with modest rooms for about $18 a night.

The next village, Waiohinu, has always been pleasing to me because it is sleepy, with old wooden houses and green lawns with flowers in the yards. A pre-war church watches over the parishioners. Mark Twain planted a monkeypod tree when he passed through here a long time ago.

Nearby on the highway is the turnoff to South Point, Ka Lae, the southernmost piece of land in the United States, but the road is broken and driving is slow. Good for adventuring if you have the time because here are caves used perhaps by the first Polynesians to land in Hawaii. Also a beach with green sand from olivines.

Look for Manuka State Park along the highway for a pit stop where there is an aboretum and clean restrooms.

We didn't go to South Point or stop at Manuka because the Lady Navigator insisted on driving the two hours it takes to reach the old Hawaiian fishing village of Milolii. The road is narrow and tortuous and Milolii is no longer the film version of a grass shack community. Instead, it is a hodgepodge of old pieces of lumber shaped into shacks, abandoned buses, lean-tos modernized with blue plastic shelter add-ons.

The natives who are left in Milolii fish for their supper. From their attitude, they don't enjoy the intrusion by rental car occupants who come to their village and stare and snap pictures. Who would?

But the ocean front is lovely with tidal pools swishing into calm lava-lined coves. A circular park at land's end has palm-covered tables and benches. The water teases you to swim. A peaceful, but not too comfortable, spot.

When we were there on a sunny morning, looking across the bluest of waters, without a sound to be heard except the gurgle of water in the tidal pools and the whisper of tradewinds in the overhead palm trees, the huge white shape of the *S.S. Constitution* appeared offshore, heading for Kona. Standing in the shade at Milolii, a backwater of Hawaii, the cruise ship might as well have come from another world.

After regaining Highway-11, we were then heading straight north. We passed through lava flows from past eruptions off the flank of Mauna Loa: 1926, 1919, three separate eruptions from 1950. As the road climbed higher above the coastline we came into the coffee trees of Kona.

This is the only coffee grown in the U.S. and its success is due to the crumbly lava soil, the faithful moisture, and the afternoon cloud cover, unique factors that combine to give the area the ideal situation for growing coffee beans with a rich, full flavor. And very expensive.

At one time, a special school holiday in October allowed students whose parents grew coffee the free time to help harvest the crop, because the "cherries" with two beans in every cherry had to be picked by hand. But the custom was ended as being a child labor abuse. (The students' grade average didn't improve after the holiday custom was rescinded. In fact it fell.)

The cost of hired labor drove many of the coffee farmers out of business. Orchards were abandoned. But today, orchards are being revived because the Kona coffee is in demand, especially in Japan, and farmers at the present market levels can make $6,000 an acre.

Two Scenes: One of Forgiveness, One of Murder

Ninety miles beyond the Volcanoes National Park is a turnoff to Hookena Beach Park, and beyond that, a sign to Honaunau, on Highway-160. At the bottom of the hill is the intriguing former palace grounds, Pu'uhonua o Honaunau, or as we know it today, the City of Refuge, a national historical park.

This well restored site was a place of safety for Hawaiians who had fallen from grace for any infraction of the many Hawaiian rules, *if* they made it inside the almost impenetrably 10- by 17-foot lava walls that extended 1,000 feet along the shoreline.

The society in the pre-Cook days was structured for the survival of the rulers. There was a great chief, served by minor chiefs, served by family, served by commoners. Various priests, or kahunas, were interwoven into the society with religious tabus.

Offenses were severely dealt with. The death penalty was not uncommon, nor was human sacrifice, to serve religious customs.

The escape clause in the society's contract was the Place of Refuge.

Prisoners of war, tabu breakers, criminals ... all who had reached the area and were blessed by a kahuna could return to their families, even after one day, and remain safe.

Being there was one thing. Getting there was another. Honaunau was a palace area which meant vigilant guards to get past. The other entry was by the sea, and those formidable walls.

The park is open from 8AM until dusk, and there are rangers to answer questions, printed folders to guide you on walk-throughs of the park. Or you may rent a taped narration about the City of Refuge at the Visitor Center entrance.

Note: before going all the way down the hill, look for a side road to the right which leads to one of the Big Island's famous "painted churches." Here is St. Benedict's, the parish church of a Belgian priest who never forgot the glories of the European churches, and attempted to capture the color and the majesty of the ancient cathedrals by painting the walls and the ceilings of his modest little mountainside church in Kona. It was repainted and restored in 1985.

After the City of Refuge, stay along the small coast road to Napoopoo, a name which sounds like it came from a Gilbert and Sullivan operetta. Look across Kealakekua Bay to the white monument marking the place where Captain James Cook, the Western discoverer of Hawaii and much of the Pacific, was killed on his third voyage. The date was February 14, 1779.

Cook, the son of a farm foreman in Yorkshire, went to sea on coal-hauling vessels as a boy where he served and learned until becoming a marine officer, and then joined the British Navy.

Despite his humble origins and lack of formal education, Cook was an astonishing man. He was a self-taught mathematician, astronomer and navigator. In North America, where the British were fighting the French for control of Canada, the Yorkshire lad became a respected Naval surveyor and map maker.

His experience and contributions to the Royal Society gained him the command of an expedition to Tahiti to measure the eclipse of Venus—and, covertly, to seek the Southern Continent. The first successful enterprise led to a second voyage and then a third, this time with the mission to discover the northwest passage from the Pacific to the Atlantic which, if found, would win a heady prize of twenty thousand pounds.

On the third mission, on his way north from Tahiti which he now knew very well from the previous two voyages, he found Kauai. From there Captain Cook sailed to the northern coast of America, up to Alaska, through the Bering Sea until his ships were finally turned back by a wall of ice.

He returned to the warm waters and islands which he called the Sandwich Islands, to put in for rest and repairs before striking north again.

Safe anchorage was found at Kealakekua Bay in the autumn time where Cook was received as the priests thought him to be—a god. Specifically the god Lono.

The creaking abused ships, the *Resolution* and the *Discovery*, were put in order. Stores and water were plentiful and the natives generous ... including the women with all favors.

After a month of such hospitality, the expedition set off again for the north.

But shortly after leaving the bay, the *Resolution* sprang its main mast. No anchorage could be found and the ships reluctantly returned to Kealakekua. The reception of the natives who had given almost everything they had to the English ships during the former visit lacked the same aloha spirit.

Stealing, always a problem in Polynesia, increased and led to friction.

Culmination came when the line of a pinnace, a small sailing tender, was found severed one morning, the boat gone.

Cook took matters in his own hands and, following his custom in similar situations, he gave orders to blockade the harbor and went ashore with a contingent of marines to take the chief into custody aboard the *Resolution* until the pinnace was returned.

A crowd formed. The hysterical wife of the chief begged him not to go with Cook. In the meantime, a minor chief attempting to leave the bay was killed and the news spread through the now hostile crowd which began arming.

Shots were fired. The crowd charged. Cook was felled. Marines were killed. An English boat manned by Williamson with back-up troops retreated instead of closing to shore.

Cook was clubbed down in the water and then dragged up on shore and stabbed again and again to the horror of the English sailors.

Cook was dead.

Later, parts of his body were returned and were buried at sea at Kealakekua Bay.

For years I have been a confessed "Cooky Groupy." I have stood at Point Venus where he established his celestial observatory in Tahiti, visited his first landing place at Poverty Bay in New Zealand, toured as he toured the villages of Tonga, walked the shores of the river in Australia's Queensland where he beached to repair his ship after putting a hole in its side on a coral head off the Great Barrier Reef.

I have journeyed to Marton-on-Cleveland, his birthplace in England, visited his second story schoolroom at the Postgate School at Ayton, spent days in the research rooms of the Public Library outside of London reading original logs, and my library is filled with Cookmania including the journals in four major volumes, published by the Hakluyt Society.

For me, to just look across the bay to the obelisk erected and maintained by Britain was not enough.

The easiest way to visit the monument is by boat. I had an ambition to be at the site, as he was, as dawn arrived on February 14.

Chartering a boat to lay off the shore overnight proved to be too difficult.

I contacted Peter Fithian who organizes the Billfish Tournament in Kona and told him my ambition. Peter called one of his billfish lieutenants, Ken Michaels, in Kona who in turn contacted a school teacher friend who lives near the village of Captain Cook above Kealakekua Bay.

So it was that the Lady Navigator and I went to the home of Tojiro and Satsuki Motoki, complete strangers, in Captain Cook where they not only gave us a bedroom to spend the night but also had guests in to drink and eat with us. In addition, Tojiro borrowed a neighbor's four-wheel jeep to drive us down the rutted trail to the monument site before sunrise.

To arrive before the sun did, we had to be up at 4AM, but we had a call at 3.

"You shouldn't miss this," said the quiet Tojiro. "At this time of year you can see the Southern Cross. Come and look."

There to the south, clear on the night's starlit horizon, was the Southern Cross, brilliant in the sky.

After coffee and rolls, we bundled into the jeep and bumped our way down the mountain and finally reached the edge of the water and waited for the dawn.

The first light edged over the mountain and slowly the bay filled with a tint of gold; it grew stronger and stronger until a vivid yellow light slashed across the water. Then the sun inched over the shoulder of Mauna Loa.

Behind us were the stone walls of the ancient village of Kaawaloa. Ahead was the bay. Was it this quiet, this still, two hundred years ago? Could such a calm dawn be the opening curtain for such a morning of violence?

Near the white monument that is visible from the far shore and just under the tidal water is a plaque with bronze letters set in stone which reads: "Near this spot Captain Cook was slain on February 14, 1779."

The 27-foot white memorial erected by the British has similar wording and was erected in 1877, replacing an earlier memorial. The land under the monument was ceded to the British government by Princess Miriam Likelike on January 26, 1877 in a letter of conveyance to Major James Hay Woodhouse, Her Majesty's British Commissioner and Consul to Hawaii.

We took pictures, inspected the lava walls and finally left the area.

It was my last Cook pilgrimage.

Kailua-Kona, the Sea of the Big Fish

On the other side of the Pali from Honolulu is the bedroom community of Kailua.

To save confusion at the post office, Kailua on the Big Island is called Kailua-Kona. It is a major resort destination area with major hotels, fast food stops, shopping malls and arcades, historical sites and the best deep sea fishing for the famous blue marlin in the islands ... some say "in the world."

We had gone to Kona as spectators of the annual Hawaiian International Billfish Tournament in August. It is another of those special events that is a bonus, should you be visiting the Big Island during August.

The Hawaiian International Billfish Tournament is not publicized as a spectator event but it should be because, from pierside, the visitor gets to enjoy much of the excitement and the color without spending the large sums invested by the fishermen contestants—and doesn't get seasick.

Invitations are eagerly sought by fishing clubs from around the world. Seventy 4-person teams from 19 nations participated that year, coming from South Africa, the Orient, Australia, New Zealand, Tahiti, Guam, Mexico, Canada, and almost every country known for fishing you could name. Representing the United States, besides Hawaii, were teams from California, Alaska, and even non-coastal states such as Nevada, Utah and Nebraska.

The tournament registration starts on a Friday and contestants leave ten days later, having spent five days fishing and five days partying. Fisherman, you've probably heard, like to party.

Headquarters for the event is the King Kamehameha Hotel, on Kamakahonu Bay and immediately behind the pier. From an elevated control tower back of the beachfront, tournament officials keep in close radio contact with the fishing boats and post current marlin catches throughout the day.

We arrived on Sunday, the opening ceremony day.

First there was a parade of the contestants down Alii Drive, the waterfront main street. The teams rode in flower bedecked convertibles interspersed with floats by supportive merchants and grateful community groups, and music by school and military bands. The Lady Navigator said it reminded her of her high school homecoming parades in Center, Texas.

The pier ceremonies followed under a sweltering mid-afternoon sun. In the square formed by bleachers reserved for all participants, a representative team from each country was introduced, his national flag raised as his national anthem was played. Nineteen flags were raised. Nineteen taped national anthems were played. Nineteen thousand photographs were snapped. A favorite: a burly, blond Australian holding a small, stuffed kangaroo.

That night there was a Meet-The-Teams cocktail party and buffet outdoors, lighted by luau torches and featuring Hawaiian music.

The action started on the pier at dawn the next morning, an exciting place for a spectator to be, as 70 teams boarded and loaded 70 boats in a carefully orchestrated, well rehearsed drill that required less than ten minutes per boat. Maximum. Just to watch the captains jockey their crafts into reverse, home into pre-assigned numbered docking positions as if they were magnetized, swiftly board contestants and their gear, and throttle out again—as the next boat was coming in—was thrilling.

Rods and reels worth a fortune were hand carried on board by the fishermen, some rather heavy-eyed, together with refreshments and lunch. Conversations, and indeed official communications, were conducted in Japanese, Chinese, Tahitian, French, and all versions of English from clipped British and slangy Aussie to local pidgin.

The contestants would be fishing from 8AM until 4PM.

We boarded a huge Captain Bean glass bottom boat that stood just outside the harbor to watch the boats come across the starting line designated as being between a U.S. Coast Guard cutter and the Kailua lighthouse.

The countdown started. The hour hand crept closer. Now the boat captains were counting off the seconds.

It was a pretty sight in the typically Kona morning sunshine. Seventy white-hulled boats creeping towards the starting line across the calm and sparkling blue waters of the bay.

Promptly at the 60th second, the fleet charged out of the bay like a pack of racing boats.

I had thought they would cruise leisurely to the fishing grounds but, no, each captain had his favorite spot and he wanted to be the first to reach it. It was full throttle for every boat, leaving behind 70 streams of white water. A stirring panorama.

We returned to the pier and I went to the control tower to chat with the father of the Billfish tournament, Peter Fithian, who started the event in 1959.

"What makes Kailua-Kona such a famous fishing area for blue marlin?"

"When you look at a map of the island," said Peter, "you can see how the two shoulders of the Big Island, Mauna Kea to the north and Mauna Loa on the south, produce two circles of wind and water, one coming from the south and the other from the north, that converge here at Kona.

"The action brings all of the fish together which makes for ideal fishing grounds.

"Interestingly, the fishermen are always on the lookout for porpoise because the porpoise and the tuna have a symbiotic relationship and feed on the same fish. A marlin feeds on tuna and can spear a 150-pound fish with its bill.

"Contestants in our tournament can use live bait, usually small tuna, or a lure. The lure developed in Kona has become world famous and is copied everywhere there is fishing for billfish. The 'kona lure' is now generic for a plastic lure with a skirt.

"We don't know as much about marlin as we should so we started in 1983 a Pacific Gamefish Foundation with a laboratory and office here in Kona where statistics can be compiled and studied. If you are on the pier this afternoon to watch the weigh-in, note that we take a sample of blood and a specimen of muscle from every fish which will be studied at the lab. Through this research, we hope to learn more of the basics about the marlin.

"Starting next year, contestants in the tournament will tag and release all marlin weighing less than 100 pounds, not just a step toward conservation but, hopefully, one that will supply us with data about the migratory habits of the marlin."

The best of the spectator events starts just after 4PM daily with the weigh-in of the day's catches. Boats loaded with marlin are backed into the pier and the giant fish are lofted by block and tackle to a scale, weighed, the poundage recorded on placards that then are pinned to the fish so that each crew and Miss Billfish Tournament, in a very skimpy bathing suit and the highest high-heeled shoes, may have their photos taken.

I'd rather land the girl than the marlin. A 2P shot.

Free bleachers are provided for spectators.

As the tournament continues throughout the week, teams are ranked every day according to the total pounds of marlin they have caught. Bonuses are added for marlin caught on lighter than 80 pound test.

Officials test the rod, reel, tackle and gaff of every successful fisherman of the day upon return to the dock for adherence to the tournament rules.

Our sympathies went to the disqualified participant who landed a 987-pound marlin—71 pounds heavier than the tournament record—but on a line that tested out at "substantially more" than the allowable 80 pound test. A real no-no.

The Big Islander at least got to keep his prize. But even that presented problems.

"The longest wall in our house is 15 feet long and 9 feet high. The fish is over 14 feet long and 6 feet in girth. It makes for lively conversation."

We stayed for most of the week at the Kona Surf Hotel, seven miles south of Kailua-Kona at the small boat harbor of Keauhou where there is a new shopping center and 27 holes of golf. A favorite because it is so open and white—Moorish almost. Its five-wing architecture is very dramatic against the black lava point on which it was built and the blue of the sea. It has the best public saltwater swimming pool in the islands.

Two historical places in Kaiula-Kona are within a block of the King Kamehameha Hotel on Alii Drive.

The first is the coral and lava rock Hulihee Palace, built by the Hawaiian governor of the island, John Adams Kuakini, in 1838 and decorated by King Kalakaua as a summer residence. It was in use until 1916.

The "Summer Palace" was restored in 1927 by the Daughters of Hawaii who operate it as a museum.

The rooms are rather small and stuffed with Victorian furniture but it is a heritage of another time in the life of Hawaii and shouldn't be missed.

Across the street is the Mokuaikaua Church built by the missionaries of black lava blocks and ohia beams in 1837. An earlier church was built on the site by Governor Kuakini from timbers taken from the forest area called Mokuaikaua, above Kona town. The cutting of timber and the building of the original church took

4,000 workers. The roof was thatched with pandanus leaves and the foundation stones came from an old heiau. It was destroyed by a fire in 1835.

We consider the Ocean View Inn another historical institution. The floor is bare, the tables linenless but the food is reliable and reasonable, and it is very local.

The street above Alii Drive, Kuakini Highway, has the Kona Ranch House where we go to see Bill Brye, the manager, share a Bloody Mary and have good fish. Tell Bill we sent you, and you don't want the fish unless its fresh.

Speaking of food, we have to backtrack to Highway-11 coming into Kona from the south.

Just up the hill at Honalo is Teshima's, a Japanese restaurant owned and operated by the sweetest lady in the Kailua-Kona area, Mary Teshima. At 75, Mary has been running the family business for over forty years.

"The more people I hire, the harder I work," she told us.

Her steak dinner with rice and garden vegetables is $8.

After a delicious Japanese dinner, we returned the next morning for breakfast because she promised to do homemade hash brown potatoes. She presented us with two kinds of hash browns—hers and a commercial portion. No comparison. Then she served pink papaya from her backyard. Delicious.

Ask for a piece of local pineapple. Incredibly sweet. Almost as sweet as she is.

Another sporting event to look for in October is the Bud Light Ironman Triathlon World Championship which will attract about 1,000 contestants who will start by swimming 2.4 miles, then bicycle 112 miles, followed by running another 26.2 miles.

Isn't that wild?

The triathlon started in Honolulu in 1978 but the traffic demands were too horrendous, like in dangerous, and the event was moved to the Big Island in 1980. It is now a major tourist attraction and Kailua-Kona has become the mecca of triathlon professionals.

On the road to the airport and beyond towards Waimea you'll see cylists in training.

The event starts at 7AM and, under ordinary conditions, the first finishers stagger into view about nine hours later.

In less than ten years the popularity of triathlon has steadily grown; today there are about 1,000 annual triathlon events staged around the world—which shows you that there is no limit to self-flagellation.

To learn more about a less demanding sports activity in the area, scuba diving, we checked in with Tina Clothier, the attractive brunette proprietress of Jack's Diving Locker in the Kona Inn Shopping Village.

Incidentally the best bar in the Kailua-Kona district is in the old Kona Inn facing the ocean.

"Diving in this area is fantastic," Tina said. "The water is warm and clear. We have lots of protected areas to dive where there are schools of reef fish, eels, manta rays, even a whale now and then.

"We have been in business for over three years and so many people come back to us and say the diving in Kona has been the highlight of their Hawaiian vacation."

Jack's two boats, 30- and 45-foot vessels, provide a two-tank dive that leaves at 9AM and returns at 3:30 for $50. An introductory dive ($35) starts in waist-high water and the student is gradually led down to about 20 feet. The shop publishes a free snorkeling/diving map of the Kona Coast and offers a complete assortment of diving gear for rent or sale.

"One of our best dives is a night dive near the Kona Surf," Tina reported.

"I'd go night diving with her anytime," I later, innocently, remarked to the Lady Navigator.

"You'll not even go diving with her in the daytime," was the firm response.

There goes another mermaid.

Walking the Shoreline Trail

The relatively new (1970's) highway north from Kailua-Kona is Highway-19, the Queen Kaahumanu Highway, a straight-arrow road bulldozed over old lava flows.

Before the highway opened there were only two resorts, the Kona Village, reached only by boat or small airplane at its private strip, and Mauna Kea Beach Hotel, reached from Kona via a mountainside road (Highway-190) which went through Waimea and down to the beach.

Now it is a straight shot up the coast.

I did a piece for a national magazine that began with the proposition that newcomers to Hawaii arriving at the Kona airport and driving north would think they were in another world, certainly not the coffee table version—the lushly green world—of Hawaii.

Kona's award winning airport at Keahole is pleasant, open, not too crowded. The way all tropical airports should be.

But once the newly arrived visitor—and some visitors fly directly to Kona from the Mainland—leaves the airport and drives north, what must he think?

On either side of the road are old lava flows, so desolate that only the occasional tuft of blond pili grass survives. No housing. No hot dog stands. Not even a grazing cow.

To the east are high but rounded mountains, often cloud shrouded, and to the west, at least a mile away, is a beachless coastline occasionally punctuated by a cluster of palm trees.

Where is the Hawaii of the postcards?

We were to discover that coast abounds with the beauty and fertility of Hawaii, but you cannot see it from the Kona-Kohala roadway.

You have to walk it.

Hawaiian Walkways conducts three- and five-day hikes along the Kona-Kohala coast.

We signed on for a three-day journey on the Ala Kahakai Trail, The Shoreline Trail, which starts at the small boat harbor south of the airport and ends at Kiholo, an important commercial bay in the last century, 26 miles north.

Hawaiian Walkways treks go from south to north in the winter to put the sun at the hikers' backs and north to south in the summer. Our November hike would go from south to north.

Our baggage consisted of a swimming suit, a towel, a snorkeling mask but no fins (too heavy), extra shirts, shorts and socks, a flashlight and toilet gear. We wore hiking shorts, a light shirt, a hat, and heavy tennis shoes.

We were advised that hiking boots were too heavy and not flexible enough for walking over lava.

We flew to Kona on Aloha Airlines arriving on schedule at 11:50 and were met by Ken Sanborn, the operator of Hawaiian Walkways. He was a surprise. I expected a lean, deeply tanned, craggy-faced mountaineering type. Instead, we were greeted by a large, bespectacled, sandy-haired bear of a man given to easy, almost drawling, carefully considered speech, whose gait was that of a shuffling bear. He had the air more of a philosopher than of a hiking guide.

It was too incongruous. I had to get this straightened out in my mind.

I quickly found out that Ken Sanborn was Dr. Sanborn, a psychologist with a practice in Kailua-Kona, who created Hawaiian Walkways because he enjoys being out in the open, taking people through a scenic, historic portion of Hawaii more than he enjoys unraveling people's emotional problems in an office. Earlier in life, he had retreated from the winter snows of New Hampshire, gained his doctor's degree in psychology at the University of Texas, had worked with the Peace Corps in Waipio Valley on the remote northern shore of the Big Island, and, now, alternated between his hobby and his profession.

At the airport we joined our fellow travelers, a pleasant thirtyish engineer from South Africa, now residing in London, and the housewife of a prominent Honolulu businessman, older than thirty, out for a stroll.

We piled into a battered van and went immediately to the small boat harbor at Honokohau, eight miles south of the airport, where we met Esther, Ken's wife who would meet us every afternoon at a setup camp, and Steve Yeaton, the driver of a truck that looked ready for the junk heap but reliably carried all camp equipment and our extra luggage.

We were issued plastic canteens of water and lightweight backpacks to carry our swim togs, towel and whatever extras we wanted on the trail.

There wasn't time to inspect the harbor which had been dug out of shoreline lava to provide a safe anchorage for the extensive fleet of charter boats used for deep sea fishing. We commenced the first leg of the journey, a 15-minute hike to Honokohau Beach and the Amakapa Pond where we stopped for a sandwich and apple lunch.

The beach, interestingly, is known as a nude beach although, officially, there are no nude beaches in Hawaii. (Very poor nudes. Mostly balding men with gray beards.)

The pond was more interesting because it is one of several along the coast protected as sanctuaries for over 200 kinds of birds such as ducks, coote, stilt.

After lunch, we started on the coastline trail, one of several historic trails which connected ancient seaside communities and intersected trails to upland settlements, the trading routes for exchanging fish and salt for taro and adzes.

The blue waters on Honokohau Bay were almost motionless. The sun-filled day under skies without clouds was comfortable for strolling.

At the end of the bay, Ken led us inland over somewhat smoothed lava paths marked by mounds of small lava stones which the Hawaiians use as landmarks. At the end of the path was a pool of fresh water in a lava basin about 15 feet round and about shoulder deep.

"This is known as Queen's Bath," Ken explained. "It is said that Queen Kaahumanu would come from Kailua-Kona by canoe and be hand carried here to the clear fresh waters for her private bath."

"Can we swim?"

"That's why you are here," said Ken.

Each of us found a convenient lava outcropping to duck behind to change into swim suits. The water was cool, freshly fed from underground springs. What an incongruous lark ... swimming in the middle of a lava field.

The whole hike was to follow the same pattern. Walk a bit, swim, walk a bit, eat, swim.

After toweling off, we changed and dawdled back to the coastline path, now marked by football-sized chunks of white coral and continued north over lava fields, on sandy beaches, sometimes following jeep tracks, stopping at a fisherman's camp on the beach, stumbling onto an isolated but occupied shack (one had a television aerial and a rude no trespass sign).

We walked by other ponds reserved for the birds but filled with fish.

Along a lava cliff bordering the ocean and about 20 feet above it, we peered down into a wide hole which the sea would fill with swirling white foam through an underground tunnel, and then the hole would empty with a loud sucking noise as the waves receded. The hole had no name, and having just swum in the Queen's Bath, we called it the King's Toilet.

A man-made walled compound nearby formed with lava rocks obviously once served a purpose. Had it been a heiau ... or a house site?

Our South African member said that it would be a *kraal* in his country, where cattle would be placed at night to protect them against the lions.

Our first day easy stroll ended at a campsite on the beach where two-person tents with plastic floors and padded sleeping mats were in place. We were issued a sleeping bag, sheets and pillows.

Cooking and serving tables had been set up and a large mat spread on the sand for communal lounging and dining. Sand chairs were neatly arranged around the mat's perimeter.

We had covered four miles and it was still only four in the afternoon.

After straightening out our gear and having cold drinks out of an ice chest, Ken piled us into the truck and drove us two miles farther up beach to the state governmental research facility Ocean Thermal Energy Conversion, (OTEC). The hope is to generate electricity by bringing up cold water from an offshore pipe deep in the ocean.

The nutrient-rich cold ocean waters are also ideal for aquaculture and experiments are being conducted in various phases of fish farming for lobsters and abalone.

The modern frame two-story office building was off limits to visitors but we could see the scattered pipe around the yard and the tanks used for fish experimentation.

It was, obviously, a government funded exercise. Cold water into electricity, lobster and abalone farming in Hawaii?

We returned to a campfire and the smell of potatoes roasting over coals. A jug of red wine was uncorked, beer and soft drinks were offered and a tray of raw vegetables with a creamy dip were placed in the middle of the community mat.

Dinner, later, consisted of barbecued steak, cole slaw and potatoes. Really roughing it.

Kristi, an attractive blond colleague of Esther's in a Kailua real estate office, joined the party to become a hiker for the next two days. Her husband, an attorney in Kona, stayed for dinner only and spoke knowingly of the still prevalent Hawaiian custom of public ownership—and access—of all beaches.

As the stars came out, we had another offshore sight of the *S.S. Constitution*, heading for Maui after the afternoon in Kailua-Kona. Like the reaction at Milolii, we had the feeling that we were looking at another world. To hikers huddled around a beach campfire, the huge ship ablaze with festive lights might have come from another planet.

Oh, yes, off in the encompassing darkness, away from the beach, was a portable flush potty. It was very civilized hike.

The next morning, after juice, fresh papaya and banana bread and coffee, we were on the trail before eight. Ester and Guy stayed behind to break camp.

The sky to the north was darkly ominous and heading in our direction, and soon we were in a light rain. It was refreshing, one of the rare rains in Kona. An hour later, the patter of drops stopped and the sky gradually cleared into another fully sunny day.

"Tomorrow," Ken had said at dinner. "We will experience three kinds of lava. Aa, pahoehoe, and too much."

We walked for miles across lava of every description and color.

"Aa" (ah-ah) is a clinker type of lava resulting when a wall of slowly moving lava crushes itself into fine bits under the pressure of its own weight.

"Pahoehoe" (pah-hoy-hoy) is a shiney black, swirled and coiled pavement of lava that once was a river of hot molten lava, frozen in place as it cooled.

From an overhead airplane, it looks like the end of the earth but on foot, the pahoehoe is a fascinating blend of patterns, natural sculpture, and tones of black. Walking through it provided an endless change of scenery.

This was the lava flow of 1801 stopped finally, according to legend, by Kamehameha the Great. Taken by canoe to the spot where the lava had entered the sea, he cut off a portion of his hair and threw it into the ocean to appease the fire goddess, Pele. How could she refuse? The lava flow halted immediately.

The lava came from the mountain of Hualalai which has not

erupted since that time and had been declared inactive until recently when volcanologists detected trembling in the mountain. Hualalai has been reclassified as "dormant."

At one rest stop on a plateau of lava above the ocean, we detected agitation upon the water and then we were treated to a passing aquamarine show put on by a school of twirling dolphins who leaped, spun on their tails and frolicked just offshore.

After hiking through three miles of lava, we returned to the beach again, a white sand beach, and traversing a point of land, came to a cove and Magoon's Beach, shaded by palm trees where we stopped and lunched and swam and napped and swam again before pushing on.

After another small stretch of lava we came to the pristine white, lonely beach of Makalawena Bay in back of which is a fresh water pond, perhaps only 15 feet long, but so refreshing. We first dipped in the pond and then played in the modest ocean surf, and then returned to rinse off in the cold clean water of the pond again. Terrific.

These perfect little beaches, hidden from view of the highway, just a mile away, were ours alone. We encountered not another human being.

Circling the bay whose beachfront lands are owned by the Bishop Estate and kept for Hawaiian civic groups—Boy Scouts and the like—we found camp set up on the far side. We settled down to relax, do notes, eat an orange and enjoy the scenery. Behind Makalawena Bay is another bird sanctuary pond.

Want to know how much "roughing it" this trek involved?

At every camp a waterproof solar heated bag of fresh water with a shower spray nozzle attachment hung from a tree at a remote spot. No shower curtain. No privacy walls. No need. The honor system prevailed.

At sunset we all stood like children peering into a candy store window, all in a row, watching the sun being swallowed by the ocean, waiting until the last tip of gold disappeared, hoping to see the green flash. No green flash.

Kristi and Evelyn, the Honolulu matron, wanted to sleep out in the open, but not alone. They persuaded the South African engineer to sleep between them. The hilarity was worthy of a Boy Scout camp, and a typical incident of what happens with the instant friendships formed in group hiking.

We had come 13 miles in a day and a half.

One blessed factor had made itself evident.

When we told our friends in Honolulu about our upcoming expedition, they all said we would be fried alive.

Not so. The protective elevation of Mauna Kea's 13,863 feet allows the tradewinds to blow over the Kona coastline but the heat of the land draws the fresh breezes in from the sea, saving the hikers from heat exhaustion.

We were never too hot.

The next day we did nine miles in eight hours.

We'd walk and swim, walk and swim.

Every swimming spot seemed to be better than the last one, but Kua Bay, completely isolated, with silken white sand, turquoise green water and an easy roller coaster surf is unmatched.

It was hard to leave.

Our luncheon stop was at the empty picnic grounds for the cowboys of Huehue Ranch where there were clean outhouses with toilet paper, fresh water, benches and tables, and a natural saltwater swimming pool protected by a large outcropping of rock at the entrance to the sea, around which reef fish played.

It was a two-hour break, a two-hour do-your-own-thing. Swim, snorkel, munch a sandwich, nap, swim, snorkel, eat an apple, nap again. Quiet. Peaceful. Contemplative.

Two miles later we were at Kona Village Resort.

It was a little bit like Robinson Crusoe walking into New York City.

Kona Village is a resort of a hundred or so "native" huts—in truth, very modern individual houses patterned after the housing of nine different Pacific island nations. No telephones, radios or television sets. The accent is on peace and isolation.

Breakfast, lunch and dinner are provided because it is not expected that the guests will ever leave the property. They will sun, swim, snorkel, sail a boat, eat and drink—and pay from $100 to $300 a day for this Polynesian peace and tranquility.

Kona Village's clientele is fiercely loyal.

My favorite story about the resort concerns the divorce of a couple who had been patrons for years. As part of the divorce settlement, she got the standing Christmas reservations one year; he got it the next.

Fred Duerr, the genial manager, appeared, not to throw out this knapsacked mob, but to direct us to the restrooms and bar.

Fred is a survivor. The Kona Village has gone through four owners, each one having more money than the last and each willing to pour additional millions into refurbishing and upgrading—and keeping Fred, who goes back to the days when you could reach the complex only by sea or by air or by walking in over the lava.

He regaled us with stories of his action-hungry days when the isolated resort first opened, and he would jog into Kona at dusk and return before dawn.

Now bordering on the portly, he added, "I was a bit younger then."

We went to the "Shipwreck Bar," actually the hull of a boat put on a reef by the original builder, Johnno Johnson.

Having a drink out of a tall glass with tinkling ice in it was a welcome break.

After the contrasting touch of resort living, we strapped our knapsacks on again and picked our way carefully across the crumbling coastline, now a series of giant jagged lava pinnacles and valleys besieged by a constant and angry surf which had reduced portions of the lava to black sand beaches. We had reached an ancient track whose stepping stones had been placed by hands hundreds of years before.

The thrill of the dramatic coastline waned as the stretch of black seemed endless around Mahewalu Point. Finally, the vegetation of Mano Point, our last campsite, appeared. The flat beachless plateau, elevated about 12 feet above the sea, was well known to the ancients for its tidal pools and salt pans.

We had gone 22 miles and except for a couple of toe blisters, everyone was in good shape.

Ken said they'd had, as hikers, a woman who could have been the fat lady in a circus, another with a dislocated shoulder, a man with a wooden leg and no one had any trouble.

Dinner that night was Hawaiian. Lau-lau, a butterfish and pork combination cooked with the tops of taro leaves inside a sack of ti leaves; poi, a paste of the taro root and water; lomilomi, bits of salmon mixed with onion and tomato; and coals-roasted yams.

The South African who was on his first visit to Hawaii, thought it fantastic.

That night there was a half moon and a blanket of touch-me stars. The lights of Waikoloa and Waimea could just be discerned in the distance. We were halfway between heaven and civilization with the soft sound of waves sweeping over rocks and swirling into foaming waters in the tidal pools.

The entire camp was asleep by nine and not a body stirred until six the next morning when the distant mountains of Kohala, Mauna Kea and Hualalai were framed in black against the new gold of the morning sky.

After a breakfast of Portuguese sausage, French toasted sweet bread, slices of papaya and strong black coffee, we were on the last trail.

Not more than a mile later we were having our first swim at Luahinewai, a black sand beach, behind which is the prettiest fresh water pool we had seen. Encircled by high cliff walls tufted with greenery and topped by coconut palms that filtered the sunlight, it was at least 40 feet long with a shallow black sandy bottom which deepened to about 20 feet at the opposite end.

The water was "chicken skin" cool and clear. With the aid of snorkeling masks, the sight of underwater green plants gave us the sense of swimming in an aquarium garden. A charming spot.

After the swim, we went on to the edge of Kiholo Bay, past a house site being prepared for Loretta Lynn, the country western singer, to another freshwater pond, only this one was inside a lava tube and we had to go down a short ladder to the water. Some of us swam from one opening through the lava tube to a second opening and explored the depths of a cave at the far end. Exciting.

At the center of Kiholo Bay there were a few scattered houses facing the black sand beach, groves of neatly kept coconut trees and a proliferation of "Keep Out" signs. We heard the barking of a dog for the first time in three days and the cackling sound of chickens.

Ken said the bay was formerly a terminus for cattle driven to the harbor over the King's Trail by paniolos. (Paniolo is a bastard word taken from the word "espanol" meaning "Spanish" and refers to the Mexican cowboys brought to Hawaii in 1831 to teach ranching expertise to the Hawaiians.)

The cattle were herded into the sea, to swim to an offshore

freighter, then hoisted by slings onto the ship on their way to market in Honolulu.

At one time there was a one-room hotel at the the south side of the bay where the innkeeper sold fresh water to the thirsty cowboys for a penny a glass.

The bay is home to green turtles and a breeding ground for barracuda. Friendly barracuda, Ken assured, but everybody still refused the last chance for a swim.

We pushed through scrub at the north end of Kiholo Bay to find the King's Trail. The faint trail over pahoehoe lava marked on either side by white stones originally was a footpath for communication around the island, but was broadened into a "highway" on the Kona-Kohala coast to herd cattle to market.

A half mile over the trail, at the 26-mile highway marker, Ken shaded his eyes against the noon sun, spotted the van on the highway, and led us over a virginal field of twisted, tortured lava the last two miles to the highway.

Ken had told Esther that we would meet her past Kiholo where the lava reached the highway at 12:30PM.

Promptly at 12:30 we climbed the embankment, sweaty but triumphant. As we drove to the airport, it was a time of re-discovery.

"Oh, there is where we camped the second night. There is where we had lunch. There's Makalawena Bay where the tidal pool was freezing cold."

It was, in summary, a fine experience. Easy physically. Exhilarating mentally. The exploring and finding and enjoying an area I thought I knew and discovered I didn't know at all was a revelation.

We chuckled over the incongruity of imagining ourselves so far removed from the real world when, in reality, we were always within sight or sound of civilization. For the first two days, the airplanes arriving or departing Kona were always overhead. We could see the automobiles on Queen Kaahumanu highway most of the time, but they, like the fishing boats, the luxury liner, and the sightseeing helicopters, appeared as mirages ... momentary and fleeting reminders of a familiar world easily shucked for the world we were discovering.

My only regret was the exercise wasn't longer, continuing north up the historic Kohala coast.

Our companions, who can make or break such an adventure, were all of good humor, complaisant and cooperative.

The only sour note that must be written concerns litter, the incredible amount of thoughtless trash left behind by local fishermen and surfers. In magnificent, tucked away places of virginal beauty, we inevitably found aluminum cans, wrappers, plastic bottles, beer bottles and other containers ... junk, junk, junk, thrown aside indiscriminately. It was, and is, a nest-fouling disgrace to the people of the island and to the state.

The Kona-Kohala tour by Hawaiian Walkways usually requires a minimum group of ten walkers. A maximum group is 18. If the outdoors appeals, or you would like to experience a Hawaii that few even know about, form your own group. When inquiring about reservations include your age: Hawaiian Walkways, P.O. Box 1264, Kailua-Kona, Hawaii 96745. Telephone (808) 322-2042. Cost is about $100 a day per person.

The Greening of the Kohala Coast

The next resort along Highway-19 north of Kona Village is Waikoloa.

Actually there are two Waikoloas. One is on the ocean at Anaehoomalu Bay, a 3P lagoon, where Sheraton has a 548-room hotel and a fine golf course and tennis courts. The other Waikoloa is up the hill where there are condominiums and private homes and another golf course which is to be redesigned by Jack Nicklaus into championship links. (I thought it was pretty good the way it was, particularly when the wind wasn't blowing.)

Behind the crescent beach of Anaehoomalu and fronting the Sheraton Royal Waikoloa is an ancient fishpond preserved by the developers, along with the remains of old Hawaiian houses and caves in the area. Herb Kane, a famous Kona artist and Hawaiiana authority was responsible for the descriptive informational signs on the property.

A new airstrip services the area with scheduled flights provided by Princeville Airways in twin-engine Otters.

The biggest news at Waikoloa was the announcement in the Fall of 1984 that Chris Hemmeter, the Jack Armstrong of Hawaii hotel development, was going to build a 1,260-room Hyatt Regency Waikoloa Hotel costing something more than $300 million. Of course that includes canals, an indoor ice-skating rink, a monorail, a sports medicine center, a skeet range and other trinkets to amuse the guests.

The Mauna Lani Resort is the next occupant along this stretch of coast which Governor John A. Burns named "The Gold Coast" when he approved the straight arrow highway and other improvements to make the area accessible.

Its Francis Ii Brown Golf Course, named after Hawaii's most famous golfer who owned the site, is the prettiest golf course in the state. It should be. The cost was about three-quarters of a million dollars *per hole*. Carved out of black lava, the green fairways and the oceanside holes are simply magnificent. Not a difficult course. Just beautiful. 5P shots from a helicopter.

The golf course is matched by the hotel's lobby, the highlight of which is a magnificent multi-story waterfall that cascades through the lobby into outdoor waterways and ponds, visually bringing into focus the nearby historical fish ponds. It is highly unusual and highly successful.

There is no registration counter. Guests are seated at private desks and discreetly registered.

The beach is largely manmade.

Efforts such as these take megabucks and the money for Mauna Lani came from the Japanese Tokyu Group, a multi-billion dollar conglomerate with lots of staying power.

Tours of the grounds and the ancient fishponds are worthwhile and so is lunch on property, especially at the golf clubhouse if you can get in.

To speak of lunch on the Kohala Coast is to speak of the buffet at the Mauna Kea Beach Resort, the most famous lunch open to visitors, and our favorite hotel in Hawaii.

The buffet is opulent with cold dishes and hot dishes and salads and hors d'oeuvres, all of which are just a teasing prelude to the pastry table. The pastry chefs of Mauna Kea are trained at Calorie Paradise University and receive diplomas written in whippped cream on chocolate pastry parchment.

Once a week the hotel stages a luau, also open to visitors, where guests are treated to local Hawaiian specialities including a fernshoot salad you will not believe—steak if you want it—and low key, genuine Big Island entertainment that you'll never find in Las Vegas.

Both the buffet and the luau are expensive but a way to share the feeling of the place if you are staying elsewhere.

Mauna Kea opened in 1965, after Laurance S. Rockefeller had searched statewide for the ideal spot to build: remote, beautiful, a depressed area in need of a new industry where a ready labor pool could be employed. He found that site at Kaunaoa Bay.

The sweetly curved beach of white sand, the gentle weather of constant sunshine and languid tradewinds were easy persuaders and Kaunaoa was where the great hotel was built. What God didn't provide, Rockefeller did.

The landscaping, the architecture, the understated room decorations, the millions of dollars in folk and antique art collected from throughout the Pacific and displayed in lobby and halls, the staff—including the chefs—reflected not only Rockefeller's fortune but his discerning eye and trained palate.

As the first rays of sun shoot through the sprinklers on the golf course and illuminate the tops of the coconut trees then flood the beach with gold and light the long white line of surf as it rolls toward shore, it is one of the most enjoyable spots on earth.

The magic returns at dusk.

To me, it is even more memorable because one evening at North Pointe (now the Luau Garden), at the edge of the sea as the sun touched the blue horizon, the Lady Navigator became my legal companion.

We have returned time and time again to play golf on the Robert Trent Jones Sr. golf course, a toughy, but with an overwater third hole that is a 3P postcard shot even for a box Brownie photographer.

We have ridden around Buster Brown Hill overlooking the cowtown of Waimea from the Mauna Kea stables.

After I received my diving certificate, I made a two-tank dive off the Mauna Kea catamaran where Andy, the guide, showed us how to crack open a sea urchin with a piece of coral and feed the sudden swarm of wrasse and other reef fish.

On the sail back, a fur wholesaler from Chicago introduced me to his private drink at the open bar: dark rum, Fresca and lime juice.

"I had four the last trip and fell in the ocean when I tried to get in the dingy."

Also I learned that a "Bloody Shame" is a Bloody Mary without vodka.

Scuba diving and snorkeling are two of the favorite pastimes of guests, perhaps due to the variety of diving spots along the coast. Tennis is another.

When Adi Kohler, the general manager, came to the hotel in 1973, there were two tennis courts and he couldn't hit a backhand to save his life. Now he has 13 courts to practice on, can beat the resident pro, and takes fiendish delight in humiliating visiting travel writers.

We arranged for two new excursions the last time we stayed at Mauna Kea. We'd heartily recommend taking the first ... and reading about the second.

The flight with Kenai Helicopters was a thriller. Kenai flies out of the Kona airport, and from helipads at Sheraton Waikoloa and just off the fourth green at Mauna Kea.

Scott Shupe, our pilot, opened with what is the standard line of helicopter pilots.

"Have you flown in helicopters before?"

Yes, you nod.

"That's good," he says. "This is my first trip."

"There are only two things we have to worry about," Scott added. "Oil in the transmission and our stereo headsets.

"If the stereo quits, we immediately go home."

We flew over the lower end of Kohala on a bright morning when the tradewinds were blowing so hard that our air speed was not much faster than the ground speed of cars on the Queen Kaahumanu Highway. Scott had time to describe the lava flows from past eruptions underneath us.

Not far away was the crater of an eruption of Mauna Loa, the first in several years, and a subject of intense study by scientists. Which brought up the subject of Madame Pele.

"One of our pilots was given the job of bringing out scientists who were stuck on an observation post where the lava activity was getting too intense.

"This pilot is one of the straightest arrow men I know. Completely serious. As he approached the observation post, he spotted the two men and a lady sitting on a bench. When the chopper landed, the two men piled into the aircraft and the pilot asked, 'Where's the lady?'

" 'What lady?' responded the scientists. 'There is nobody here but us.' "

Pele.

The more you hear, the more you believe.

We flew over the scrub brush country of the Parker Ranch, the largest privately-owned ranch in the United States with some 220,000 acres and 50,000 head of cattle. Miserable country. At one point we spotted dusty army units on dry-run maneuvers. Miserable job.

The country improved as we approached Waimea, population 1,179 in 1980, headquarters for the Parker Ranch and a major truck farming community.

Now the scenery underwing turned to rain forest, green on green, then—whoom—over a cliff we flew and dropped into the luxurious verdant valley of Waipio.

Waipio was once the home of royalty. Kamehameha grew up here as a boy, hidden from those in power because it was prophesied that he would become a great chief one day and such a prediction put his life in danger.

At another time of drought on the island, it was said that the rich land of the valley supported 40,000 people.

The tidal wave of 1946 swept most of the buildings away and a giant rain in 1970 covered the valley from wall to wall in four feet of water. Now only a handful of people reside in the valley.

Scott circled the little inn where we were booked to spend a couple of nights as soon as we left Mauna Kea. (Mauna Kea for $300 a night and the Waipio inn for $8 a night.)

From the helicopter we could see the jeep track descending at a 45-degree angle into the valley. Spooky road.

Scott flew out over the beach.

"The next valley is Waimanu. It is completely uninhabited. The people left in 1940 before the tsunami of '46. Almost impossible to get into except by sea or by that trail you see going over the hill from Waipio."

We flew very low over the lonely grass covered valley.

"Sometimes we flush a wild boar. They'll weigh up to 300

pounds. No sense of humor at all. Charge at a helicopter or anything else in sight."

In one of the farthest reaches of the valley, we flew into "The Hole", a nameless dark shaft of lava rock carved by a waterfall that fell 1900 feet from the cliff above. We circled just above the floor of the waterfall, looked straight up through the plexiglass canopy at the blue sky far, far away while symphonic music poured through the headsets. A five-wow experience.

Out of the valley again we flew along the cliff face to witness myriad shoreline waterfalls and holes in the sides of the cliffs. "Some of those are royal burial caves," said Scott. "I don't fool around with burial caves too much. They are sacred to the Hawaiians so they are sacred to me." We liked him for that.

Out to sea the helicopter circled sea stacks, piles of basalt rocks standing like sentinels in the ocean. One of them, Mokupuku, had a hole drilled through by the waves, like a giant molar with a cavity.

Back along the cliffs we hovered just above ground level beside Lapahoehoenui, a small flat of land where a waterfall, Paopao, cascaded down to a pond. We could see remnants of an ancient trail.

"We are forbidden to set down at any beach or park now," said Scott, "but in the past we have had unique weddings here."

With that romantic thought, we whirled up the cliff, leveled out over the sugar cane plantation, and skirted Waimea town again.

"See that rectangle of forest over there?" Scott directed our attention to a singular area on an otherwise barren plain. "The trees were planted by the railroad company to use as railroad ties. But the strong winds of Waimea bent the trees so much that the timber was useless."

The same strong winds were now pushing us toward home and we were soon back on the ground.

Great flight.

The second expedition was to the summit of Mauna Kea, the mountain, for a Saturday night open house at one of the observatories to look at the stars and the planets through a giant telescope.

The whole thing was a fiasco. We had gone to the expense of

renting a four-wheel drive, enclosed station wagon. The hotel had gone to the trouble of preparing an elaborate picnic supper. We had brought along ski jackets and gloves to ward off the weather at almost 14,000 feet.

Shortly after leaving Waimea we ran across thick ground fog. And then we ran across the army in full maneuvers. Lines of trucks with cannons. Lines of jeeps with radios.

We were supposed to be on top of the mountain at six o'clock for the open house, which happens only during the summertime.

We made it. The view from the summit was an airplane view from outside the airplane. It was so cold. We shivered and shook inside of our heatless station wagon. Any adventuring outside left us breathing in short panting gasps because of the high altitude.

At 6PM nothing had happened. Finally a woman with a decidedly German accent appeared and led us to one of the six observatories on the mountain top, all of which are unheated because the temperature inside must be the same as the temperature outside to prevent the instruments from fogging over.

The zero temperatures and the high altitude pressures created new demands on one's bladder. There were no restroom facilities.

A frantic Japanese astronomer who had a limited two-week access at this particular telescope broke his glasses ten minutes before starting his first assignment.

By threading our way through a maze of wires and cables, we were able to get one peak at Saturn through the telescope. It looks better on the pages of National Geographic. We couldn't flee the mountain fast enough.

Mauna Kea Observatory open house? Don't go.

However, it should be noted that Mauna Kea is a candidate for the Astronomical Capital of the World. With six observatories in place and two under construction, Caltech in Pasadena has announced a new $70 million project for Mauna Kea which is already creating more than 200 jobs for scientists, local and visiting, plus the support staff. Not a little industry on the Big Island.

We had talked two New Zealand friends, Michael Brett and wife Angela, into sharing the observatory experience with us and, as we sat in our Mauna Kea hotel room having our late picnic, they were giving us strange looks.

"Never mind," we said. "We'll make it up to you. We are going to take you into Waipio Valley for the adventure of your lives."

All fingers were crossed.

Note, Mauna Kea, the mountain, is also the scene of the most unusual skiing in the world. Snows come late to the peak and stay as late as June. No ski tows or chair lifts, of course. You ski down corn snow and your jeep takes you back up.

The Lady Navigator has had the experience. During her ski trip one member of the party passed out and had to be revived with bottled oxygen.

Ski Shop Hawaii in Waimea rents clothes and ski gear and operates transportation to the mountain during the season. The Waimea number is 885-4188.

Waimea: Cowtown, Science City, Horse Heaven

Waimea is a mixed up little town.

It can't even get its name straight. Because it becomes confused with Waimea on Kauai, it has another name, Kamuela, Hawaiian for Samuel as in Samuel Parker, the second generation of Parkers who established the giant ranch. The post office is Waimea-Kamuela and the local airport in Kamuela.

The present Parker Ranch owner and a direct descendant is Richard Smart who starred with Nanette Fabray in musical comedies on Broadway, and who has added sweet curlicues to the local architecture and built a $2.5 million theater to indulge in one of his favorite hobbies.

Mr. Smart, a tall handsome character who looks like a musical comedy star, also built a small museum in his shopping center and opened the Parker Ranch Broiler where you can get Parker Ranch grass-fed beef.

Add to the local scene the French accents of scientists who are responsible for one of the Mauna Kea observatories plus those of other countries, add the local Japanese cabbage farmers and the Mexican-Portuguese cowboys, add the moneyed gentry from Honolulu who have elected to retire to one of Hawaii's few upland communities to play horsemen and horsewomen ... and Waimea becomes a very curious but enjoyable stew of people indeed.

Together with the Bretts we stopped in Waimea to shop for groceries because the inn where we were spending two nights in Waipio does not serve food but provides kitchens with running water and Coleman stoves. No lights. No electricity. No telephone.

Between the baskets of food we bought and the luxury items that the hotel had packed for us, we were foddered for a week and proceeded around the corner of the island to Honokaa, a small sugar town. Honokaa is also the site of the processing plant of the Hawaiian Holiday Macadamia Nut Company with an operation similar to the Mauna Loa plant outside of Hilo: see-through windows to watch the operations of roasting, mixing and packaging. A large showroom offers a variety of macadamia nut products for sale.

Road signs point north on the side road to the Waipio Lookout and the little town of Kukuihaele (or House of Light after the coastal lighthouse which used to be there).

Next to the Last Chance store—and it *is* the last chance store—is the office of the Waipio Valley Shuttle, operators of a fleet of British Land Rovers into the valley. Two earnest young men, Al Shattuck and Brian Nelson, former pilots and real estate brokers, retired from their other occupations to become owners of Hawaii's most unique transportation company.

The Waipio Shuttle is a professional, if laid back, business which doesn't intrude on the peace and serenity of the valley.

Primarily, the Land Rovers take visitors down the steep jeep road for an hour and a half tour of the valley for $15 a person. Half or full-day jeep and hiking tours into the valley, with a light lunch included, are priced at $50 and $80.

The shuttles begin at the end of the road, at the Waipio Lookout. A 3P stop.

A few visitors, tempted by the great scenery, take their rented Japanese cars down the road to the valley floor despite the signs warning drivers not to do so. Don't be tempted. Your car will not make it back up. It's dangerous. And expensive. The haul-out can cost you $200.

As you stand at the Lookout, you have to imagine how this lush valley, a mile wide and six miles deep, used to be when it held one English school, three Hawaiian schools, five stores, four restaurants, one hotel, two jails, a post office, four billiard halls, five churches, and a lot of homes.

Additionally, the taro and rice fields flourished and the trees were thick with fruit.

Off the Waipio Valley beach, the first naval battle in Hawaiian history occurred when Kamehameha used cannon for the first time. The battle, still famous in Hawaii, was known as the battle of the red-mouthed guns.

Our guide and chauffeur into the valley was David (Kawika) Fujimoto, a Waipio native of Japanese, Chinese, Hawaiian ancestry. He took us the two miles into the valley and a hundred years back in history.

"The zig-zag trail that led into the valley was a thousand years old. When the government put the road in and farmers could bring jeeps into the valley and haul their taro out, they let their horses go. You'll find wild horses throughout the valley. And wild pigs.

"Heiaus date back to 680 A.D. There were four of them. One of them was a place of refuge like the City of Refuge in Kona. Another was a place for human sacrifice, and it was said that a former chief, Umi, sacrificed eighty lives at one time.

"Kamehameha grew up in the valley from the time he was three months old until he was 15."

The road down was a throat filler. Cars going down are requested to give the right-of-way to cars coming up.

"It's not dangerous as long as you keep moving," said David. "People who don't know how to drive can get stuck coming up. They stall. Put on the brake, start to slide and away they go."

How many times had David made this trip?

He laughed. "Thousands. Don't worry."

How many people have been killed on the road?

"About twenty."

I worried.

Once at the bottom and breathing more easily, we went to the beach where large waves pounded the shore. David picked up an empty beer can. "We are garbage collectors. We want to keep the valley clean." He pointed to the surf. "Not a day for good swimming. Good fishing though."

"See that trail on the other side of the valley. That goes over the hill to Waimanu Valley. One night I was fishing here with some friends, there were five of us, and we saw a line of torches going up the path and we could hear the chanting. They were Night Marchers. Only time I ever saw them.''

Night Marchers are the ghosts of former Hawaiian warriors who walk at night throughout the Kohala district. They are seldom seen, but often heard.

And this was where we were going to spend two nights. Our friends, the Bretts, looked askance at us.

It was less than a mile up a dirt road to our funky little inn. Tom Araki, a wispy moustached, 75-year-old taro farmer and proprietor, was there.

The ''inn'' was a plantation type building with five bedrooms side by side behind a porch, and separate rooms for the WC and a cold water shower at the end of the building.

Below, but still at ground level, were two kitchens equipped with Coleman stoves and kerosene lamps.

Fronting the building was a patch of lawn, plumeria and fruit trees, and a wet plot of taro. In the distance we could hear the surf pounding the beach. We had told the Bretts to ''think rustic'' but we could sense their doubts for having left the luxury of Mauna Kea.

David departed, promising to return that night with anything we wanted from the Last Chance store.

We made sandwiches for lunch and then strolled up the dirt road. Fruit of every kind was growing on either side. A river, running strongly from recent rains, was only a hundred yards from the house. ''Lots of fresh-water prawns in the river,'' David had said. ''You never have to go hungry in Waipio.''

That night before dinner Tom and David returned to ''talk story'' and share in the wine. (It is most important that if you go to Tom's inn in Waipio that you take plenty of wine.)

Tom brought over a plate of freshwater prawns sauted in a shoyu sauce. Delicious. He lives next to the ''hotel'' in a small house that used to be a schoolhouse and was used by the Peace Corps when Waipio was a training center.

''You know, back in the old days,'' Tom said, ''here in Waipio, everybody would pitch in and help with the work. If your taro plantings needed weeding or cutting, everyone would bring a sickle or machete and food and make a day of it. Next week you might help someone else in their taro patch. Ho'olaulima it's called in Hawaiian, to get together, to cooperate. Laulima means many hands. But today there aren't so many people and it's every man for himself.

"At one time the beach was filled with bad hippies. They stole everything from me but sheets. Now they are gone. Some haoles from the Mainland live on the other side of the valley. They smoke marijuana and take nude baths but they don't give me any trouble.

"There are about forty people living in the valley now. Part time taro farmers who come down and work on the weekend, like my son. The old Chinese who came as immigrants and planted rice in the valley are gone. The Hawaiians are all gone. Just a few of us old timers left."

With a valley so rich in history, there must be a thousand legends, we suggested.

"Oh, yes. You know that Waipio is the legendary doorway to the Lua O Milu, the nether regions to the Hawaiians. It is said that every year a great procession of ghosts winds its way through the valley and enters the mysterious underworld at an unknown part of the beach.

"Back in the valley," David said, "is the tallest waterfall in Hawaii. It is called Hiilawe and is named for a princess who fell in love with Kakalaoa but their families refused to let them get married. She wept and wept and created the waterfall and he changed himself into a large rock now found in the pond at the bottom of the cascade of water so that Hiilawe's tears could fall on him."

By now it had grown dark and the long porch fronting the bedrooms where we gathered at a table was lit by kerosene lights. Electric lights would have been out of place.

"What's the official name for your place?" we asked Tom.

"It doesn't have one. Use any name you want. Waipio Hilton. Tom Araki's Sheraton. If I use a name, I have to register it. Send me a check for the Waipio Hotel, I have to send it back.

"But you have to make a reservation. I live part time in Hilo, you know. You have to have a reservation."

What about a deposit?

"No deposit. The people say they come, they come. If they don't come, they don't come. Simple."

For 32 years Tom was in the construction business, building

breakwaters, office buildings, homes. He could bring electricity into his inn but he doesn't chose to. He has a telephone in his house. That's enough.

Sometime in 1985 he was closing down the hotel to redo the floors. "They are like me," he said. "About to fall in."

Dinner that night was out of the ice chests sent by the Mauna Kea Hotel and included the fern shoot salad featured at their luaus. Fantastic.

The next day was centered around a horseback ride offered by Waipio Ranch, an operation run jointly by Sherri Hannum and her partner Wayne Teves.

They picked us up in a van, having already made a run to the top of the hill to pick up two day visitors, and took us to a riverside camp where our saddled, rugged, valley ponies were waiting.

It was a return to the old tradition of four-legged transportation in Waipio.

We first rode down a dirt trail, crossed the river at a shallow spot and headed north to the end of the valley and Neneuwe Falls, home of the shark god. Our ride took us past mango trees, lilikoi, guava, strawberry guava, wild coffee trees, java plum for fruit jelly, elderberry, mountain apple, grapefruit, breadfruit, wild taro, bitter melon, kukui nut used by the ancient Hawaiians for torches, papaya, poha and noni, a small fruit that smells like Limburger cheese and is used as an antiseptic medicine.

There were also birds. Doves, singing birds, tiny yellow birds.

We also passed make-shift houses—good make-shift houses, bad make-shift houses—one house with a television aerial and another house that must have cost a lot of money.

Alongside the path at one point was a naked man pouring buckets of water over his head and body. He didn't say anything in greeting ... just continued to face us and pour the water. We didn't say anything either. Like: "Nice day for a naked shower."

Once we came across a group of wild horses dominated by a handsome stallion.

"Keep your horse away from the stallion," warned Sherri.

Our horses were more interested in feasting on the fallen mangoes.

After thinking we had seen all of the fruit in the valley we came across avocados, navel oranges, tapioca, persimmon and lychee.

It was a Hawaiian Brigadoon, a lost valley, bulging with everything, a place without time, without clocks, where you lived forever.

"That's a bunch of hooey," said Tom Araki later. "You die, you die. That's it."

We rode down to the beach for a picnic and watched the waves. The honeymooning couple riding with us locked hands and walked over the sands to a cave at the far end of beach while we lounged on a grassy knoll under a shade tree.

After lunch we remounted horses and attempted to cross the river at its mouth. Too deep that day. We rode upstream a couple of hundred yards and followed Sherri across with our feet held as high as the saddle horn to keep them dry. The experienced horses delicately picked their way over the sunken river boulders to the other side. A Japanese touring group clicked off a thousand pictures of our crossing.

We slowly rode up the south side of the valley and then crossed the valley floor, once filled with rice paddies, passed one of the few remaining houses that had survived the tidal wave and the flood, and were back at the ranch.

A nice ride.

In the afternoon the Lady Navigator and the Bretts took off to find the aluminum and glass "teahouse" cantilevered over the valley facing the Hiilawe waterfall put up by Howard Butcher, a Philadelphia millionaire and investor in Hawaiian companies who wanted to have a small restaurant in the valley. Permission denied. He turned the building over to the Bishop Museum. The museum, strapped for money, doesn't know what to do with it either. A waste.

The hikers also came back with armfuls of fruit.

That night Michael and I found enough dry wood to make a fire in the small barbecue pit in the back of the inn and we grilled steaks over charcoal and drank red wine by kerosene light. A million miles away from everything.

Eight dollars a night each. Bring your own towel.

You do have to have reservations. Waipio has become a "find" among travel writers in the last two years. Jerry Hulse, syndicated by the Los Angeles Times, did a feature on the valley and Tom Araki, who was also "discovered" by the Chicago Tribune and several TV network shows. Michael Brett, a tough man to please, was even smiling when he left and intended to reveal Waipio to his readers in the Auckland Star.

For reservations at Tom Araki's You-Name-It Inn, write 25 Malama Place, Hilo, Hawaii or telephone (808) 935-7466 in Hilo or (808) 775-0368 in the Waipio Valley.

The Waipio Valley Shuttle is P.O. Box 128, Kukuihaele, Hawaii 96727. (808) 775-7121

Waipio Ranch, Box 1283, Honokaa, Hawaii 96727. (808) 775-0373.

The Big Island Backwater

We would recommend to anyone with the time not to leave the north end of the Big Island and the district of Kohala without making the loop drive from the Mauna Kea Hotel up the coast road (270) to Hawi and across the top of the Kohala Mountains to Waimea on 250.

Just north of the hotel is a huge, somber temple of brooding lava rocks. Puukohola.

You want to make up a story to match its visual mood?

Try this: The young Kamehameha, ambitious to conquer all of the islands, conferred with his most trustworthy priest who advised him to build a massive heiau to the war god Ku at the point of land overlooking the sea.

After the completion of the temple, he was to make the most important human sacrifice he could.

Kamehameha had the perfect candidate. His arch rival was invited to the opening ceremonies not knowing what an important role he was to play in the ritual. As his canoe approached the beach, a Kamehameha chief ran to the canoe and put a spear through the rival's body, killing him. His body was carried to the temple as the important sacrifice.

Below the Puukohola Heiau, now under control of the National Park Service, is the happier scene of Spencer Park with white sands, shallow waters for romping kids, good changing rooms with showers and a camping ground for those with permits.

Going north past the harbor of Kawaihae is the state park of Lapakahi. Stop. Take a half hour and roam through this site of a former Hawaiian fishing community. Guides are available.

You learn how the people lived, worked, fished, farmed and played. Interesting place.

Continuing on Highway 270 you pass Mahukona Beach Park, formerly a harbor. The camp ground is filled with litter, the blight of the Big Island.

If you feel adventurous you can leave the highway and take the highway down to Upolu Airport, an emergency strip which, it has been suggested, is used for secret flights out of illegal agricultural products. Turn left at the airport to Mookini Heiau, another temple built to the war god Ku, but this temple, according to legend, was built in one night with stones from a quarry 14 miles away. A.D. 480, says the sign.

Not far from here is a place where Kamehameha was born, now marked by a simple stone enclosure erected by the Sons of Kamehameha, a respected Hawaiian fraternity.

Next is Hawi, once a dozing town that has gone to sleep. Hawi was an important sugar community but when the plantation was closed and the mill shut down, the income spigot was turned off and, gradually, the stores closed and the buildings were abandoned.

Little boutiques of this and that are slowly coming into being because it is a peaceful corner of the island and an attractive place to live. I always feel good in Hawi. Luke's Hotel and Restaurant ("No Drinking in the Parking Lot") at the main intersection is still there but has changed owners. Friends say that it is clean and inexpensive. One day Hawi will be born again with people who discover what a pleasant place it is.

The oddity of the area is in front of the courthouse at Kapaau beyond Hawi.

"Oh," you'll say. "A bad reproduction of the Kamehameha statue in front of the Hawaii State Supreme Court building in Honolulu."

No, this is the original we mentioned back in the first chapter.

The statue was commissioned by the Hawaii Legislature in 1878 and a fortune of $10,000 was appropriated for the project. The original clay model was finished in Florence, Italy by Thomas R. Gould, the sculptor, and was cast in Paris.

The ship carrying the bronze statue caught fire off the Falkland Islands, burned and sank, carrying Kamehameha to the bottom.

A second statue was commissioned to the same sculptor, this

time for $7,500, and arrived in time for the centennial celebration of Captain Cook's discovery of the islands.

The unbelievable happened. A ship arrived in port and, on board, was the original Kamehameha statue which had been retrieved from the sea, bought by the sea captain and brought to Hawaii. Slightly abused with a hand and spear missing.

King Kalakaua bought the damaged statue for a knocked down price, repaired it and had it shipped to North Kohala, the birthplace of Kamehameha, and the rightful place for the original.

Continue on to the end of the road for great views into the Pololu Valley, a hikable gorge 300 feet below.

I remember the last time I stood on that cliff looking down at the black sand beach of the valley and seeing a lone horseman riding by the water followed by his dog. How did he get there? What was he doing?

When you take Highway-250 from Hawi across the Kohalas to Waimea, you almost forget that you are in Hawaii. This is cow country with herds of Herefords and Holsteins mooing at you from alongside the road.

If you want to ride this range, make a reservation with Ironwood Outfitters whose stables are in the middle of Kahua Ranch, a mountainside 23,000-acre cattle ranch that reaches up to rain forests, through pasture lands, by old water ditches that once carried water from the wet side of the island to the dry side.

We signed on with Iowa-born Judy Ellis, a no-nonsense horsewoman who has been running her successful stables since 1981, taking riders for two hours into the green hills of Kahua. Noble views. Good horses. Except when they relieve themselves. "Oh, gross!" exclaimed a twelve-year-old companion.

Kahua Ranch is managed by Monty Richards, a solid rancher, who is afraid not to experiment in all directions. He has launched a successful carnation nursery, started raising sheep and supplying Mauna Kea with fresh lamb, stages professional visits for visiting farmers ... does anything to create a dollar to save the land.

The most unusual success was forged from what could be a problem: constant winds. The windy top lands have proven ideal for generating electricity. Over 200 windmills with monstrous propellers are now whirling in the gales of Kohala, providing new income for the ranch and reducing the cost of importing oil to the island.

You'll stop along the road for all kinds of pictures. 3P country.

If you return to Hilo along the east side of the Big Island, you'll drive through miles of sugar cane as the area is filled with sugar plantations. It is known as the Scottish coast because many of the original engineers in the sugar mills where cane is reduced to raw sugar were Scots, former marine engineers who jumped ship and brought the technique of ship boilers to the sugar factories.

When you live in Hawaii, you are asked two first questions by visitors. One: "How long have you lived here?" Two: "What is your favorite island."

As professional travelers logging over 100,000 miles a year, we naturally whimper with gratitude when we return to our nest on Oahu to lick our weary wounds, catch up with our friends, play tennis at Waialae and golf at Oahu, transcribe our notes and do our laundry, walk down to the Outrigger Canoe Club for the Wednesday ox-tail special, and have sam see noodles at King's Garden.

But when we go adventuring at home, we tend to lean toward the Big Island; to the horseback rides in unusual places, scuba dive at Mauna Kea, hiking and tramping, camping and poke-around-driving.

And while the festivals of all the islands are unique, the Big Island's tend to be a little more so: The Merry Monarch Festival in celebration of the hula, the Billfish tournament in Kona in pursuit of the giant marlin, festivals honoring Kona coffee and the noble macadamia nut, or the rodeos that celebrate the spirit of the paniolo country.

We never tire of the Volcanoes National Park or the peace of Hawi.

There are resorts on Hawaii which invite a shoes-off vacation. But all islands offer such vacation resorts.

What the Big Island has is the variety. Take time to taste it. And meet all of those people on the Big Island with the Big Hearts.

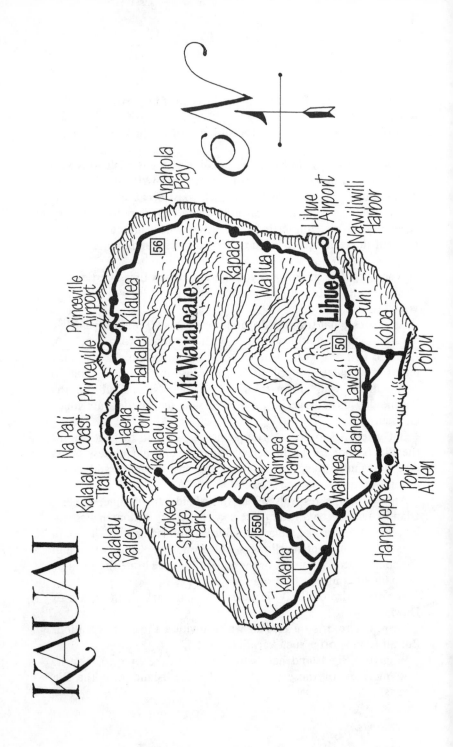

5. Kauai—
The Motion Picture Island

The South Sea helicopter rises slowly from the parking pad, side-slips easily over to the runway and then twirls down the white line faster and faster as the theme music from "Chariots of Fire" rises dramatically in the stereo headsets.

At the end of the runway the helicopter swoops into the sky as the orchestration hits its crescendo, booming in your ears and—wow—below, the panoply of Kauai unfolds.

Holy Wow. It is all 3P country.

Kauai is called the "Garden Island" and you can see immediately why from a helicopter. Sugar cane plants sway rhythmically over miles of sea green acres, volcanic mountains poke towering peaks into a halo of clouds, green forests are punctuated with majestic canyons and Fantasy Island waterfalls inland, and the island is surrounded by fingers of turquoise bays with fingernails of white sand beaches.

Small wonder so many motion pictures are shot here.

Put it at the head of your Hawaii vacation list: "I will take a helicopter trip on Kauai."

Kauai is the oldest of the principal Hawaiian islands. Perhaps that is why it is so pretty. It has had more time in the beauty parlor.

The island, statistically the fourth largest in the state, being something over 500 square miles, has a total population of about 40,000. The capital, Lihue, claims 4,000 residents. The rest of the populace is well scattered because the economy is still agriculturally based, although tourism is now the island's leading money earner.

Not too many years ago, Lihue had the simple characteristics of a small farm plantation town: a small coterie of merchants and service facilities catering to the people who came to shop on Saturdays and worship on Sundays. A simple, disciplined community with predictable tomorrows.

Although still small, the character of Lihue is changing. There are now traffic lights and fast food shops and small shopping centers within town and a major shopping complex, Kukui Grove Shopping Center, outside of town.

The old motion picture house and the traditional car salesroom are closed, and supermarkets are replacing the mom-and-pop stores.

But the most apparent evidence of change is seen weekday mornings when the crawl of cars bringing people to work extends out to the municipal golf course, seven miles away. The times, they are a'changing.

The Tip Top Bakery on Akahi Street used to be famous for its macadamia nut cookies but they can no longer afford to make them by hand. Still, the little restaurant with its linoleum floors and a counter full of loyal followers, serves superb macadamia nut pancakes.

It's a favorite gathering place for morning coffee and gossip.

Upstairs are clean air-conditioned motel rooms for tourists on economy budgets.

Just outside of town, next to Nawiliwili Harbor, is the Kauai Surf Hotel, 10 stories, restaurants, lovely gardens, tennis courts and the only hotel on Kauai with its own 18-hole golf course. The Surf faces on Kalapaki, a nice beach with good waves. (Once upon a time a group of us capsized a small outrigger canoe while riding one of those good waves to shore. The best advice in such a situation is to dive to the bottom and wait for the bodies and oars and canoe to clear out of the way.)

The Kauai Surf and the Maui Surf were bought from Inter-Island Resorts at the end of 1984 by Chris Hemmeter, the developer of the Hyatt Regency hotels in Hawaii whose characteristics of imagination and boldness undoubtedly will soon be imprinted on his new toys. The Kauai Surf alone is going to take 16 months to go through a $70 million restoration. A new wing. A swimming pool only slightly smaller than a football field with slides and waterfalls.

The Club Jetty at the end of the wharf is a Kauai institution, successfully combining a family-style atmosphere with good Chinese food during the early hours, and a swinging style with live entertainment after-hours. Lately, we have heard that the Jetty has become somewhat rougher in the evening. But a Kauai resident said that fights, when they occur, take place outside. Oh, good.

Part of Lihue's new image is a growth of international restaurants, JJ's Broiler featuring Slavonic steak, Casa Italiana, La

Luna, Rosita's, plus old standbys like the Barbecue Inn and the Hamura "Please don't stick your gum under the counter" Ichi Ban Saimin Stand.

We tell our friends to be sure and visit the Kauai Museum, a small brownstone building on the main thoroughfare, Rice Street. Looks like a former public library which, indeed, it was.

Lots of little goodies inside. For example, do you remember the impossible-to-pronounce name of the highway on Oahu leading to Hawaii Kai: Kah-lah-nee-ana-oh-lee? Here in the museum is an elaborate cut glass cordial dispenser which belonged to Prince Jonah Kuhio Kalanianaole, delegate to Congress for twenty years, who was born on Kauai.

As you get into Hawaiiana, you'll appreciate more and more the beauty of the warm, textured wooden bowls, or calabashes. There is a fortune in good examples in the Kauai museum, including a lathe-turned calabash made for Kamehameha III. This immense vessel was used as a poi bowl according to the exhibit legend. (It's probably not true because bowls made of koa, which impart a bad flavor, weren't used for food.)

A newer second building of the museum, named for William Hyde Rice, gives the visitor an excellent background of the early history of the island through ethnical and geological exhibits. One such is the phenomenon of the Alakai Swamp at 4,000 feet, the only such oddity in Hawaii. Another exhibit dramatizes Mt. Waialeale, the wettest spot on earth with annual rainfalls ranging between 400 and 600 inches.

History? Much on Hawaiian and pre-European customs of the Polynesians: sports, agriculture, tapa making, religion.

One exhibit is devoted to Captain James Cook who made his first landing in Hawaii on Kauai at Waimea in January, 1778.

Did you know there once was a Russian flag-flying fort on Kauai? Three, in fact. One lava rock fortification at Waimea at the same river mouth where Cook landed and two earthwork forts on Hanalei Bay on the north shore. An intriguing story. An exhibit in the museum recalls the incident:

On January 10, 1814, a Russian-American Company merchant ship, trading guns for sandalwood and food, was pushed ashore by a gale at Waimea. The Hawaiians confiscated the valuable cargo and the desirable metal from the capsized vessel.

In an effort to recapture the lost cargo, a German-born physician, Dr. Georg Scheffer, was sent from the Russian company's headquarters in Sitka, Alaska to gain the confidence of Kamehameha and to persuade the monarch to command the return of the confiscated goods.

Scheffer was a man of contradictory talents. Charming and abusive, a pragmatist and dreamer, able and inept. He gained the goodwill of Kamehameha but not the trust of Kamehameha's lieutenants and he eventually sailed to Kauai with no assurances of help from the king.

But the chief of Kauai, Kaumualii, who had been forced to give his allegiance to Kamehameha, saw in Scheffer the opportunity to get the backing of the Russians and, not only regain his own sovereignty, but also to capture Oahu and Maui.

Such ambitions fitted the grandiose mentality of Scheffer who became the quasi-ruler of Kauai, assuring Kaumualii of Russian military support.

He built the fortress at the head of the river, flew his country's flag and named the fortification after Queen Elizabeth of Russia.

Two more fortifications were thrown up at Hanalei which became a Scheffer fiefdom and which he named "Schefferthal."

But the Russian government never approved of any military alliances ... and Kamehameha was angered. "Throw the baggage out," in effect was his message, "or else."

Scheffer was forced to flee for his life and the Russian episode was ended. The Waimea fort, however, was not dismantled until 1864 when some 36 cannons were removed. Remains of the fort can still be seen overlooking the Waimea River.

Up a Lazy River

At Lihue we took part in a kayak river adventure that starts in Nawiliwili Harbor and explores the lower reaches of the Huleia River, a part of the Huleia National Wildlife Refuge.

We met with a dozen other paddlers at the Lady Ann Charter Fishing office at the entrance to the small boat harbor with the guides from Island Adventures who took us to the launch site where a flotilla of strange yellow crafts was moored.

The crafts were called "Royaks," a $700 cross between a kayak and a canoe. The occupant sits in an open depression in the plastic vessel, about 12 feet long, with slotted spaces for his legs. Its synthetic construction material, lexan, is bullet-proof strong and can stand the abrasions of sand and even coral reefs. We were assured that they were seaworthy and virtually capsize-proof.

The first Hawaiian word taught the paddlers by the guides was "okole"—or posterior—because to get into the Royak one has to place a hand on each side of the gunwale, holding the ship in place, and then slide one's okole into the seat.

A two-bladed oar with an aluminum shaft and yellow plastic blades provides the tool for propelling.

After experimenting with the ability to turn, to glide forward, go backward, the fleet took off upriver looking a little like a family of yellow ducks skimming over the water single file.

Usually, the river water is transparent—"Clear enough to see the bottom and the river fish, mullet and tilapia" but a recent storm had brought mud downstream and it was the color of cafe au lait.

We were off at 9:26, according to my watch, and back before noon.

Phil, our curly headed guide-informant, volunteered a bit more about the river and the island as we skimmed along.

"Kauai has seven rivers and we operated boats on three of them until Hurricane Iwa, in 1982, destroyed almost everything we had afloat. All the small boats in this harbor were sunk or swept on shore. Those boats you see over there on cradles are still being repaired.

"The fishermen you see in the motorboat are checking their crab pots. They take Samoan crabs out of the river that are sometimes as big as three feet across ... bigger than Alaskan crab.

"As a wildlife refuge you can see all sorts of birds: shearwater, blue heron, gallinule."

Gallinule?

"It's a Hawaiian bird, slate gray about a foot long with white feathers on the flanks and tail. Once upon a time the bird was native to all islands, but has disappeared from the Big Island and Maui."

The paddling was easy. A trick to learn is to keep the blades low coming out of the water so that the water doesn't run down the paddle and into your boat and soak your okole.

"We are now opposite the Menehune Fish Ponds. According to

the legend, the Menehunes, the little people of Kauai who appeared only at night, built the fishpond in one night. If you ever see a Menehune, don't look at it. You'll turn into stone.''

The river beyond the harbor opens up on each side and we could see the mountains on the south shore and Queen Victoria's profile with her mouth open. She is supposedly chastising her relative, Kaiser Wilhelm, by saying, "Now, Willy, Willy" which, according to one version, is where the harbor gets its name, Nawiliwili. (According to Mary Pukui, Hawaii's language authority, the harbor is named after the wiliwili tree, a native tree bearing red seeds.)

"Kahunas, the priest of old Hawaii, were an important part of the society," said Phil. "They all had different powers. Some of them could even throw bolts of fire. Over there you can see where a kahuna threw firebolts against the side of the cliff. It looks like an outline of an angel holding a candle.

"The mountain land between here and the coast is all but inaccessible and where you'll find the biggest boar in Hawaii.

"Ahead of us is where they filmed the opening scenes in the "Raiders of the Lost Ark." Remember where the natives were chasing Indiana Jones through the tall grass? That was over there. When they were skirting the river bank, it took place on the other side, over there. The pontoon plane was stationed right here and he swung out from the river bank to the plane on a vine to escape, remember? The vine is all gone now because tourists have cut away pieces of it for souvenirs and there is none left. Parts of "King Kong" were filmed here also, and so was "Uncommon Valor."

At mid-morning, we stopped in mid-river in accordance to our guides' instructions in a lateral line. By placing a leg over the gunwale into the next Royak, the line-up remained stable. A guide anchored each end.

A platter of pineapple chunks, hunks of cheese and honeywheat bread from Jacques Bakery in Kilauea was passed down the line, followed by plastic cups of guava-orange juice.

"Usually the tradewinds are strong enough to push the royaks upriver without paddling, but it is calm today so we have to work."

It was very little work. Towards the end of the river as it started to narrow down to a 20-foot width, the jungle foliage growing on either bank covered much of the river and we had to snake our way through the tunnel of leaves, vines and branches, and through much faster flowing water. That was little-boy fun.

In a pool before an impassable shallow rapids we stepped out of the boats the same way we got in, okole first, and followed a path a hundred yards inland to a van waiting to return us to the harbor. The countryside was munificent with apple bananas, breadfruit, wild coffee, mango, papaya, avocado, guava, lilikoi (passion fruit).

A pleasant adventure for about $25. And you get a certificate enrolling you as a member of the "Wet Okole Club."

Island Adventures, P.O. Box 3370, Lihue, Kauai, Hawaii 96766. Telephone (808) 245-9662.

The Plantation Life of Yesterday

The river-rafting-royaking-kayaking experience is unique in the islands. Can't do it anywhere else in Hawaii.

So is the experience above the harbor.

At a homestead on a calm plateau five minutes from Lihue is an historical museum of plantation life on Kauai, the headquarters of Grove Farm, one of the first and most successful of the sugar plantation operations on the island.

Also it is a monument, though it is never implied or presented as such, to an unusually dedicated, intelligent man named George N. Wilcox.

Wilcox was one of six children born to Abner and Lucy Wilcox, missionary teachers, who had arrived in Hanalei in 1846. Young Wilcox was educated at Punahou and, like his father, at Yale. After working at various jobs for other people, he bought an embryo plantation, Grove Farm, in 1870 for the immense sum of $12,000, most of which was borrowed. He was 24.

In four years Wilcox had 200 acres under cultivation and the cane was milled and the profits shared with the Lihue factory. Almost immediately he bought more than 10,000 acres from a member of royalty and, with a keen intellect and a born engineering ability, he was among the first to replace ox carts with railroads, to use steam plows for oxen-pulled plows, and irrigation ditches for rain.

Ten years after buying Grove Farm, Wilcox was a partner in an irrigation company capitalized at $600,000.

As the Hawaiian chiefs faded from power, dead from the white-man diseases or politically exiled, men like Wilcox became the *de facto* chiefs, the new *alii*.

When you visit Grove Farm—and you should—you are not just visiting a highly interesting, self-sufficient, successful plantation homestead, you are also entering the palace grounds of a small kingdom.

Grove Farm is located off Nawiliwili Road on Highway-58. A small sign indicates the entrance driveway and a sign directs you to the parking area.

A caution: you cannot visit the homestead without a tour reservation. At the present time, tours are conducted Mondays, Wednesdays and Thursdays. The morning tour begins at 10, the afternoon tour at 1:15. Promptly. This was, and is, a very punctual kingdom. Arrive early. Cross the large lawn and go to the plantation office to the right where you are greeted by your guide.

The office has the air of still being operative. On the wall is a picture of Wilcox as a young man, sitting on a photographer's couch with the bootlegs crossed, hands folded across his lap. A handsome bearded face looking straight into the camera. A dedicated but shy young man who never married.

He brought a brother into his sugar plantation and the brother's daughters, Elsie and Mabel, were born and lived at the homestead throughout their lives. In the Wilcox tradition, they took responsible, serious roles in the community, devoting themselves to educational and public health tasks.

Also on the wall is a pre sugar-cane train picture of oxen pulling giant carts filled with hand-cut sugar cane.

A corner safe bearing the insignia "Wilshire Safe & Scale Co." has a bucolic scene painted on its door and a cannonball resting on its top. At one time the plantation payroll came by ship from Honolulu and the cash to pay the workers was kept in this safe.

When the headquarters for Grove Farm was moved to its new location at Puhi, the safe remained unopened for many years, its combination lost. Old papers were searched. Every obscure niche probed. No trace of it. Finally a legal safecracker was brought in and after many futile attempts, he cracked the combination.

What was it? "B-A-L-L" of course. The cannonball on top had provided the obvious, visible clue all along. Nothing was found inside except an old kerosene lamp, canceled checks, and a few receipts.

The conducted tour is a leisurely walk around the property, initially around the grounds to see the first rain gauge on Kauai, mounted in the middle of the lawn, and then to the buildings, starting with the Old Shed. Nothing was ever thrown away. The Old Shed was filled with ancient farm equipment and such abandoned household devices as an antique washing machine from Buckfalls, Illinois, patented in 1899.

Housing for plantation workers was provided and is still occupied by faithful servants of the family. We visited the home of the laundress for Grove Farm where she had lived for 52 years. A simple frame house with a living room, bedroom and kitchen, its assorted objects reflecting both the Western tradition of her adopted nation and her Oriental ancestry.

Another small cottage served the peculiar dual combination of a trunk storage room and Mabel Wilcox's Public Health Office.

The homestead was self-sufficient. There were poultry pens for hens, ducks and turkeys, vegetable gardens, fruit trees, flower gardens. Beef and dairy cows grazed in the pastures. In the back of the compound, under a knoll, there even is a bomb shelter, built at the the beginning of World War II.

The Wilcox home was a mansion in its day, a palace for entertaining other plantation royalty, a home for his nieces until Mabel died in 1978. Her clothes still hang in her closet. The wood-paneled rooms, the book-filled library, the flower-filled parlor, the satin-polished entryway, all immaculately kept, seem to await the footsteps of the former residents in a they-will-return-momentarily atmosphere.

The house still lives. We even stopped in the kitchen, which is separated from the living rooms by a wide verandah, to enjoy homemade cookies and mint tea prepared by Hisae Mashita, a cook at Grove Farm for over forty years.

Next to the main house are two more buildings. One is the guest cottage with two bedrooms to house business associates as well as friends. There were no hotels in those days. Adjacent to the guest cottage is the George Wilcox personal cottage/den/bedroom dwelling where he lived a solitary life among a collection of hats and canoes.

His den was filled with agronomic books, engineering books, weather records, evidence of his basic professionalism.

A second bedroom with large screened windows had been built for the warmer summer weather.

The plantation museum is also now a research center with farm records faithfully preserved together with a library of information of historical artifacts and botanical specimen.

A biography of the plantation and George N. Wilcox, *Grove Farm Plantation*, written by the popular, able columnist of the *Honolulu Advertiser*, Bob Krauss, is available in paperback at most bookstores, and, of course, at the plantation office.

Call 245-3202 to confirm the current visiting days and hours, and to make reservations. A small admission charge. Written requests may be sent to Grove Farm Homestead, P.O. Box 1631, Lihue, Kauai, Hawaii, 96766.

The Left Arm of Kauai

Kauai is an easy island to explore.

Look at the Kauai map.

One day you can go left, to the west, on Highway-50, ducking off the highway to the coast to visit the resort area of Poipu, then continuing west to Kehaka where you turn north to the "Grand Canyon of the Pacific," Waimea Canyon, and beyond to the Kokee State Park.

The next day you take the right arm, Highway-56, and drive to the north end of the island, to Princeville, Hanalei Bay, and at the end of the road, find the caves beyond Haena Point.

Our itinerary was to go first to the end of the left arm, to the state cabins at Kokee Park for a two-night stay, visiting areas of interest along the way and then doubling back, picking up places we missed, to stay and play at Poipu.

One of our first stops was at the Kauai office of the Hawaii State Parks Department's Outdoor Recreation and Historic Sites.

My primary question was regarding the safety of hiking.

An unpleasant fact is that Hawaii's verdant, hidden valleys have become ideal garden patches of highly profitable and illegal marijuana. Formerly the hobby of hippies, the farming of marijuana has now become the province of gun-carrying criminals.

A unsuspecting hiker stumbling onto a "farm" is in danger of losing his life. It has happened and it has happened on Kauai.

The advice given to me by the parks department was to always stay on the main trails. Always travel with someone. (Women, especially, should never travel alone).

Sign in and sign out in the registration books found at the head of trails. Wear proper footwear and watch the weather.

Our second mission was to have lunch with Jan TenBruggencate, Kauai correspondent for the *Advertiser,* to catch up on the latest gossip and contacts.

(Jan, a tall, blond Dutchman was born in Holland but raised on Molokai from the age of nine, the son of an agricultural researcher. Locals don't believe he is local. (His name is remembered by saying "ten broken gates." He once received a telephone call to "Ten Weddings Cakes." Wrong.)

After victualing ourselves for the cabin life at Kokee, we took Jan's advice and made our first stop at Puhi, headquarters for Grove Farm, and the location of Puhi Lanai Restaurant, the only place you can buy Sereno Portuguese Sausage.

If you are very lucky at Puhi, you might find a cloudless day and see Mt. Waialeale, elevation 5080 feet, in the distance.

We continued west on Hwy-50, passing the attractive tree-lined road to Poipu (Hwy-52). At Lawai, Hailima Road (Hwy-360) intersects from the southeast, and leads to the unmarked entrance of the Pacific Tropical Botanical Gardens, a most unusual place.

In 1964, Congress, in an act of rare wisdom, chartered the garden to fulfill a need for botanical research, particularly in identifying plants with medicinal values.

Today the former dry and dusty valley has been changed into a 186-acre garden of rare and endangered trees and plants from around the world. It is a treasure retreat of beauty and scientific achievement which you can tour Monday through Friday, but only with a reservation. Tours are $10. Write P.O. Box 340, Lawai, Kauai, Hawaii 96765. The garden, unfortunately, is not on many visitor agendas. Put it on yours.

Of additional interest and impact is that the son of a Chicago cattleman, Robert Allerton, had previously turned the adjacent property, acreage once owned by the Hawaiian Queen Emma, into a showplace of flowers and fountains and reflecting pools. His protege and adopted son, John Gregg Allerton, now in his eighties, is expected to donate his estate to the gardens.

We passed through hilltop Kalaheo, making a note to stop in at the Kukuiolono Golf Course on the way back and went on to the Hanapepe Lookout, a scenic river valley, a 2P stop.

We scheduled a stop at Hanapepe. (I have favorite Hawaiian names that sound pretty on the tongue and this is one of them. "Hah-nah-pay-pay".)

Another thing that is pretty on the tongue is the lilikoi chiffon pie at the Hanapepe's Green Garden Restaurant, a favorite eatery with Kauai families, run by the Hamabata ladies, Sue and Gwen, who wear awesome strands of perfectly matched Niihau shell leis. You will learn more about these "pearls" of the islands in the following chapter. The restaurant is large, pleasant, filled with plants and people enjoying steaks and fish and desserts. Actually, we returned to the Green Garden Restaurant because we were told by an informant that the bar serves one of the two best mai tais on Kauai. Good mai tais. Our dinner consisted of mai tai sampling, a glass of wine, soup and salad, fresh fish with rice and vegetables and then a slice each—in the name of anything-for-the-readers research—lilikoi, macadamia cream and chocolate cream pie. The cost was less that $20.

Approaching Waimea, we turned into the Russian fort. Actually, there is little left of the star-shaped fortification. You can read that it had walls 17-feet wide and was 20-feet high in places, and you can step inside the remaining walls where there was once an armory and barracks and officers' quarters but, factually, it is more fun to read about than visit in its present state. A badly weathered and stained short history of the fort with statistics was posted at the site when we were there. A 1P satisfy-your-curiosity stop.

From the fort you can look across the Waimea River to the location of Captain Cook's landing in 1778. A marker from the highway points to the location in a public park but, disappointingly, there is nothing there but a memorial stone.

Still, if Captain Cook, the Great Navigator, is one of your heroes, it is worthy of a visit. A ZERO-P stop.

At the time of Cook's landing, Waimea was a prosperous, agrarian community with neatly tended taro farms irrigated by an ingeniously engineered, stone lined ditch, said to be built by the Menehunes, the little elves that tour guides love to dwell on. Before taking what you hear too seriously, you should read about the Menehunes in a well written, thoroughly researched book, *Kauai*, by Edward Joesting, a local author who maintains, along with other scholars, that the Menehunes were probably the first of the Polynesians to arrive in the islands. Later they were sub-jugated by the second wave of immigrants from Tahiti who referred to conquered people as "manahune." The appellation "little people" came from their social category, Joesting claims, and not their physical size. No archaeological evidence of "little people" has ever been found.

The next day we would spend a couple of profitable hours in the small but absorbing museum at Kokee State Park just beyond the Waimea State Park.

Among the museum's exhibits was a quote from the journal of one of Cook's more perceptive officers, Lt. James King, who had walked into the valley above the river mouth:

> "The inhabitants far surpass all neighboring island-
> ers" (By 'neighboring' he was referring to Tahitians,
> Tongans and Samoans) "in their management of their
> plantations. These plantations are divided by low and
> regular ditches ... the fences were made with a neatness
> approaching elegance, and the roads through them
> were thrown up and finished in a manner that would
> have done credit to any European engineer."

From the little seaside sugar mill town of Kekaha, you turn right on Highway-65 to drive 11 miles uphill to the Waimea Canyon lookouts and the Kokee State Park with its modest but comfortable cabins, restaurant and small museum.

The park also offers extensive walks, hunting and trout fishing. *Trout fishing in Hawaii?* Yes, trout fishing, but only on Kauai.

In contrast to nature's exhibit of mountain scenery, there is a satellite and missile tracking station at the top.

(If you are going to drive to Waimea Canyon just for the day, go first thing in the morning when the light is quite dramatic. The other rationale for getting an early start is to beat the tour buses to the best spots.)

There are several lookouts over the 10-mile slash in the earth that plunges to depths of more than 3,000 feet in spots. The walls are cut by wind and rain and present different shadow patterns at different times of the day. Best at dawn and sunset. Worst at noon.

The serrated levels of rock are multi-colored—moss green atop a rust strata, below which are layers of grayish greens and brownish gray streaked frequently with lines of solid coral and coral-pink combinations.

The problem, I find, at Waimea Canyon is that once you get there, you look down at the colors, perhaps you can see the glint of a running creek at the bottom, you look at the birds. If you are lucky you might sight a feral goat or two, and that is it. You take your picture, usually a 2P, and leave. A passive happening.

Despite the publicity, it is not the Grand Canyon.

On the other hand, if you know that the adjacent Kokee State Park encompasses 4,345 acres with a dozen good hiking trails, and if you come prepared to walk about in one of Hawaii's rarest nature scenes, you'll turn a passive morning or afternoon into an active, happy, memorable experience.

Our day was waning and a light mist was falling so we hurried on to Kokee State Park.

I have to share with you the exhilaration a resident of Honolulu gets on a mountain peak where the air smells of woods and is cool on the cheek, where you inhale deep, refreshing, invigorating breaths, where you can light a fire in a fireplace when the evening turns cool. Hey, that's high stuff.

The activity center of the Kokee State Park is in a lush meadow, an abrupt contrast to the densely forested area surrounding it. Here you find the Kokee Lodge, a properly rustic restaurant that serves breakfast, lunch and dinner—hot corn meal is a house specialty—has a liquor license and a small shop where you can buy a few necessities and the inevitable logo tee-shirt. It also dispenses hunting and fishing licenses and, under contract, provides the only accommodations permitted in the park.

Next door is the Kokee Natural History Museum (open 10 to 4 daily). At the entrance to the compound is a small Park Ranger's office. The ranger is usually out but his bulletin board contains useful, current information.

At the edge of the meadow, in a shaded area, are facilities for tent campers holding permits and picnickers: tables, outdoor stoves, covered pavilions and restrooms.

We checked in at the Lodge, picked up the key and directions to one of the dozen cabins tucked back into the woods, invisible from the Lodge, and ordered firewood for two nights for $6.

The Lodge and cabins are 20-year concessions, won by bid.

Originally there were four cabins, a small grocery store and the museum, run by Territorial Park personnel. More cabins were constructed and the first concession was granted in 1961.

In 1982, when new bids were solicited, the concession was won by two Honolulu couples who had made a hobby of going to Kokee on weekends.

But before the bids were opened and awarded, Hurricane Iwa huffed and puffed and blew the house down—in fact blew houses down all over Kauai. The park was without power for several months which hampered renovation work by the new operators. It was spring of 1983 before they reopened with a remodeled kitchen and modern equipment, new furniture, dinnerware and tableware.

One memento of the hurricane is the 16-foot slab of koa wood topping the bar in the lounge, taken from a tree knocked over by the wind.

The cabins were refurbished—one was rebuilt—and housekeeping equipment replaced.

Our cabin had a double bed in the living room, two small bedrooms with twin beds and a hot-water shower/bathroom. Sheets, towels, blankets and pillows were provided. The kitchen, separated from the living room by a roomy storage compartment topped by a dining counter, had an electric range and oven, a large refrigerator with many trays of ice, and all necessary cooking utensils.

No condiments were to be found. Bring salt and pepper.

The cost of the cabin, for two *or* six, was $25 a night, plus tax. One of the best accommodation deals in the state. Of course there are restrictions on how long you can stay; the maximum number of allowable nights per stay is five, according to park regulations.

We shooed aside a flock of what looked like barnyard chickens to get to our door. Actually they were "moa," descendants of fowl brought to Hawaii by the ancient Polynesians prior to Captain Cook's arrival. Brightly plumed creatures, once used as food and sacrificial animals, their feathers valued for capes and other ornaments, they were also prized as fighting birds by Hawaiians of yesteryear.

Moa, also called Jungle Fowl, existed on all islands until the mongoose was imported in 1883 to destroy rats in the cane fields but the rats slept in the daytime and the mongoose slept throughout the night. The mongoose, however, fed well on the ground-nesting birds, destroying the bird life on all islands except Kauai where the shipment of mongoose was shoved into the sea and drowned.

Every time we stepped outside the door, the moa congregated. They are accustomed to being fed by the cabin occupants. Do not look at them as potential roasted drumsticks. They are protected by the park. It is illegal to harass them much less injure them. That includes eating them.

We had just enough light left in the day to make a quick ten minute trip to the end of the road, to one of our favorite places—a 3P stop—at the Kalalau Lookout. You stand on the edge of a 4,000-foot cliff and look down into the verdant, near inaccessible valley of Kalalau, once densely cultivated by Hawaiians but now abandoned, a Shangri-la with waterfalls and fruit trees and a clear ocean that sweeps up onto a pristine beach in long, lingering lacy white waves.

Perhaps it is because of the action of the sea and the waterfalls and the beckoning charm of the carpet of green below you, but the Kalalau Lookout is more satisfying than the Waimea Canyon Lookout.

A few minutes beyond, at the very end of the road, is a different perspective of Kalalau. It also marks the start of the Pihea Trail, one of the 17 hiking and hunting trails in the park. At the head of the trail there's a park logbook for hikers to sign as they enter and exit for their own security.

Registrations on the first two pages included hikers from Finland, New Zealand, New York, Germany, Illinois, California and Australia, together with such remarks as "Trippy!" "Beautiful." "God's country!" "Great." "Tough but worth it." "Spectacular—to heck with Maui." "Like walking on a cloud."

Among the 45 miles of trails are easy nature walks and rugged to treacherous hikes to distant lookouts. The local people are challenged by the unusual Alakai Swamp Trail, a Dr. Jekyll and Mr. Hyde trek through wild brush and black bogs, that extends to a lookout over Hanalei Bay. The treachery comes from the weather. The local people know not to attempt the bog after a sizable rain, and never to go in when it is raining.

We ducked back to our cabin, built a roaring fire, grilled a steak and drank red wine in the warmth of the flickering light, and listened to the pitty-pat of the rain on the roof.

The next day we caught up with Mac Hori, the current park ranger, a young looking 55-year-old, who previously had been stationed in Kalalau and was still in love with the valley.

"At one time Kalalau became overrun with hippies and they created problems. Unhygienic, too much pot, too much nudism. So we had to get them to move out. No trouble. The make-shift camps were burned or torn down and now the valley is pretty much protected. Only 80 campers with permits can be in the valley at one time, and they can only stay for five nights. If they go in without a permit or overstay their permit time, we confiscate their equipment and they have to appear in court to get it back.

"I tell the campers that the valley is like a woman. At the top is the head formed by ohia trees, its lehua blossoms decorating the hair. If you pick a lehua blossom, it is going to rain, you know that, don't you?"

Mac paused for the expected reassurance, then continued on with his litany of love.

"The two eyes are Twin Falls, those towering waterfalls toward the back of the valley. The mouth is the Big Pond. The belly button, I call 'Smokers' Rock' because, I tell the campers, that is where I go to spot them smoking marijuana.

"Where the two legs come together is the Little Pond.

"I wrote a poem about Kalalau. Would you like to hear it?"

Oh, yes, we said, and I pulled out my miniature tape recorder. Our stalwart ranger immediately had stage fright.

Finally, we got him started. He put his feet up and looked out of window speaking slowly: "I call it 'Kalalau Inspiration.'

'When you hike into Kalalau,
    'Enjoy nature.
    'Look at the mountains and the hanging valleys of
the Na Pali Coast.
    'Smell the breeze from the wild surf dashing against
the cliffs.

'Listen to the running water from the falls above.

'The vibrations you feel at certain places will be good or bad.

'But Mother Nature will tune into you and give you an inspirational feeling.

'It is a magical valley ... where I like to be.' "

A map of Kokee's hiking trails is available at the ranger's office.

Commercial hiking guide books are sold at the Kokee Natural History Museum which has a small but engrossing collection of exhibits pertaining to the park.

Good museum. I was dismayed to learn that it took 80,000 birds such as the apapane, a red breasted bird common to the area, to make a feather cape for Kamehameha. Especially so, since the Audubon Society counted only 106 apapane in their December, 1983 census.

Our spirits lifted with the description of the ohia tree as being "carmine" colored.

We learned in the museum that the "Pacific" plate on which Hawaii floats is one of the earth's twelve plates, which we didn't know, although we did know that the ridge line of undersea mountains making up Hawaii extends to Siberia and Hawaii sits on a "hot spot" of magma that stills bubbles up through volcanoes on the Big Island, creating new land.

Also news was the fact that the longhorn cattle brought to Hawaii by Vancouver in 1793 had no natural enemies and the herds increased so rapidly that the over grazing resulted in such serious erosion of forest cover that professional hunters were hired in 1900 to eliminate the animals. By 1916, all of the feral cattle were gone, including cattle with huge platter-like hooves, an evolutionary result of living in Alakai Swamp.

Wild pig and goats still abound on the island and can be hunted with a license. Rainbow trout swim in the streams of Kokee and Waimea, trout which are stocked every year because the waters are not cold enough to encourage spawning. The record trout, according to Lodge records, is over six pounds. The trout fishing season is August and September.

The cabins at Kokee are 40 percent occupied by overseas visitors and the remainder about half and half between Kauai and Honolulu residents who come primarily in the summer months for the harvest of wild Methley plums, a delicacy, and the fishing season, or for holiday weekends.

A $25 deposit will confirm a written reservation. Write Kokee Lodge, P.O. Box 819, Waimea, Kauai 96796. Telephone (808) 335-6061.

Niihau, the Mystery Island

At the Puuhinahina Lookout on the rim of Waimea Canyon, one of the two view points ignores the canyon, focusing instead on the offshore island of Niihau.

In 1864, the island was bought by a lady from Scotland, Elizabeth McHutchinson Sinclair, who had been widowed in New Zealand and came to Hawaii to buy agricultural land.

Eliza, as she was called, was offered land on Oahu but turned it down, including, it is said, all the land between Honolulu Harbor and Diamond Head.

Discouraged, she was about to depart for other countries when the king offered her Niihau for $10,000. She took it.

Niihau is barren land with a scarcity of water and Eliza, realizing that she had a marginal operation, subsequently bought over 21,000 acres of land on south Kauai as a backup, for $15,000.

The Sinclair daughters married into the families of Knudsen, Gay and Robinson, names which are still prominent on Kauai today. Niihau remains in the firm hands of the Robinson family and the Hawaiians there are protected from all outside influences. Visitors are forbidden. Hawaiian is still the first language of the 200 or so inhabitants of the island.

Many titles for the island have been created by travel writers since that time. "Island of Yesterday" is on the plaque at the Puuhinahina Lookout.

"Forbidden Island" is another favorite.

The little island is only five miles wide and 18 miles long. There is no permanent stream and very little rain. Sheep and cattle are raised on the island, but the island is famous locally for the exquisite—and expensive—shell necklaces. The Lady Navigator is bullish on Niihau leis and will tell you more than you want to know about them in the chapter on Kauai shopping.

The Action at Poipu

The only thing that comes closer to giving a travel writer great pleasure than an advance payment check is the discovery, no matter how small, of a person, a place, a thing which is rare ... unusual ... the writer's own.

I found one on the way back from the canyon at Hanapepe. On the mauka (mountain) side of the road is a small white building, Swiss-neat, bearing a sign "Lappert's Aloha Ice Cream, Factory Outlet, Wholesale & Retail."

It was late morning and time for a scoop.

What a find. The little factory creates some 50 flavors of ice cream, all of which contain 16% butterfat. The normal store-bought ice cream contains 11%. Special products are imported like Madagascar vacuum-distilled Bourbon vanilla and Guittard chocolate from San Francisco.

The factory now uses 1,500 pounds of macadamia nuts a month and takes advantage of the fresh tropical fruits processed in Kalaheo, the village next door.

Creator of this enterprise is Walter Lappert, a cheerful, sixtyish, white-bearded Viennese, an ex-liquor distiller in Central and South America, who retired to Kauai and took up ice cream making as a hobby. His hobby now employs 14 people and customers come from as far as Lihue to buy a double dip. A son has opened an Aloha Ice Cream outlet in Sausalito, California.

But I stray from the subject: Hula Pie Ice Cream. You must try the hula pie. It is a gooey, fattening, okole-broadening combination of Kona coffee ice cream streaked with dark chocolate fudge, mixed with just a tantalizing touch of coconut and speckled with macadamia nuts. Not those little tiny bits and pieces of macadamia nuts, but big, chunky macadamia nut bits. You'll never forget it.

Promise yourself two treat of treats: "I will go to Kauai and (1) I will take a helicopter ride and (2) I will have a double scoop of Lappert's hula pie ice cream."

Our next stop was a return visit to Kukuiolono. Follow the signs off Highway-50 at Kalaheo. Kukuiolono was once the estate of the McBryde family of the nearby McBryde sugar plantation. The wrought-iron gates, concrete drive and castiron deer on the lawn are still there but instead of a mansion, there is a 9-hole plantation golf course with hilltop, sweeping views in all directions.

The first time we ever played Kukuiolono there was a large coffee can to receive the 50¢ cents for the green fee. Honor system.

Today there is a proper clubhouse. Green fees are about $5 and there are a few beaten-up, gasoline-powered carts.

"You'd better have good legs if you take a cart," said the groundskeeper, "because you'll probably walk home."

The king-of-the-mountain feeling you get atop Kukuiolono, looking up and down the south coast of Kauai, is worth the visit and even the walk home, if necessary.

There are several challenging holes as well.

In the winter months when the "snowbirds," (condominium owners from Canada and the frozen north in the United States), come to spend January to March in their apartments at Poipu, Kukuiolono gets a lot of play.

At the clubhouse, chatting with the starter, we also found Evie Warner who runs a statewide bed-and-breakfast association from headquarters on Kauai.

If you'd like to share a home in the islands with an island family, write Evie for a directory. Box 449, Kapaa, Kauai, Hawaii 96746. Telephone 822-7771.

We took the back road through Koloa to the beach resorts of Poipu and were soon in an oceanfront suite at the Sheraton Kauai.

Our game plan had been to check in, find a lonely beach nearby as a picnic site, and loll away the afternoon. But when we arrived in our room, on the beach a few feet from the water, we took a pleasant, refreshing swim and spread out our goodies on the coffee table in air-conditioned comfort and, with the manager's complimentary bottle of white wine, had a feast. Isn't that terrible?

The 1982 Hurricane Iwa struck the western end of the Hawaiian Islands and devastated Kauai. What the winds didn't tear down, the thundering waves on the south coast tore up.

The area of Poipu was bombed. The two-story wooden units of the Sheraton Kauai were blasted off their foundations and pushed into the lobby of the newer, concrete Sheraton wing across the street. The street was littered with bed sheets, busted television sets, broken furniture.

Waiohai, the adjacent major hotel, had its lower floors flooded while guests kept safe upstairs.

Seaside restaurants like the Beachhouse, an institution since the '70s, were smashed and disappeared into the raging surf. Beaches were denuded of sand including Brennecke's Beach, which has the best known body surfing on the coast.

Two years later, you wouldn't have known anything had happened. The Sheraton replaced its oceanside units and added a new restaurant complex. Waiohai's lobby was recreated, as good as ever. Even Brennecke's sand has almost returned, although boulders rolled in by the storm make surfing there rather dicey now.

The nearby town of Koloa, said to be the earliest sugar plantation town, has undergone a rebirth and a championship golf course designed by Robert Trent Jones Jr. has opened.

As a result, Poipu with its six crescent beaches protected in the lee of the island from the tradewinds, and with a low rainfall matching that of Waikiki, is more of a complete resort entity than it was before the hurricane. In 1985, it had over 2,000 hotel and condo units, 18 restaurants and 30 tennis courts available for a tribe of faithful followers.

In its former prosperity, Old Koloa Town had its own sugar mill. It was the site of Hawaii's first successful sugar plantation started by three Irish immigrants who leased 9,000 acres from Kamehameha III in 1833. Two years later the township of Koloa was established, becoming the center of commercial activity for all of southern Kauai.

Over a period of time the sugar industry diminished. The lands were incorporated in those of Grove Farm. The mill burned down. So did the local theater. The buildings sagged.

In a glorious understatement, the new father of born-again Koloa, Bob Gerrell said, "There was a lot of deferred maintenance."

Gerrell obtained a 67-year lease from the trust holding the title to the major land area and buildings in the town and initiated a $3 million renovation program which required intensive surgery to replace termite eaten timbers, redesigning, remodeling, repainting, and re-leasing ... without losing the character of the Old Koloa Town.

It was all coming together when we were there, not complete but on the way—an upgraded, colorful, authentic addition to Poipu's pleasure portfolio where visitors can shop and sip and eat in an alternate place.

Around the corner from the main street next to the Chevron station is a ramshackle two-story building with a kite shop on the top floor. Downstairs is the home of Fathom Five (Terry O'Halloran, proprietor), where I signed up for a morning dive at Koloa Landing.

Like a nervous bridegroom not finding the ring, I couldn't find my PADI diving certificate and had to answer a lot of probing questions to satisfy the shoptenders that I—honest—was certified. I signed releases, crossed my heart . . . Later, of course, the certificate was found in my dive bag, the logical place for it.

Early the next morning I was back in the shop, nervously wishing I were taking kite flying lessons instead of a guided scuba dive. After I was fitted into a rubberized jacket, given a respirator, tank and weight belt, the precise lass asked:

"How many pounds do you take?"

"Eight," I answered, guessing at the number but hoping to sound experienced.

Outfitted, we boarded an old Navy van and drove down to Koloa Landing, two and a half miles away.

More than a hundred years ago this tiny niche in the land was an important harbor shipping yams to gold miners in California and, later, fresh meat and vegetables to the Honolulu market and processed sugar to the Mainland. Eight cargo ships and schooners with passengers and goods were unloaded every day.

Faded photographs show the harbor surrounded by horses and carriages and the wharves piled with wares.

Still later, it became a small boat launching harbor with a concrete apron extending from the shore into the shallows of the water ... until Hurricane Iwa filled the landing with giant boulders and took away a beach, a pavilion, a restaurant and a waterfront condominium.

Enough of the harbor had been cleared of rocks to allow us to walk carefully down the slippery concrete runway into the shallow water and put on our fins and test our equipment.

Our professional diver/guide, Mark, a sun-washed blond, calm, lean, unflappable, had only one rule, repeated twice: "Let me know as soon as your tank gauge reads 1200 pounds."

My dive companion was from California and had every device known to divers including a dive timing clock which started running automatically as soon as it was immersed in water. I felt rather inadequate with my $3.95 high-yellow diving gloves.

Masks in place and breathing oxygen, we slipped under the water and out the harbor barely clearing a last barrier of rocks mounded at the entrance.

In deeper water, I released the last air from my flotation vest but couldn't sink. Not enough weight. Mark, underwater, took weights from his belt, undid my belt and added the additional lead, and down I went.

Mark carried smelt in a bag attached to his belt and, almost instantly, he attracted a school of yellow reef fish that never left him during the dive. Later I learned they were "taape," imported from Tahiti as a reef fish.

We first ventured along a coral face hugging the coast where Mark found his first pet eel. Like the accompanying reef fish, they were old friends. Mark put his hand to the eel's gaping mouth to say hello. I backed off ten feet.

Leaving the shore we ventured into deeper water and first saw a small spotted ray, gracefully undulating its bat-like wings. This was not an old acquaintance of Mark's. It took one look at us and disappeared into the hidden reaches of the sea.

Schools of many colored fish swam by us or we swam through them. Many red young goat fish, "oama" in Hawaiian. Then we saw a papio that would grow into a skipjack tuna and weigh over a hundred pounds.

We swam over clusters of dull colored coral, leisurely, slowly cruising underwater, propelled forward by the easy kicking of our giant rubber fins, the only sound being my own inhaling and exhaling. Streams of air bubbles rising from the heads of my companions seem to have a life of their own.

A huge school of dark fish swam by, Achilles Tang, the largest school of fish I was to see in my short, ten dive scuba career.

Mark would go down to an algae covered rock, tap it with his knife and the fish, knowing the drill, reacted as if they had heard a dinner bell. He then would scrape off the algae with his knife and the fish would dive into the scrapings like the Lady Navigator into Lappert's hula pie ice cream.

My gauge read 1200 pounds which I signaled to Mark. We turned back to the shore and reached the reef where Mark had found the first eel. This time there were two.

On shore Mark would assure us, "They are only about four feet long. They are not gnashing their teeth at you. That's how they get water through their gills."

They may not have been long but they were as big around as my thighs. He fed them bits of smelt, pushing away the yellow-fin taape.

Mark beckoned for me to come closer and held out a piece of smelt in my direction. "Come feed the eels," he was coaxing.

"Non, non, non," I replied by wagging my Naughty Marietta finger at him. "I need these digits for tapping out copy on my word processor. I am not about to lose my living playing feed-the-eels in an underwater zoo."

Forty-five minutes after leaving the harbor we were slipping back over the rocks into the shallow water.

Good dive. Not great visibility. No multi-colored coral heads. But good fish life, great performances by the eels and a solid guide.

Recommended.

Kiahuna Golf Village

The missing ingredient of a modern vacation resort at Poipu for many years was a world-class golf course. This was rectified with the completion in 1984 of the Kiahuna Golf Village, an 18-hole, par-70 course that is short but interesting visually because of its varied terrain and holes, and historically because the developers have left intact the remnants of a former Hawaiian village—lava rock walls, caves, tombs—and have integrated these physical vestiges of the past into the golf course.

(You are allowed a free drop from any rock wall that interferes with your swing but you are charged one stroke if you go into a tomb or an ancient stone oven.)

Robert Trent Jones, Jr. did not follow in the footsteps of his father whose courses were designed to send the golfer weeping back to the hotel. The Kiahuna links are not difficult but they are narrow. Hit it straight and you'll do very well.

One unusual feature of the course is that it has the only green shared by two holes in Hawaii, a la St. Andrews. The green for the 3-par 13th across the water going north and the 3-par 16th across the water coming south are the same, but the holes are so far apart that most golfers don't even realize it.

A new white, wide, rambling clubhouse has been opened, looking as if it had been transplated from Palm Springs.

All together, an enjoyable layout for the recreational, vacationing golfer.

We can't leave Poipu without mentioning one of the great weekly attractions: the Sunday morning brunch at the Waiohai Hotel. It starts at 10AM, but the line starts at 9AM. People come with their Sunday newspapers and read while waiting. No reservations, unless you have a party of ten.

Fresh made omelettes, seafood, pastries, sausages, hot dishes, cold salads, fresh fruit crepes ... a tummy-popping table and a great local favorite that compares with Mauna Kea's buffet lunch. Expensive but worth the money if you enjoy fabulous spreads.

The Right Arm, North to Hanalei

You leave Lihue on Highway-56 going north and seven miles later you are at the Wailua Golf Course, perhaps the best municipal golf course in the state. A par-72 course today, it was first opened in 1920 with nine holes which now comprise the back nine. The shade trees and the developed manicured fairways and greens give evidence of the nine's maturity. The front nine was developed in the 50's and, being on the ocean, was slow to take hold. Flat, windy, tough. Today, the maturing trees give the front nine a kinder look.

Farther on, a road off the highway to the right leads to Lydgate Park, a recommended place for snorkeling but no longer for camping due to an ugly incident a few years ago when a bunch of local thugs abused—to put it lightly—some camping tourists.

When you get to the Wailua River bridge, to the left will be the Wailua River Marina with a major dock for giant-sized scows taking giant-sized loads of tourist to the Fern Grotto.

Yesteryear when the Smith family ran small boats up the river and a family member sang the "Hawaiian Wedding Song" in the fern-filled grotto, the sweet melody reverberating off the walls, it was hand-squeezing time with your friend, and an experience you encouraged your visitors to share.

Today, I have a hard time with the Fern Grotto trip.

Perhaps the charm of it remains in spite of the mobs of people, but I'd doubt it. If you take the river trip, let me know.

(Since I wrote the above impression, I went to the airport to pick up a houseguest who had been in the islands on her first trip five years before. She had been at Poipu on Kauai and at the Kona Village on the Big Island.

"What do you remember the most?" I asked her.

"Oh, it was a river ride where we went to this big cave ..."

"Fern Grotto?" I asked.

"Oh, yes, the Fern Grotto. It was unforgettable."

There you are. Sometimes our local feelings are not in tune with the visitor's impressions.)

What you shouldn't miss knowing about Wailua is that the area was once the hallowed ground of the *alii*, the royalty of the island. Known as Wailua Nui Hoano, or Great Sacred Wailua, it was one of the two most sacred areas in the islands. Even in the times when travel was still being made to and from Tahiti, the place of Wailua Nui Hoano was known throughout the regions of the Central Pacific.

Commoners were not allowed to traffic in this wide valley which extended two miles south of the river and three miles north. It was rich with fruit and taro from the land and fish from the sea.

Royalty, men and women, surfed in the waves at the beach near the river. When a great chief arrived by canoe, the canoe, with the chief in it, was transported litter fashion by carriers to his hut.

On the south side of the river are the remains of an important giant heiau, the Temple of the Rising Sun or Hikinaakala, said to be a place of refuge for sinners, criminals, escaped prisoners. Once inside the walls, they would be exonerated.

Farther inland was an even larger heiau, almost a hundred yards square. Little remains of these walls of greatness but across the river, within walking distance of the Coconut Palms Hotel, there's a royal reminder still visible: the Birthing Stones. A mother-to-be would place her back against a stone and spread her legs on another stone to give birth. It was only for royal births. A commoner touching or stepping over the stones would be executed.

Down by the river bank was another heiau, small, but most sacred because here monthly human sacrifices were conducted. The victims' bodies were hung from an oracle tower until morning when they were placed on the sacrificial altar to remain until the flesh rotted off the bones.

Now would you like to step over to the Coco Palms Hotel for lunch?

(If you would like more background on Wailua, we again refer you to Ed Joesting's book, *Kauai).*

The Coco Palms is a tradition now in Hawaii but, what seems like only yesterday, it was the first post-war hotel on a Neighbor Island, and for Honolulu people, it was a thing to do—run away to the Coco Palms for the weekend.

What made Coco Palms work was the unusual abilities of two people, Lyle "Gus" Guslander and Grace Buscher.

Gus was a tough guy. The first time I ever saw him was as manager of the then Matson-owned Moana Hotel in Waikiki and its sister hotel, the new (1951) Surfrider Hotel, now a wing of the Moana.

An important community function involving Bob Hope and Ann Blythe was scheduled to take place at the Surfrider during Gus's absence in San Francisco, and he stood, surrounded by his staff, barking orders at them like the ex-Marine he was, emphasizing every command with stabs of a lighted cigar. Tough, muscular, demanding.

Coco Palms was his first hotel, and Grace Buscher, his first manager. In contrast to his generalissimo tendencies, she was the perennial pixie but with the ability to take charge of a staff, create and inspire innovation while charming the socks off guests.

She started the custom in Hawaii of blowing the conch shell at sunset to summon guests to watch the loin-clothed beachboys run barefoot through the property lighting luau torches. It became an instant "ancient" tradition. The conch-shell-beachboy-tiki-torch-lighting-routine is now an established custom at practically every hotel property in the islands.

She put visiting celebrities to planting coconut trees on the hotel grounds, stocked the streams with fish and gave her adolescent guests fishing poles, an enchantment for both parents and kids.

She had lambs or pigs roasting on spits as guests arrived, installed giant clam shells as bathroom lavatories, outrigger canoes as beds—among other Hawaiian-gimmicked decor. Nothing was too schmaltzy to try ... and everything worked. Guests from Honolulu and Des Moines loved the Coco Palms.

Gus went on to create a successful chain of hotels, sold the chain to AmFac for millions, gave a hunk of money to the Travel Industry Management School at the University of Hawaii, and married Grace. Gus is dead now and Grace recently retired, but her touch will always be the heritage of the Coco Palms. That's one of the nicer Hawaiian success stories.

Farther along the highway in the direction of Kapaa is The Market Place at Coconut Plantation, a major tourist-oriented bazaar with many fast-food outlets, shops and hotels.

Kapaa used to be the center of the pineapple industry on Kauai with its own cannery, now closed. It's population in 1980, according to the census, was 4,467—larger than Lihue's. Kapaa is going through a familiar metamorphosis, from an agricultural community to a service-oriented center built primarily around the visitor industry. The old buildings, faded and sometimes leaning, are being taken over by arty folk and converted into cute restaurants, bars, boutiques. It is a new world for Kapaa with new tomorrows.

Along the eastern shore of Kauai are many fine beaches that are made for picnicking, swimming, snorkeling, surfing and just sunning. An annual Mainland visitor, Lenore W. Horowitz, who has been coming to Kauai for years with her children, publishes an annual booklet called *Kauai, Underground Guide* in which she gives details about all the beaches of the island. It is a good car book for anyone spending much time on Kauai.

We don't agree with her negative comments about many of the restaurants but her information on beaches is unmatched by any other guide.

For example, one of the most spectacular beaches on Kauai is at Anahola Bay, north of Kapaa, and the guide devotes an entire page to the beach, adding advice on where to get the best hamburgers to take to the beach. (Duane's Ono Burger next to the Anahola Store.)

Anahola Beach is immense, uncrowded, and has places for children, surf fishermen, snorkelers, surfers and picnickers eating Duane's Ono Burger with avocado and bean sprouts.

A sign on Highway-56 points to Anahola Bay less than a mile off the highway.

The next sign to watch for on the right is to the town and lighthouse of Kilauea—"kill-ah-way-ah." Kilauea is more a village than a town with its general store billing itself as the "Gumps of the Cane Fields" which it isn't, and also Jacques Bakery. Jacques has been "discovered" by a legion of travel writers. The dark headed little Frenchman told the Lady Navigator that he could tell which publication she had read by which pastry she ordered because that was what that particular magazine's travel editor had picked to rave about.

"Chocolate eclair," she challenged.

"Modern Bride," he replied immediately. "And that is the worst thing I make."

What he makes are good croissants and some breads such as the honeywheat bread we tasted on the kayak trip. His success in the cane fields led to the opening of a Honolulu branch where the competition is keener.

Towards the coast on a bumpity-bumpity road, slightly paved, is the Kilauea Lighthouse which attracts major numbers of tourists because it is the only lighthouse in Hawaii prepared to receive visitors.

In 1908, a Congressional act appropriated $75,000 for construction of the lighthouse at Kilauea. The land was purchased, as was a 4-ton French prism lens, the largest of its kind in the world, capable of creating a concentrated beam visible for 20 miles at sea.

Five years later the lighthouse and keeper's quarters were completed. Hundreds of people lined the coast on May 6, 1913 when the manager of the Kilauea Sugar Company set the light in operation.

In 1975, the original light developed a series of mechanical problems and was replaced by an automated light which is mounted several yards in front of the old light.

Touring the lighthouse grounds includes a lesson in the indigenous plant life and its neighboring bird sanctuary. The area is under control of the U.S. Fish and Wildlife Service because the surrounding cliff area abounds in sea bird colonies: red footed boobies, shearwaters who come in at sunset by the thousands, frigate birds and tropical birds.

In winter, migrating whales pass in front of the area.

The grounds of the Kilauea Lighthouse are open from noon to four and closed on Saturdays. Bilingual volunteers serve as guides and operate the bookstore.

As you approach Princeville across a cattle-strewn plateau of grazing land, you will see on your left an airfield built by the Colorado developers of Princeville who felt that their luxurious but remote resort needed a faster gate for transportation than the Lihue airport provided. They, therefore, built their own airport and organized their own airline with reliable twin-engine jet-prop Otters. Besides the frequent scheduled flights to Honolulu, the airline currently maintains service to a new airstrip near Waikoloa on the Big Island, linking the prestigious Kohala Coast resorts more closely to the Princeville destination.

The airport at Princeville is also headquarters for Papillon Helicopters, probably the largest helicopter operation in Hawaii and a leader in touring visitors over and around Kauai in a never-to-be-forgotten experience. The French word 'papillon' (butterfly) connotes an ethereal quality of flight for pleasure and sensual enjoyment. That's what the press kit said.

We'd buy that, particularly after checking in and being seated at a table containing two carafes, one for fruit juice, the other for white wine. A ground host (it could have been a hostess) briefed us, assigned seats and passed out a sheet with boarding instructions and a flight map.

Everything at Papillon is tightly but lightly organized. There is never, never a hint of carelessness but, at the same time, the operators make sure that the atmosphere is joyful and pleasant.

Beautifully thought out and expertly executed.

We took off, six passengers and the pilot, in a Bell helicopter. Sticking to the established script for helicopter pilots, our whirly-bird jockey said he didn't want us to be nervous, that it was *already* his second professional flight.

Symphonic music swelled through our big stereophonic earphones, occasionally interrupted by our captain pointing to areas of interest. We passed over Hanalei Valley, swooped into the Valley of Rainbows with its multiple waterfalls. No rainbows but the day was so clear that, to the east, we could see the faint silhouette of Oahu on the horizon. The pilot said that was indeed rare.

He flew the "butterfly" into the bowels of Mt. Waialeale, to the bottom of a towering waterfall. The dark gray cliffs encased us like a giant tube. It was difficult to see the top of the mountain.

We flew down the Valley of Fertility and made a turn around an isolated, Hollywood-perfect waterfall where a Carol Burnett film was scheduled to be shot.

Along the shoulders of the mountain we could see wild goats and, near Olokele Canyon, an isolated hunting lodge which belongs to the Robinson family.

The helicopter skimmed a ridge and dropped into Waimea Canyon—it looks more impressive standing on the rim—past waterfalls and over the Alakai Swamp, then climbed over another ridge to the Na Pali Coast and flew into the Valley of the Lost Tribes where traces of 600-year-old terraces gave mute evidence of a long-ago Hawaiian farm system.

Flying along the spectacularly scenic Na Pali Coast, we could see the 11-mile, cliff-hanging trail into Kalalau Valley and I made a mental note to take that off any proposed braver-than-thou adventure itinerary. Hairy.

A Zodiac boat was anchored at an isolated beach, the occupants snorkeling in the vicinity. That looked do-able and fun. It went on the must-do list.

We flew over the north end of Kauai, past Haena Point and the Bali Hai beach, over Hanalei Bay—looking exactly like the motion picture set for "South Pacific" (which it was). The bay is an extraordinarily wide, armful of green to blue water, combed with gently rolling white waves that end at a semicircle of creamy sand.

The pilot then headed upland and inland, circled a grassy valley and landed the twirly bird, like a giant insect, gently onto a knoll. We disembarked, helped him unload a couple of hampers, and followed him down a short path to a clear water stream, one of God's perfectly landscaped, natural swimming pools. He opened a bottle of champagne and passed around a modest nibbly. Nice touch.

During our brief touchdown with nature, we remarked that other air tours we had taken on Kauai ended with the dramatic flight inside Mt. Waialeale, and wondered why Papillon started their tour there. His answer of "starting where the others stop" was predictable, of course, but he went on to volunteer that Princeville, being closer to all of the scenic wonders of Kauai, gave Papillon an advantage over the other companies whose headquarters were the Lihue airport. Quite true.

Five minutes after reboarding we were back at the airport where the Lady Navigator pronounced the gift shop's "logo" merchandise among the finest quality in the Islands. She bought enough Papillon sports shirts for six Christmases to come.

All helicopter operations have a similar menu of flights. Dawn flights. Around the Island flights. Champagne flights. That sort of offering. Papillon has a special trip which takes a couple to the mountain slope stream where we had sipped champagne, leaves the loving pair by an isolated swimming hole/waterfall with water floats, games, picnic lunch and bubbly, then disappears until the scheduled afternoon pick-up time. Sounds like a four-star romp.

The Adam-and-Eve retreat is on a private lease negotiated exclusively for Papillon passengers and is also the location for many weddings arranged by the company. The wedding package includes helicoptering a party of six—"don't forget the minister" the instruction sheet warns—and champagne compliments of the company. Or, Papillon will arrange for a minister or priest or rabbi, photographer, limo service, flowers, wedding cake, etc. For a price.

A friend of ours staged such an all-out wedding for his son and said it cost him a fortune, but it was worth it.

One caveat: the six-passenger Bell helicopters are configured so that two people behind the pilot ride backwards. Bad. You don't see as much and, like the young bride sitting opposite us, you tend to get airsick. Don't go if you are assigned a seat where you must fly backwards.

Princeville is a complete resort. Sitting on top of the plateau overlooking Hanalei Bay, it is one of the prettiest sights in the islands.

The 27-hole golf course on a non-windy, non-rainy day is a joy. The three nine-hole segments suggest the difference of their scenery by their names. The Ocean Nine is the most spectacular with two par-3 holes the most fun. One plays from an elevated tee down to a polka dot of green flanked by water and sand. The other crosses an awesome inlet to an isolated slice of green in another world. The Lake Nine sees a lot of water and grabs a lot of balls, particularly on the final hole. The Woods Nine is made for scholars and gentlemen.

The whole complex is another creation of Robert Trent Jones Jr., the dominant resort golf course architect of Hawaiian courses. He has a home at Princeville and if he takes his fees out in houses, he owns a lot of real estate in Hawaii.

A thousand condominiums are available for vacation rentals at Princeville, many including a car in the package. On a recent trip, we stayed at the Hanalei Bay Resort in a one bedroom apartment with a gourmet challenging kitchen overlooking the bay. Two swimming pools, 11 tennis courts and cart transport service to deliver you to the beach at the bottom of the hill if you are too fatigued to walk. Lovely.

Princeville had been opened for more than ten years before it finally got its first hotel in 1985 with the opening of the Sheraton Princeville, a deluxe hotel demanding the economic reach and expense account flexibility of the same caliber of guests who inhabit Sheraton's Royal Hawaiian Hotel.

We toured the property before it was opened and came away impressed. Sited on a bluff facing Hanalei Bay and its Hollywood-come-true panorama, the hotel is built on descending levels down the hill. Rooms costing $150,000 each are decorated in early Hawaiian motifs. It has to be one of Sheraton's finest properties in the Pacific. Certainly the most costly.

Princeville has the look of a moneyed suburb with expensive new homes and gardens and swimming pools. The shopping center complex reflects the neighborhood and includes restaurants and a huge Foodland supermarket.

The view toward the mountains, weeping with waterfalls, has a different mood than that overlooking Hanalei Bay. It is quieter, more introspective, more peaceful. Nicer, in a way.

Friends of ours, the Larry Prichers, built a home in Princeville. With a choice of any lot looking at the ocean or the bay or the golf course, they chose a location with a full vista of the mountains.

Princeville is surrounded by 3P opportunities, but the mother of all 3P photographs is a short distance down the road.

Just after leaving the Princeville entrance toward Hanalei there is a lookout over Hanalei Valley. Stop. Even in the glare of high noon, Hanalei Valley presents a gold-medal award shot. A peaceful green valley of taro and rice in their many stages of growth, a river meandering between fields and a million birds feeding, some atop the buffalo performing their grooming duties, Hanalei Valley evokes the same emotional reaction that a person has on seeing a beautiful baby. "Ahhhhhh."

The road drops to the valley floor and you cross over a wooden one-way bridge that in time of heavy rain disappears under water, isolating the Princeville school children at their classrooms in Hanalei. In a "make do" fashion, they sleep in the gym until the floods subside ... but the teachers project VHS movies, bring in hot dogs and hamburgers and the kids love it. It's only the parents and teachers who suffer anxieties.

Hanalei is a village with its own personality. Once a missionary headquarters and dominated briefly by the infamous Georg Scheffer who built two earthwork forts flying Russian flags, Hanalei is now prosperous, servicing the visitor industry.

Near the town entrance, you'll pass the Tahiti Nui, dominated by Louise Marston, a legend in her own time, where you might spend an afternoon on the porch, leaning back in your chair as Walter Cronkite did, sipping and "talking story." It does have the flavor of Tahiti.

A sure reflection of prosperity is that the village's traditional Chinese store, Ching Young, is now a mini shopping center that includes a variety of visitor-oriented stores. One such is a sports shop for rental camping equipment, should you suddenly be inspired to get a permit and hike into Kalalau Valley.

Beyond Ching Young's on the left is a lava rock Protestant

church and behind the church, reached by the next driveway to the left, is the Waioli Mission House. Go. It will give you a flavor of missionary life in the 1840's, and a feeling of great tranquility in the 1980's.

Park in the shade of trees planted a century ago, walk beyond a picket fence across the expanse of lawn and you feel yourself entering the time warp.

A docent in missionary dress meets you at the door and guides you through the two-story, wood-framed building, giving you a brief background of its history and answering questions.

"The first missionaries came in 1834 in a canoe from Waimea," said Barbara Morrison, our attractive volunteer hostess, "and first lived in a new grass house. Much of the present house was shipped around the Horn from Boston and erected in 1837 by William Alexander, the first missionary, with the help of half a dozen Hawaiians. It cost $4,000."

In 1846, Abner and Lucy Wilcox, parents of George N. Wilcox, the proprietor of Grove Farm, came to Hanalei as teachers. Their grandchildren, Etta Wilcox Sloggett and Elsie and Mabel Wilcox, were responsible in 1974 for restoring the house and opening it as a non-profit museum.

The small but charming house has the memorabilia of the three missionary families who occupied it until the mission was officially closed.

On one wall is William Alexander's Passport, No. 4461, issued by the Department of State on July 9, 1836.

Here is a clock brought from Boston. Cost $8.

There, a picture of the St. Louis courthouse where the Dred Scott verdict leading to the abolition of slavery was handed down.

One bedroom was dominated by a gracious four-poster bed, so high off the floor that it had holes in the sideboards to hold a rope ladder for occupants.

One kitchen wall was lined with Chinese dishes which had been placed in mud and used as ballast in ships returning from trading in China. The mud was washed off and the dishes sold.

Spend an hour at the Mission House and find your own nuggets of intrigue. Open Tuesdays through Saturdays, 9AM to 3PM.

Adjacent to the Ching Young complex is a line of tottering buildings housing a number of enterprises, including a hodgepodge museum-cum-popcorn-stand, a small restaurant, and the headquarters of "Captain Zodiac" of the Na Pali Zodiac Company, originator of the rubber raft trips to the almost inaccessible Na Pali Coast.

Captain Zodiac is Clancy Greff, 31, a sea captain's son, slim, sun bleached, who, in seven years, has turned a hobby into a million dollar operation with a fleet of sleek, French-made Zodiac inflatable crafts ($35,000 each) with engine.

"At one time our family lived in Hawaii and I returned on a college vacation. Never went back. I started fooling around Na Pali in a 12-foot dingy. Over the years people heard about this damn kid going out to the Na Pali coast in a wooden boat and photographers and writers started asking for rides. So I went into business.

"A wooden boat is dangerous because it won't bend with the waves like a rubber raft will. Safety comes first. And that means the wind is critical. If you have no wind, it is perfectly safe in a Zodiac even with waves of six to seven feet. But if we have strong winds, we won't take passengers out in a four-foot swell."

Na Pali Zodiac offers three tours. The first tour is a half-day excursion, out to the coast to explore the sea caves, swim over the side depending on the ocean, picture-taking and a mini history lesson by the captain.

Tour "B" is a full day trip, a longer tour of the coast, past Kalalau to the ancient fishing village of Nualolo Kai, landing on the beach, snorkeling, hunting for shells, riding under waterfalls.

Tour "C" is for the very active, physically fit person who can swim through small surf and has the stamina to tour seven hours without strain.

"We also take hikers and campers in and out of Kalalau. Every morning we leave at 6:30 and drop off or pick up as many as twelve people a day. That cost $50 a person, one way, or we take out backpacks for $40.

"We are also volunteer garbage collectors. We bring out litter. Keeping the whole coast clean is a responsibility we have to assume because it is a virgin area that mustn't be allowed to be fouled. Greed and garbage are our two biggest problems.

"The element of greed comes from the fact that the tours to the coast are becoming too popular. The number of operators is growing. Somewhere along the line, the government has to limit the number of boats allowed along the Na Pali Coast or we can become another Wailua River—with the added factor that without proper licensing, it can be hazardous.''

In summer, when the seas are flat, Captain Zodiac and his crew of 32 take adventure seekers out on cruises from dawn to sunset. It is a major industry in tiny Hanalei.

In winter, winds and high surf can cut the number of tours to eight in a month. We tried to go twice on half-day morning trips because the wind is quieter in the morning, and twice we were canceled out by 15-foot waves which came up suddenly. Both times, the day was sunny, balmy, made-in-heaven weather. Only the surf was uncooperative, which underlines the necessity for not only having reservations but also confirming them at 7AM the morning of your trip.

Na Pali Zodiac, P.O. Box 456, Hanalei, Kauai, Hawaii 96714. Two telephone numbers: (808) 826-9371 or 826-9772.

The following summer, on our third attempt, we succeeded in making the trip. It was unforgettable. Barefooted, we climbed aboard the 21-foot rubber raft powered by two powerful engines. As we headed out of Hanalei Bay into open ocean, giant turtles floated by or dived for quieter waters. Our Zodiac captain talked of playful porpoise which we were not destined to see. We looked back into verdant valleys that you cannot see from the road, spotted goats on impossibly steep precipices and hikers on the cliff-suspended 11-mile trail to Kalalau Valley, and cruised around and under waterfalls into lava-tube caves.

Beyond the beachcamp at Kalalau we entered a tunnel leading to an open-to-the-sky grotto. The water's rare cobalt translucence enticed most of the passengers into swimming.

The ride home against the wind and the current was like riding a bucking bronco. (Hint: Sit midship on the starboard side for the best viewing going down the coast and the drier ride coming back.)

After our second winter washout—and before the summer tour—we followed the advice solicited from a group of action-oriented Yuppies after a sumptuous Cinco de Mayo dinner created by Lydia McCoy, my favorite Mexican food chef. They said not to miss the experience of the first two-mile segment of the Kalalau Valley Trail. A breeze, they said.

We decided to try the trail. A breeze, right? We drove to Kee

Beach at the deadend of a winding paved road that is punctuated with several one-way bridges and many pretty beaches, through jungley growths—you might think you are in Tahiti—past Bali Hai Beach, the launching spot for the Zodiac trips, and finally, past the wet caves of Waikapalae and Waikanaloa, and the dry cave of Maniniholo.

We found the last parking space in the crowded area behind the beach, and without taking water with us (mistake) or a candy bar for energy (mistake two), I put the keys to the car and the condominium into the pocket of my swimming trunks (mistake three), and we set off.

The first part of the trail is strenuous. It is a rather steep climb over small boulders, a heart-testing, heavy breathing quarter of a mile until you reach a spot looking back at Kee Beach and the reefs off Haena Point.

From there on, the path is well above the surf, marked with golden guava dropped from overhead fruit trees and 2P views of the Na Pali Coast as it bends around curves.

Half way to Hanakapiai we met a middle-aged couple with full backpacks hiking out from Kalalau.

"Was it rugged?" we asked.

The bearded man replied, "Look, I am in good shape. I jog. I play a lot of tennis. Good shape." (He was panting.) "But I have had to lie down and rest along this trail. Yes, it is rugged."

I mentally underlined again the resolution not to hike into Kalalau.

The two miles were not too easy either but the trail is not dangerous; it is not the cliff-hanging, acrophobic portion I had seen from the helicopter.

After a bit more than the hour the Kalalau Trail map indicated the hike should take, we descended to the Hanakapiai Stream and clambered over the giant rocks to the beach.

Wearing swim trunks had been a near useless idea. The surf crashed 15-foot waves (the reason the zodiac trip had been washed) onto the beach. We were reduced to splashing around in tidal pools, even then being shoved back to the rocks by a few surging large waves.

Our park map warned that experienced swimmers had drowned at this beach. We believed.

A scattering of other people were sunning on the rocks.

It is possible, according to park rules, to camp at Hanakapiai for one of the five nights a permit allows on the Na Pali Coast, but not for two consecutive nights.

For the serious hiker, the second "camp" on the trail is Hanakoa, four miles away, and then Kalalau, another five miles.

Day trippers have the option at Hanakapiai to hike a two-mile trail up to a spectacular waterfall. The first half is easy, the second half is rugged, the map advised. Also there is a danger of flash floods and falling rocks.

We headed back.

A return hike always seems easier than the outward bound trip for some reason. We were half way back when we stopped for a breather. I do not know why but, suddenly, I realized that something was wrong. Terribly wrong.

The weight of the keys in my swimming shorts pocket was gone. The pocket was a nylon sack sewn inside the shorts and the weight had torn the sack loose and it had vanished. Disappeared.

"I-have-lost-the-keys-to-the-car," I said. The key to the apartment didn't matter. Easily replaceable. The keys to the car at the end of the telephoneless Haena Road was another matter.

The Lady Navigator gave me that "I-Hope-They-Find-You-Frozen-In-An-Iceberg-Some-Day-But-Not-Soon" look.

It was a frantic moment. Had I dropped the sack and the keys on the trail? Would it do any good to go back searching the ground? Had I dropped them playing around the tidal pools? Would it do any good?—no, of course, not. There was no solution.

After a most depressing ten minutes we decided to push on and try to jump the ignition wires to start the rented car without the vaguest idea about how to do it.

Then I made a last search of my body. In the bottom of the liner of my swim trunks I found the frayed sack.

The look on the face of the Lady Navigator was one of incredulity.

"Didn't you *feel* anything?"

The remaining hellish mile hike to the parking area was punctuated with off-stage remarks to the clouds, the trees, the gods revolving around the phrase, "He must have felt *something*." It was the sound of smothered laughter that really hurt.

I knew the Kalalau Trail was dangerous.

6. The Lady Navigator's Shopping Secrets

Hawaii is a swinging door between East and West ... and South. Visitors from the East come here to buy wares from the West. Travelers from the West stop over en route back to their Oriental sanctuaries to buy stranger-than-logic items from the East. Kiawe charcoal. Packaged sauce mixes and spices. American-made bed and bath linens are just as popular with shoppers from the South Pacific as Oriental art objects are with our Mainland friends.

And nearly all visitors buy apparel, if only to wear while they are in Hawaii's warm and sometimes humid climate.

Then there's the matter of souvenirs—memory joggers for ourselves and gifts for folks at home. Our personal inclination when traveling is to seek the indigenous item: a work of art, an antique artifact, books about the area, handicrafts, clothing specialties—items to make recall stronger.

This roster has been compiled with the help of friends whose tastes and opinions we trust, and reflects those shops we patronize, and shops that have some special reason why you might like to make the effort to visit them.

But first, let's get a feel for the marketplaces available.

Every island offers interesting, sometimes different, often offbeat shopping experiences, but none can compare with Honolulu. It is, quite simply, the Mighty Mango.

Ala Moana Center installed the first hinge on Hawaii's swinging door as a shopping mecca just after statehood came to Hawaii.

We have friends who come to Honolulu not for the sun, sand, sea or surf of Waikiki, but for the 9AM to 9PM shopping action at this monument to merchandising. I chuckle a bit when I compare Reading, Pennsylvania and Orlando, Florida, against Ala Moana Center. Those East Coast cities created huge *discount* shopping centers with factory outlet stores to woo out-of-town visitors by the busloads, but Ala Moana Center—a *full retail* operation—attracts shoppers by the planeloads. The complex of 155 shops and restaurants has become, in travel industry jargon, "a destination unto itself."

I remember being impressed with it even as it was under construction in 1959. I had been in the islands about six months when Ed Sheehan, a Celtic bard who has a way with words, offered me the temporary assignment of helping to publicize the opening of the regional shopping center. Influenced by his melodious Irish voice, and, in truth, itching to get back into professional gear, I jumped at the opportunity.

In those pre-opening days, Sheehan and I billed Ala Moana as the world's largest open air shopping center. (It does look somewhat like an aircraft carrier.) Factually, it was in a class with three other shopping complexes in size, but it was—and still is—the world's largest "open air" shopping center having been expanded, renovated, enhanced and upgraded dozens of times.

It is a wonderful place to spend the day, as many people do.

Fountains and massive fanciful sculptures decorate the tree-lined mall. Tables with sun umbrellas are provided for people's people-watching pleasures. Center stage comes alive with entertainment every day at noon and three times daily during summers and on holidays. It may be the regular "keiki" (kids) hula show, a local celebrity in a benefit appearance, or an art or crafts demonstration.

Whatever the entertainment, it takes a backseat to the galaxy of retail stars.

As anchor stores, you'll find the well-known American shopping center regulars—Sears, J.C. Penney and Woolworth—alongside Shirokiya, Japan's first major retail entry in the islands and an original tenant, and the homegrown giants, Liberty House, McInerny, and Foodland.

In addition to these biggies, there are the fascinating little shops that specialize in imports from throughout the world: India Imports, Tahiti Imports, Oriental Imports, China Silk House, Prides of New Zealand, Iida's and Hotei-Ya. And the likes of Louis Vuitton, the world famous French luggage maker.

Several of our favorite shops are in the vicinity of the ground floor Center stage: Honolulu Bookshop, the dean of the book stores in Hawaii with more of every kind of book; Compleat Kitchen whose name tells it like it really is except they also have accessories for the dining room, Francis Camera Shop, our cameras' make-it-right nanny, and Mrs. Field's Chocolate Chippery whose macadamia nut chocolate chip cookies are to die over. Buy one (enough), eat it hot; somehow they don't taste the same cold.

Around the corner is a tiny blink-your-eyes-and-you'll-miss-it

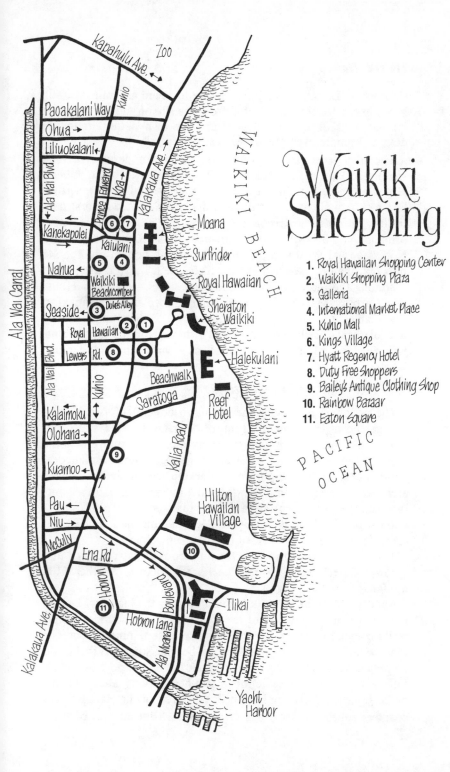

Waikiki Shopping

1. Royal Hawaiian Shopping Center
2. Waikiki Shopping Plaza
3. Galleria
4. International Market Place
5. Kuhio Mall
6. Kings Village
7. Hyatt Regency Hotel
8. Duty Free Shoppers
9. Bailey's Antique Clothing Shop
10. Rainbow Bazaar
11. Eaton Square

shop where Daughter Duffi and I love to spend an hour preening in the exotic leisurewear created from the silk of antique Japanese kimono and obi. Fumi also offers her own cottom muumuu designs—simple, well made and reasonably priced.

The mall level (second floor) is the fashion level. We send visitors seeking a wide selection of Polynesian attire to Liberty House and Sears at either end of the mall. Sears is less expensive. For men's quality, *conservative* aloha shirts (muted colors, controlled patterns), we recommend Reyn's. The Spooner reverse-print aloha shirt with button-down collar is Reyn's trademark. Not cheap. Al Wilson, a pal from Cape Cod, bought one for $48 plus tax, then refused to wear it ... because it was too nice!

Among the more fashionable fashion stores are Liberty House and Carol & Mary's (designer labels), Chocolates for Breakfast (delectables for dining/dancing evenings), Villa Roma (trendy and off-beat for the young), Ethel's (basics for the professional woman) and McInerny (Japanese new wave couture designer labels).

Waikiki: Big Action Contender

The action is no longer the exclusive domain of Ala Moana Center, however. Waikiki, font of tourism for the state, developed its own competitive shopping blend to capture a lion's share of the market. Off-street arcades, elegant hotel esplanades, multi-rise shopping emporiums, marketplaces designed around architectural themes, in addition to the independent stores fronting the main thoroughfare—at last count 1,082 operations—pushed Waikiki over the $600 million mark in 1984 to claim 15 percent of total retail business on Oahu.

That figure does not include the numerous illegal "clutter" and a few "gutter" vendors that, each year, rake in another $100 million.

Kalakaua Avenue, Waikiki's main drag, is the big roar. During retail store hours any day of the week, there will be more people walking, window shopping, watching free entertainment or buying than will be found on the famous beach. Some of them will complain about the curbside hawkers of exotic curios, the hand-billers who thrust freebie or discount coupons at them, the pedicab hustlers jangling their bells for fares, or the Hare Krishna chanters collecting donations to save souls. But enough of them

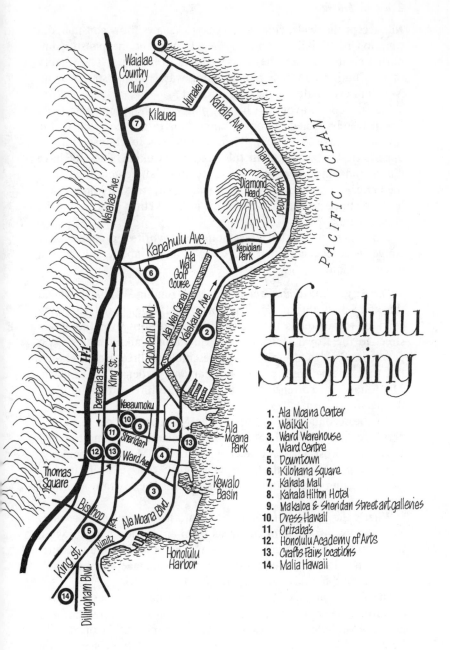

Honolulu Shopping

1. Ala Moana Center
2. Waikīkī
3. Ward Warehouse
4. Ward Centre
5. Downtown
6. Kilohana Square
7. Kahala Mall
8. Kahala Hilton Hotel
9. Makaloa & Sheridan Street art galleries
10. Dress Hawaii
11. Orizaba's
12. Honolulu Academy of Arts
13. Crafts Fairs locations
14. Malia Hawaii

PACIFIC OCEAN

Waialae Country Club
Kilauea
Diamond Head
Kapiolani Park
Kapahulu Ave.
Ala Wai Golf Course
Ala Wai Canal
Kalakaua Ave.
Kapiolani Blvd.
Waialae Ave.
Beretania St.
King St.
H-1
Keeaumoku
Sheridan
Ward Ave.
Thomas Square
Bishop
Ala Moana Blvd.
Nimitz
King St.
Dillingham Blvd.
Honolulu Harbor
Kewalo Basin
Ala Moana Park
Hunakai
Kahala Ave.
Diamond Head Road

will accept the deals, ride the bicycle-rickshaws (now considered a tradition in Waikiki!), and buy-haggle over the inexpensive, imported curios to keep the street vendors in business. The legality of distributing handbills and hawking wares on the streets as an issue will eventually be decided in court.

If you want to avoid the hassle, plot your shopping route from one privately-owned shopping emporium to the next where the curbsiders have no access. There are dozens to choose from, a baker's half dozen right in the heart of Waikiki. They all have dining and snacking spots. Several feature daily entertainment ... the better to woo a prospective crowd of buyers, you know. Each has a distinct personality based on its marketing plan, if not its architecture.

Some have shops that are among my favorites; a couple have convenience elements that are good to know about. All have a story to relate.

The Royal Hawaiian Center: "They're ruining Waikiki," wailed the kamaainas during construction of this four-tiered shopping corridor that extends three city blocks and hops over the access street to the Royal Hawaiian and Sheraton Waikiki hotels via a pedestrian bridge. Indeed, it did resemble a three-deck freeway. But that was before the trees and hanging gardens were in place. The foliage has softened the austere architecture and tranquilized the harsh criticism.

On the second level as part of the McInerny Store, there is a branch of the Friendship Store from Mainland China and the only convenient Post Office branch in Waikiki. More conveniently, there's a nearby specialty store called GBC that sells all kinds of gift packaging and mailing supplies, or will pack, wrap, and mail for you.

What's the personality of this behemoth? A tropical cakewalk. You win by just strolling along its open-air corridors or enjoying the daily entertainment hosted around the fountain courtyard—anything from hula and Hawaiian language lessons to all-out, big-time holiday extravaganzas.

The merchant mix, 120 operators, is from hot dogs to haute couture, Cartier, Chanel, and Louis Vuitton shops providing the latter. Alongside the all-too-frequent souvenir emblazoned with "HAWAII" but stamped "Made in Taiwan," there's a special little shop, the Little Hawaiian Craft Shop, on the third floor where authentic, affordable Hawaiian crafts are available. You'll not find anything made in Hong Kong or Taiwan in the place. Maybe some Tongan tapa and shells from throughout the Pacific, but most of their merchandise is strictly local.

Waikiki Shopping Plaza. In a street-oriented shopping society, this pioneer highrise mart fronting on Kalakaua knew it had to use imagination to lure customers to its five upper levels of shops. So the Plaza built escalators around a six-story water fountain then created a variety of sculptural effects by washing it with colored lights. The best sound-and-light show in Hawaii.

There are branch operations of Chocolates for Breakfast (but the focus is on daytime wear) and Villa Roma. Amid the gift, jewelry, sports clothes and equipment stores, there is also a good Waldenbooks store.

The Galleria: "Finesse" describes this newest member of Waikiki's shopping fraternity in the Waikiki Trade Center at the corner of Kuhio and Seaside. Small by comparison to its peers, it has the feel of casual elegance from the moment you set foot to its rich brown tile in spite of—or maybe because of—the sidewalk cafe smack dab in the middle of the only customer passage to the shops. Even its "career girl" apparel stores have a fashion flair, but at reasonable prices.

"Reasonable" the prices at abbraccio are not but—WOW—what a shopping experience. Classical music, rose petals in bone china saucers in pastel-toned dressing rooms that are lighted to flatter every woman, and a fuss-fuss, dress-the-fashion-model sales approach. This environment is backed with some of the most gorgeous well-bred mostly European clothes, you'll ever find. One woman's taste? Yes, but what good taste. Owner Arleen Stafford spends three months a year in Europe ferreting out fashion-wise, often yet-to-be-discovered designers who work in the natural fiber fabrics.

Yet another barometer of abbraccio's (small "a" please) class: it's once-a-year sale (in February) is "by invitation only" and patrons are given the opportunity to make appointments! There's a security guard at the door. If your name is not on his list, you don't get in. How's that for snob appeal?

Silks Honolulu, another very special shop at The Galleria, is the best upmarket cottage industry I have ever encountered. Every item of apparel, silk of course, is the handwork of a young local woman who once sold her designs at craft fairs. Gaye Pope's one-of-a-kind silks range from $35 to $400, and you will never find them anywhere else. She dyes her own fabrics with great imagination and custom tailors each and every garment personally.   The first exclusive shoe store in Waikiki—i.e., selling shoes exclusively and exclusive shoes to boot, if you can forgive the pun—is C. June Shoes. Expensive labels: Dior, Bally, Halston, Xavier Danaud and Charles Jourdan. June runs a discount store across the corridor, or will as long as the lobby space is available.

International Market Place is the granddaddy of Waikiki's off-street marketing combines. In a slower paced era, it was a gathering place for locals to share a cup of coffee, an Ed & Don's ice cream or lunch on the verandah of the colonial restaurant. I doubt that a resident sets foot on property without some commercial purpose today, not because it is less, but because it is too much. It still has a tropical feeling with its bazaars and open-front shops and its vintage banyan trees, but is now so cluttered it offends. Vendor carts consume those spaces too small to build upon ... and never in my life have I seen so many Buy-An-Oyster-To-String-A-Pearl-Necklace or Gold-Chains-By-The-Inch vendors operating so closely, and so prosperously.

It is still the most reliable place in town to get a distinctive Hawaiian T-shirt. There are dozens of vendors, including a factory-to-you manufacturer, Crazy Shirts, which has 10 other retail stores throughout the island and a factory outlet at 470 North Nimitz Highway. If they still have their "poi bag" bargain bins, take a chance. Buy, in a sealed bag marked for size only, three shirts for the price of one.

Somewhere in that maze there's a little shop where you can get a newspaper front page customized for a special friend or a special occasion. Inquire.

Kuhio Mall, directly behind International Market Place, borrows its character and merchandising concepts from its eminently successful neighbor. Nearly a hundred stores, vendor carts and restaurants operate in a three-story complex around a central courtyard which is decorated with a mixed cultural bag of Polynesian tikis, Oriental gates and Hawaiian thatched roofs, selling curios, souvenirs and handicrafts from Thailand, Indonesia, Burma and Laos. Here, you will encounter the deal maker! A free hula show is presented nightly on the second floor.

King's Village, a block east and behind the Hyatt Regency Hotel, depicts a fantasized Honolulu at the turn-of-the-century. A cobblestone street leads to 50 shops and restaurants on several levels, and walkways around turrets and Victorian balconies recall Hawaii's monarchical period.

The nightly "Changing of the Guard," a 20-minute precision rifle and marching drill won't replace Her Majesty's Coldstream Regiment but it is a festive performance and is followed by free entertainment.

An example that illustrates the importance of Waikiki in the overall retail picture is the number of Liberty House stores found on or along Kalakaua Avenue: 11 of its 19 Oahu stores! In addition to a major specialty store on Kalakaua Avenue, resort shops are found in King's Village, The Galleria (called Collections), the Hyatt Regency, Hilton Hawaiian Village, the Royal Hawaiian, the Surfrider, Sheraton-Waikiki, plus not one, but two stores in the Ilikai Hotel (one called Suits Me!).

But that doesn't compare with the ABC Discount Stores, a convenience store selling the basics for travelers—snacks, booze, film, drugs, cosmetics, etc—with 24 stores in the area!

Hyatt Regency Hotel. Before venturing to the west end of Waikiki, route yourself through another pleasure playpen.

Many of the Hyatt Regency shops encircle the hotel's tropical atrium and overlook a grand waterfall from their second floor perches. The merchandise runs the spectrum from Hawaiian gifts to imports such as Gucci.

The store we want you to visit, however, is Hyatt's Hawaii, where you will find "Aunty Malia," as she is known throughout Hawaii, or one of her daughters, Rosalind and Vivian. They mix a special blend of aloha with authentic specimens of Hawaiian crafts: weaving, shell and featherwork, Hawaiian quilting (called kapa) and its ancient predecessor, tapa. It's a place for sharing culture and warm aloha.

Aunty Malia is credited with rediscovering how and with what kinds of natural dyes the early Hawaiians made their tapa cloth. (You can see a collection of her work decorating the corridors at Mauna Kea Beach Hotel.) Because of her extensive research and efforts to bring Hawaiiana to our visitors, she is considered a

State Treasure. Her "Aloha Fridays" are festivals of Hawaiian arts, music, dance, food, and craft work. (From 10AM).

Duty Free Shop. If you hold a valid passport and an ongoing ticket to a foreign port, and if you care about making your duty free purchase selections before you get to the airport, Duty Free Shoppers maintains a showroom at 330 Royal Hawaiian Avenue, less than a block off Kalakaua.

The Hilton Hawaiian Village Rainbow Bazaar. On the westerly edge of Waikiki, three trading "villages" were created to represent the South Pacific, Imperial Japan and Hong Kong. Striving for authenticity, the builders brought many of the shops' building materials directly from their "mother" countries along with craftsmen to supervise construction. The theme is extended by the merchandise sold in each village and by the salespeople wearing, when possible, the native dress.

The Benihana of Tokyo Restaurant actually is a 400-year-old farmhouse built without nails or screws, dismantled and shipped to Hawaii for reassembly by Japanese craftsmen.

Despite this effort, the Bazaar has never done well. It is always a little distressing to encounter so little traffic.

Eaton Square. Just shy of Waikiki's western "border," Eaton Square is a combination convenience center for the residents of the luxury condominium lofting above it and an upmarket art and antique find.

Creativity figures into the name of one of the three antique shops here. Garakuta-do, in Japanese means "fine junque store." Class.

The most creative leis, along with the most imaginative presentation containers of green bamboo or fresh ti leaves, are made by Meheula Flowers. They are true works of art. I still have one which dried beautifully, a gift nearly six months ago! Not cheap nor predictably for sale to the drop-in trade since each is made to order. But worth a stop by to see any lei on hand or to order for a future occasion.

Adjacent to the Chez Michel French Restaurant, a treat of a place for lunch, is Galerie St. Martin with gifts and a gallery full of Guy Buffet paintings of Polynesia and France. They are delightful.

Built into a cul-de-sac near the Ala Wai Canal and behind Kalakaua, Eaton Square is not easy to find; go down Hobron Lane, directly in front of the traffic light at the Ilikai Hotel.

Farther Afield, But Worth It

You could spend your entire time shopping in Waikiki, so saturated it is with diverse and intriguing wares and opportunities. Don't.

You'll miss some of the best.

The Ward Two. In order of their juxtaposition to Waikiki, there is Ward Centre and its older sister, Ward Warehouse. Ward Centre is trendy, "with it." Ward Warehouse is a comfortable old shoe.

Ward Centre is new, flashing a bright new marketing concept; good California-based restaurants have been clustered on the second floor as magnets for a covey of small chic boutiques on the first floor. The formula was a success from the start.

Ward Centre contains another of my favorite apparel haunts, Susan Marie. The long-stemmed, black-eyed beauty who owns it is Marie Pagliuso. I find her merchandise choices exquisite, her prices fair. She stocks a superb collection of linens and other natural fabrics and exciting accessories.

The store itself is fabulous, reflecting the talents of Marie's architect husband, Tom, and her leanings toward the clean and understated. Get this: module clothes hangers spaced widely apart prevent any garment from getting crushed. Nice.

Trademarks of Susan Marie: a glass of wine while you browse; a red rose with every purchase. The soft keys of a piano in the background, sometimes ... predictably at holiday shopping time.

Ward Centre is where you'll find the Polo/Ralph Lauren shop, a partial collection of the Laura Ashley line at Lady Ashley's (a full-line store is going into Ala Moana), and shoes by Pappagallo.

For sweet goodness sakes, try a RoxSan savory or pastry at the Patisserie. (This mid-twenties dynamo, RoxSan, opened a cabaret at The Galleria in early 1985. It is a cafe-cum-jazz lounge that has the town a'buzzing.)

Ward Warehouse, although a comfy moccasin, has its share of

recommendables housed under its sturdily beamed five-story warehouse setting. There are bath and kitchen, art and gift and stitchery boutiques and, if you like frozen desserts, a couple of real finds: the Yami Soft Frozen Yogurt Shoppe, one of a pair in the city; and Dave's Ice Cream Parlor, featuring a 16 percent butterfat content concoction using exotic island ingredients. The ice cream has received raves from national publications. The poha (a tart berry at home in the Volcanoes National Park) was included in a book published in Boston, *The Very Best Ice Cream,* and People Magazine named Dave's coconut-macadamia nut one of the top five exotic ice creams in America. Not bad for a home-grown kid.

And speaking of books, Upstart Crow and Company is the epitome of the ole shoe philosophy, serving up books and periodicals along with a coffee/tea service in its on-premises salon. Comfortable for the browser.

Kahala Mall, a few blocks from the Kahala Hilton Hotel in the residential district of Waialae-Kahala, is our weekly provisioner. The pace is calmer. The people are local. The entire complex is under roof and air conditioned, a respite from unaccustomed humidity or an occasional shower.

Besides these attributes, Kahala Mall also has Star Market which gets most of our weekly allowance. You won't find Star Market in the tourist publications, but we have hooked several repeat visitors on it.

Our friends from Pacific nations find it fascinating. Even USA pals enjoy the comparison between Hawaiian supermarkets and their Mainland cousins. You won't find one like it in Des Moines or New York City. There are strange looking vegetables in the produce section (I promise you'll discover at least one new item!), packets and tins of exotic ingredients in the Oriental foods section, and even some unusual items in the housewares section.

Kahala Mall has many of the same stores found at Ala Moana—Liberty House, Andrade, Carol & Mary, Compleat Kitchen, India Imports, Long's Drugstore, McInerny, Reyn's, Woolworth's,—plus a bevy of individualistic apparel boutiques to cater to the taste and purse of the neighborhood. At the top of the scale, there is Alion, inside of which there is a Calvin Klein boutique; Fabrications, whose owners, Jan and Jeff Berman, are custom clothiers with a solid local following; Cotton Cargo, catering to the young with affordable around-the-clock clothes; and Wildflowers, for an even younger crowd.

Space occupied by J. C. Penney has been re-allocated to a small film theater and dining complex.

Kilohana Square. To call it a shopping center is not quite accurate. Kindred spirits and specialists have banned together in this tiny enclave behind the real world that exists on its feeder street, Kapahulu Avenue. You could pass by without knowing of Kilohana Square's existence. It would be your loss if things Oriental, Hawaiian patterns for needlepoint, European antiques, rare books and distinctive apparel appeal.

The Carriage House serves as a highbrow consignment center for local estate owners whose lifestyles have changed. Once annually, however, owner Connie Pickett heads abroad to replenish her stocks from all corners of the British Isles and France.

Antiques from France (The French Quarter), the Far East (Max Davis), and Japan (T. Fujii) might seem a bit pricey, but only if you are planning a trip to the source country to do on-site buying.

Pacific Book House also has antiques, but the specialty is out-of-print and rare books.

Needlepoint, Inc. which sells New England patchwork quilts and pillows in addition to needlepoint patterns with Hawaiian motifs, has an international clientele.

"It is not unusual," says Adelaide Kistner, "for a customer to call from the East Coast or Canada and order 'that kit with the Hawaiian flower on it on the top shelf in the back.' Mercy. Which Hawaiian flower?"

One of the assets of shopping Kilohana is its size. It is small. Intimate. Unhurried. The shops are distinctive; there is nothing modular or plastic to be seen.

When was the last time you wandered into a jewelry shop and actually met the lapidarist? You can at La Dame au Cheval. If I didn't have the best jeweler in Hawaii (no, I cannot reveal his name; he is far too busy!), I'd be tempted to give Martin Trent a commission to mount some of my rocks.

Kilohana's apparel boutiques know they have to be different to attract business to their out-of-the-way doors. They are. The Trunk specializes in clothes for the larger woman; Pomegranates in the Sun, a private co-op, features half a dozen local designers; Max Davis' backroom deals in silks from Hong Kong—both for men and women including Dynasty exotic evening attire, one-of-a-kind, one-size-fits-all silk dresses by Diane Fries, and men's silk shirts that remind you of the old Hawaiian "silkies."

(Things-I-Never-Knew-Department: the Fries collection is categorized into five levels of quality. Devotees of this ruffled and pattern-on-contrasting-pattern dress can tell, at a glance, which Fries "level" another woman is wearing. Starting price, level one, is $350. But, at least, that's the whole dress; Max's silk shirts for men are the same price—and that's the equivalent of only half a dress.)

Where Else For What?

The Catering Connection. "Shopping" on a vacation may not be limited to durable goods. Frequently, we shop for perishables ... food and beverage for a picnic, a cocktail party, maybe even a dinner party for local guests, or a simple romantic dinner for two. It's nice to have alternatives to restaurant entertaining. Box lunches from your hotel are an option. So is McDonald's or Colonel Sanders. RoxSan's Patisserie (526-9533) and JR's Upstairs at Kilohana Square (735-2204) will put something together, given a little lead time. Both have delectable pates, quiches, salads. The tourist publications can add other layers of options. But I have the definitive solution to any catering need you might have in Honolulu. Call Tad and Pat, 735-1747. Tell them what you want.

Want to have a broiled mixed grill for ten in the park? We did. A hearty menu was to reward our guests who had scaled the cliffs of Diamond Head just after dawn (easy!). I wanted palaka napkins and tablecloths to add a strictly Hawaiian touch. (Palaka is a sturdy, checkered cotton fabric akin to denim in durability that the plantation workers wore in the canefields.) Tad was up until midnight sewing my palaka, I learned later. She didn't have to; she could have said "We don't have palaka napkins." I could have been dissuaded. But I ordered palaka; I got palaka. That's typical.

They will find you the perfect location, deliver the menu, or stick around to serve and clean-up whether you order a box lunch or an all-out gala. And I promise: with my friend Conard in the kitchen working her magic, you'll never regret making that telephone call.

The Netsuke Connections. Honolulu has a reputation as a source of the netsuke, those miniature fobs made of Chinese ivory or native Japanese wood that decorated pouches and containers worn on the pocketless kimono until the mid-19th century. They hung from the obi, a utilitarian but ornamental accessory.

An antique netsuke predates 1868, when the Meiji Restoration accepted Western dress codes. After that, netsuke were carved as art objects instead of apparel accessories. In either case, they are small (an inch or less), intricately carved, and incredibly realistic. It is difficult to understand how the artist could work on such a minute surface. The subject might be an entire tableau or a single mythical, religious, or legendary object.

A major reason for Honolulu's netsuke reputation is Bernard Hurtig. His Orientwest collection at the Kahala Hilton Hotel is something special. Hurtig's encyclopedic knowledge of the art form is evident in his illustrated book, *Masterpieces in the Netsuke.* He is, additionally, the patron for a contemporary netsuke carver. His wife, Helen, has edited the *Journal of International Netsuke Collectors* for 12 years, and, together, they have a rare personal collection.

Orientwest also has a magnificent collection for sale, starting at $300 ... and many exceed six figures. (The four-color book of masterpieces is available for $125).

Other places to shop for netsuke on Oahu are Takenoya Arts at the Halekulani Hotel, Antiques Pacifica in the Royal Hawaiian Hotel where vintage pieces are sometimes available, and T. Fujii's Japanese Antiques in Kilohana Square. Or call the Hawaii Antique Dealers Association for additional sources.

Contemporary netsuke are the specialty of Takenoya, whose parent company is the oldest netsuke manufacturing company in Japan. A third-generation family member, Taiji Takenoya, and his wife, Mieko, operate the shop.

Other Asian Art. In addition to those discussed at the established shopping centers, I have my personal favorite—"favorites" being born because we find things we really like at prices we can afford to pay. It is Treasures Of The East, at 1320 Makaloa Street, parallel to Kapiolani Boulevard and mauka of Ala Moana Shopping Center, in an indoor/outdoor setting that is nearly always packed to the rafters. Dorothea Ogdemli and Kaya, her ex-Pan Am pilot husband, accumulated so many "treasures" on their travels they decided to sell some. The reception among their friends was so upbeat, they entered the trade. That was in the 1970's, and four locations ago. Their prices have kept abreast of inflation with each move, but there are good buys to be found.

How about Asian art to wear? Like antique kimonos and obis. Orizaba's, at 1149 Beretania Street near Safeway supermarket, has hundreds of them in stock. Ruby Uehara imports them by the container load in all sizes, all prices, assuring a full inventory of 400 at all times. The obi sell from $5 to $40, not bad for a 12-foot doubled length of silk that you can use as a table runner, fashion into cushions or vests or jackets or whatever. Kimonos range from $5 to $150.

Local Art. Art being a matter of personal taste, who's to say what is good or bad, which artists are the "best." I can tell you which local artists sell for the most money. Madge Tennent, once criticized for her rendering of Hawaiian women with near Negroid qualities, and muralist Jean Charlot, both now dead, are big-ticket artists, but you won't find their works just floating around. Tennent's works can be viewed at the little known Tennent Art Foundation Gallery at 203 Prospect Street. Call 531-1987 first. Open hours at the gallery are limited. Charlot's murals of Hawaiians at work decorate banks and other public places.

Prolific John Young and Peggy Hopper, who picked up the Tennant tenet of bigger-than-lifesized Hawaiian women, sell their canvases in the five-digit figures.

Names like Lloyd Sexton, Yvonne Cheng, Peter Hayward, Joe Feher, David Lee, Susan Hansen, John Wisnosky, William Stamper, Mamoru Sato, Barbara Britts, John Whyland, Marcia Morse all stand for quality.

Gallery friends tell me that "up and coming along very nicely, thank you," are ceramicists Suzanne Wolfe and Robert Young.

There are art galleries in many of the hotels and all of the shopping centers, some of which show local works. In the same vicinity with Treasures of the East are a couple of recommend-ables dealing in local artists: the Art Loft, at 637 Sheridan, and Gallery EAS, Ltd. at 1426 Makaloa. The Ward Centre Gallery also has a strong following among local art buyers.

If you visit Hawaii during November or December, and art is important to you, do not miss the annual "Artists of Hawaii" juried show at the Honolulu Academy of Art. It is considered THE most prestigious show in the islands among the artists themselves. (Incidentally, stop by the Academy gift shop to peruse folk art from around the world as well as Hawaiian crafts.

An Art Appreciation Field Trip. Visiting an artist's studio, unless you are a personal friend, is not always easy. But there are exceptions.

A visit to the Hart & Tagami Studio across the Pali in Kaneohe is possible on weekends and Mondays "before 11AM and after 1:30PM" as potter Richard Hart informs you on the telephone. It is wise to call before you make the trip out for two reasons: to get directions for getting there, and to avoid a crush of people. It is a popular field trip.

In a rural setting, Hart and Hiroshi Tagami, a pallet knife painter, have developed what one fan calls a "Country Oriental" home/garden compound complete with a rare bird walk-in aviary, a cage for the Gibbon apes they raise, a Japanese Tea House (no, they don't serve lunch; they don't even want you there between noon and 1:30), an impressive galley surrounded by gracious Oriental gardens, and separate studios for each artist. The harmony of man with his environment you sense in the setting is reflected in the art shown in the gallery. It's a dimension of art in Hawaii you don't get in the urban galleries. (For appointment, call 239-8146).

Authentic Hawaiian Crafts. In our polyglot Polynesian com-munity it is easy to understand how crafts from all other Poly-nesian societies can, mistakenly, be considered "Hawaiian." Su-perimpose over that the copious pretenders that are made in Fiji (woodenware), shell leis (the Philippines or Taiwan), the perfectly awful lava tikis, etc. Is it a wonder I get excited about sharing sources for the real McCoy?

Of course Bishop Museum has the genuine thing! So does the

Mission House and the Academy of Arts. To a lesser extent, the Polynesian Cultural Center qualifies.

You can find bona fide Hawaiian crafts at many of the art galleries and at some of the department stores (do check the bottom of the object for its country of origin, however, if authenticity is important).

The best source for originals are at the Craft Fairs that are spaced throughout the year. My vote for the best of the lot goes to the Pacific Handcrafters Guild's Christmas Fair, held at Thomas Square, across from the Academy of Arts. I can virtually do my Christmas shopping right there, have an ono (good) lunch of teriyaki meat-on-a-stick or stew 'n rice, wander among the wandering minstrels and mimes and musicians, and meet the artisans, some of whom are professionals, others hobbyists moonlighting to put a kid through college or earn a down payment on a house.

The craftspeople are highly screened by the Guild, establishing a standard of quality and excellence. Some of them take orders and will mail.

At other times during the year, the Guild holds its fairs at Ala Moana or Kapiolani Park. Four in all.

There are also annual craft fairs staged at the Mission House and at Bishop Museum.

So how does one find out when a crafts fair is scheduled? Buy a current copy of HONOLULU Magazine which publishes a calendar of cultural and special events. Most reliable.

Muumuu Mania. The muumuu will always be a staple of islander women's wardrobes. "Where is the best place to buy?" has to be answered with "How much do you want to pay?" If you want to spend little, we recommend Dress Hawaii, although there are literally hundreds of places you can shop throughout the islands.

Dress Hawaii is a factory-to-you operation with a wide selection of muumuus priced from $19, and the quality is good. Styles are produced in the hundreds but that won't matter to you back home. The showroom is located at 818 Keeaumoku, but be forewarned: there is a *singular* fitting room, in the usual discount store tradition. If stripping in front of a dozen women disturbs you, go to Sears or Watumull's or Shaheen's where there are private dressing rooms.

The pacemakers today are a couple of new-to-the-business entrepreneurs who also have eliminated the traditional middlemen, but that doesn't mean their clothes are cheap.

Mamo Howell, fashion model and premier hula dancer, turned her talents to the needle because "I got tired of seeing the same thing all over town." She protests the definition of her styles as "muumuus," suggesting instead they just happen to be made of cloth imprinted with Hawaiian patterns. The patterns, in fact, are family quilt designs that she had silk-screened. "You remember, my grandmother was a quilter when patterns were the exclusive property of the designer."

Mamo's high styled non-muumuus are available exclusively at her boutique at the Willows Restaurant, priced from $75 to $200.

Nake'u Awai was a professional dancer in New York until, as he says "I realized I wasn't that terrific." After several false starts at designing through the normal industry channels, he concluded that, to be distinctive, he also had to design his own fabric and sell his line of aloha wear direct. His workshop show and sales room is near the Bishop Museum in Kalihi at 1613 Houghtailing Street.

Nake'u also custom designs, creates a line of aloha shirts, T-shirts and sun dresses, and sells accessories and some extraordinary gift items made by friends.

The Aloha Shirt. It started back in the 1930's when a Chinese tailor made the first "silkie." A couple of pioneering garment manufacturers took the loose fitted shirt, substituted cotton and splashy floral prints to give birth to the now "indigenous" aloha shirt. A few of the early manufacturers also cranked out a limited number of the silkies.

I doubt that any of the Chinese custom tailored shirts are still around, but Bailey's Antique Clothing Shop, at 2051 Kalakaua Avenue, deals in recycled pre- and post-war manufactured silk aloha shirts.

For our 12th wedding anniversary (silk), I searched among the racks full of pass-alongs and found a big loose flowing shirt in subtle colors with an oriental design that bore the label "Liberty House." It is one of my star's favorite shirts.

A lot of other stars go to Bailey's to buy the hard to find

"silkies." Rock star Cyndi Lauper and her manager left $1,000 behind for the oldies-but-goodies. Gene Siskel, the TV movie critic and aloha shirt collector, says they cannot be too old.

But we are sidetracked ...

If the oldies are not what you're after, the stores are filled with shirts in myriad styles and patterns, even—God forbid—those that match the lady's muumuu. In addition to Reyn's that has shops at Kahala Mall and the Kahala Hilton Hotel as well as at Ala Moana Center, we like Liberty House's selections.

Other Alohaland Affectations? If it's high fashion you're interested in, and you're here on the last Wednesday of the month, go to Designer Wednesday at the Ilikai Hotel. (Lunch is $20, served at 11:45; the show starts at 12:30. Call the Ilikai, 949-3811. Extremely popular with the locals who have made it a dressy, social event.)

An inspired young woman, Mari Frey, did for some of the genteel fashion stores that which they obviously couldn't do for themselves; she put them together on the fashion runway, giving customers an overview of what's available in town. Smart.

Among the participating stores (with their top ranked or exclusive designer labels in parentheses) are Alion (Escada and Calvin Klein), Carol & Mary (Bill Blass and Geoffrey Bean), Ethel's (Joanie Char and Flora Kung), Chocolates for Breakfast (Laise Adzer and Diane Fries), McInerny (Issey Miyaki and Takezo), Gucci (Gucci!), and Chanel (who else?). Of course, the store lineup changes periodically.

You'll want to explore also: Collections, at Kahala Hilton Hotel, for resort clothes. Mandalay Import Specialty at the Halekulani for silks from Thailand. The Crest Room at Liberty House, Ala Moana. (Ask for Emily Bolton, a friend and most unusual sales lady. She tells you what not to buy as much as what to buy. I like that.)

Collections, incidentally, is a stunning boutique and carries a stunning line of hand-knit sweaters by a local lass under the label Klee Original Art. They are. Art, that is.

Malia Hawaii, a contemporary sportswear fashion label known on three continents, opened a factory outlet in 1985. Not to be confused with the factory-to-you operations that are geared to the tourist trade, Malia's retail outlet sells off overages from production for overseas stores—designs not commonly sold in Hawaii—at discounts up to 60 percent. This includes sweaters they manufacture in Hong Kong, the handmade clothes they import from Japan, and sportswear from their Los Angeles operation ... along with the occasional overruns from Mainland manufacturers. Additionally, a separate boutique carries items from the current seasonal collection. Malia does five collections each year.

It's a big break for residents, and for you too, if you are a "Malia Woman." The retail outlet is located at the factory at 2200 Kamehameha Highway.

Three Honolulu hot hautes, having tried manufacturing without satisfaction, have focused exclusively on custom designed Important-Evening-Looks only, and are reachable by appointment only. They are: Amos Kotomori, talented as a ceramicist, now designs his own fabrics in brilliant colors or uses silks from antique obi and kimono; Zsalei, self appointed arbitrator of the "Ten Best Dressed Women in Hawaii"; and Allen Akina, from whom I bought two of my favorite muumuus ten years ago. Allen took the "Big Hawaiian lady" set in tropical scenes as a trademark for his fabrics, then designed a muumuu around the art. It was a first ... and dynamite styling. He moved his operation "uptown" to the Royal Hawaiian briefly, and now, I understand Allen is sending high fashion sky high in aisle shows aboard Continental Airlines, to Pacific destinations. The kid is an innovator.

Each of these Hawaiian designers' creations have been sold in the likes of Bloomingdale's, Neiman Marcus, Marshall Field's or boutiques on Rodeo Drive.

Go on, commission a fantasy.

Hawaiian Jewelry. The "local" jewelry, referred to as "heirloom jewelry" is gold with your Hawaiian name enameled in black and encased with fancy Victorian engraved curlicues. Today, it could be a bracelet or a ring or a pendant. Its origin was as a bracelet.

Queen Victoria presented Queen Kapiolani and the then Princess Liliuokalani with such bracelets when they represented King Kalakaua at the British Queen's 50th Jubilee in London. They, in turn, had bracelets made for their ladies in waiting. Thus was born an instant tradition.

Tips from my jeweler: buy the heaviest gold you can afford because the lighter the gold, or the narrower the bracelet, the greater the risk that the bracelet will flex, breaking the enamel, a black glass fused onto the gold.

Another popular piece of Hawaiian heritage jewelry stems from Merrie Olde England as well. A design for a royal coat of arms was drawn up by the College of Arms in 1840—and every king changed it to his own whim. Sometimes the warriors face outward, sometimes inward; Kalakaua dressed them in ermine capes.

Hilgund at Dawkins Benny owns 6,000 dies for molding various versions of the Hawaiian coat of arms and turn-of-the-century company insignia. Her work is splendid, worthy of an official royal coat of arms, putting to shame the painted on enamel pendants you find all too often in gift and curio shops. Go. Look at the collection of dies, if nothing else. Downtown, at 119 Merchant Street.

Hawaiian Books. Hundreds have been written. Since our particular interest here is shopping, I'll review three. *The Bests of Honolulu,* the best of the three, is literate, well researched and a good read. Written by a fine native-born journalist, Jocelyn Fujii, the idea for the book grew out of articles she first wrote for the *Honolulu Star Bulletin.*

The other two are straightforward rosters directed to residents, *The Shopping Bag* for newcomers, and *Hawaii's Super Shopper* for bargains seekers. Check the publication date for currency before buying. As with all guide books, they tend to get outdated very quickly.

There are two more books I'll recommend, *Oahu Market Island Recipes & Shopper's Guide* is a delightful guide, history, recipe, glossary & pictorial roster of the exotic vegetables, fruit & fish sold at the 80-year-plus open market in downtown Honolulu. On sale at the Oahu Market. The other, a non-fiction, non-shopping book, *Days of '41: Pearl Harbor Remembered*, for a glimpse of life as it was by a very sensitive writer, Ed Sheehan. (Yes, that melodious voice, my first employer in Hawaii.)

Hawaiian Novelties. Scratch 'n' Sniff postcards, at various boutiques about town, feature lil' brown girls in scenes that make sense to add scents to, like banana, plumeria, coconut, ginger, pineapple. Got it?

Aloha Shirt Ties are bright floral substitutes for the shirt they are named for. At Liberty House. ($12.50)

Videotaped How-to-Hula lessons in 30 minutes. (Beta or VHS). Video House on Keeaumoku Street. ($39.95.)

Hard to find Hawaiian-inspired clothes for little boys. Giggles at Ward Warehouse.

Hawaiian hula ti or grass skirts, gourds, drums, nose flute, feather and plastic leis, hats with haku leis, and the ornamentations for those sexy Tahitian dances. Hula Supply Center, 2346 South King Street.

A genuine Hawaiian ukelele, by the Stradivari of ukeleles. In beautiful wood—koa, rosewood, spruce. One could cost more than the outfits for the entire hula troupe, or you might find a genuine bargain in factory seconds. Kamaka Hawaii, Inc., 550 South Street.

Fruits & Flowers To Go. You cannot purchase these items at any grocer or fruit stand and expect to take them out of state. The quarantine laws are rigid, for the protection of other agricultural communities. Such items will be confiscated at the airport.

Kamaainas turn to St. Louis Florist (732-1454) to pack and ship pre-inspected edible or floral gifts abroad. Select from several standard gift packs, or specify whatever fruit, leis, flowers or other Hawaiian product you want included.

There are any number of companies who pack pre-inspected papaya or pineapple and deliver it to the airport check-in counters for pickup at flight time. They will bill you by mail. Two choices: Tropical Fruits Distributors, 847-3234, or Puna Producers Enterprises, 836-2792, whom I favor because the farmers own the firm.

Should you drive around Oahu, however, pre-order/pre-pay at the Dole Pineapple Pavilion near Wahiawa for a carton of those golden nuggets. Somehow, they seem so much tastier coming from the source, and they are slightly cheaper.

Bargain priced macadamia nuts by the carton can often be found at Long's Drug Store for a smidgen over $2.00 per 5-ounce tin.

And now, for the Neighbor Islands.

The "Goodie/Damn" Syndrome

Check-in time at interisland airline counters once was a colorful parade of neat little boxes tied together for ease of carrying.

My Favorite Friend once wrote an article called "Hey, Lady, What's in the Little White Box?" ... having asked the question dozens of times, on dozens of planes, to dozens of women.

What *was* in the little white boxes were specialties of the island that friends and relatives took to friends or relatives on another island, goodies they could not buy where they were going.

These little gifts, called *omiyagi* by the Japanese, are less the interisland tradition these days because a lot of them can now be purchased in supermarkets on all the islands.

That's what our family calls a goodie/damn. "*Goodie*, I can get it whenever I want it; *damn*, it has taken an edge off the thrill of travel."

Yet, thank goodness, you still see vestiges of the tradition. A Honolulu De Lite Bakery box, hand carried on board an outbound plane, will have—you can bet your last dollar—a lighter-than-a-feather lilikoi or haupia cake inside.

Our friends in Kamuela, Bob and Charlot Butterfield, adore Chinese food which is scarce in their part of the world. When I traveled to the Big Island frequently on business, I pre-ordered and picked up Chinese take-aways for their dining pleasure, but, Bob, then general manager of Mauna Kea Beach Hotel, never let me leave without a box laden with Heaven-Can-Be-No-Sweeter white and pastel chocolate covered macadamias as my reward. I won. Now the chocolates go home by the dozens with many departing guests.

Each of the islands has its specialties. Who hasn't heard of the incredible Maui potato chip—just to hear the crunch makes you hungry. Or sweet Maui onions—so good people eat them like apples. We like them on crisp saltines slathered with mayonnaise, layered with salmon, and accompanied by a chilled bottle of champagne.

Kauai Kookies or Popo's cookies or Lappert's ice cream are incomparable edibles from the Garden Island, and the Big Island's cornucopia of take-home munchies (or to devour there, for that matter) is chock-a-block: buttery macadamia nuts, Puna papaya, Kona coffee, Hilo Cream Crackers and Hilo Saloon

Crackers, steaks from the Parker Ranch, fishcake from Sumida or Amano, and Mountain View Bakery stone cookies (now on sale at the Hilo airport).

Just as popular are the Big Island's orchids, anthuriums, and the most gorgeous and unusual flower leis you can imagine. Or the Up Country Maui leather crafts in Makawao and the strange but beautiful protea in Kula.

Kauai's premier contribution to the shopping basket comes from the sea, is perhaps the most expensive endemic and traditional souvenir you can buy in Hawaii, is called "momi o kai" (pearl of the ocean) ... but is not a pearl. It is the Niihau shell lei.

These rare garlands of the sea are made of the tiniest of shells, some as small as an eighth of an inch long, with the luster and translucence of pearls. A single strand, perfectly matched for size and color, can cost more than Elizabeth Sinclair paid King Kamehameha V for the island of their origin—$10,000, in 1864.

Niihau is still a privately owned island, is forbidden to visitors.

I'm relatively certain that the privacy policy, imposed to help retain the island's Hawaiian culture and rural lifestyle, is also responsible for Niihau's most revered cottage industry.

Can you imagine any community with radios, telephones, televisions, automobile/bus/train transportation, or any of the other luxuries we call necessities where the women and children gather sea shells by hand, often by kerosene lantern to avoid the sun bleaching or dulling the sheen of the shells? Especially, if a day's yield was likely to be limited to five or six shells and it took 250 shells to make a single 40-inch strand, and several strands are required to make a lei?

I would doubt that the women of Niihau would undertake such a lifestyle, given the option.

Can you imagine the patience required in sorting, sizing, grading for color, cleaning and hole drilling in shells that small? (The mortality at every stage is alarming. We are told it can take 10 years to complete one perfect lei.)

Can you paint yourself into a community picture like that? Hard. I spent a nervous week in a similar environment on an island in the South Pacific, fearing I would be trapped there throughout the winter hurricane months, and I assure you, it etches a new perspective, indelibly, on your conscious mind, and a new appreciation for 20th century technology.

How Much Do You Have To Pay For a Niihau Lei?

I formulated this theory: the price increases $3 per mile for every mile from the source of supply. Silly? Maybe, but it held up under intense research. The cheapest prices were in Kekaha, Kauai, the closest village to Niihau. The most expensive—in the tonier resort shops of Maui and the Big Island.

Kauai's Hidden Treasures, in Kekaha en route to Waimea Canyon, looks a disaster, outside and in. The signage assaults the senses. Garish hand painted lures such as "Stop and Save" "Free Leis" "Lowest Prices Here" clutter up the warehousey exterior. Tour buses dominate the entrance. Insipid juice in specimen-sized paper cups is dispensed by a shuffley, dispirited soul at the door from a cardboard box top serving tray, as a tacky lei is strung around your neck. The first items you see are awful shell-covered animals and boxes, some dusty with age or neglect.

Don't be put off.

As we were about to pack it in as just too insensitive, I spotted the "hidden treasure"—two counters lined with every type of Niihau lei, strung in every style, in every color, in every length. Some may not have been strung by Niihauans. A few were better than most. (Show real interest and they bring out the *hidden*, hidden treasure from locked cabinets.)

For comparative pricing, I asked for an appraisal of my lustrous 10-strand 54-inch pupu-Niihau lei. My Favorite Friend bought the gorgeous lei in the early 1970's, before the puka-shell craze (when people were paying $100 for a choker of fragmented seashells!) rocketed the price of Niihau leis to unbelievable heights.

She quoted $1,000, thinking I was a seller, but the gleam in her eye clearly revealed they would bring more.

I repeated price and appraisal comparing around the island. A couple of miles down the road in Waimea, the appraisal of $1,500 brought an unsolicited testimonial: "On the other side of the island, they'd sell it for $3,000."

My barometer was established.

She was correct. Again and again, in Poipu and on the North Shore of Kauai, in Honolulu, at Kaanapali and Wailea and Kapalua on Maui, and in Kona and the resorts along the Kohala Coast of the Big Island, prices increased, although not as dramatically as from the southwest side of Kauai to its northeast side.

You don't have to pay that much. You can buy a choker for $35 to $50, unless you seek "investment" quality, in which case you need the help of an *impartial* authority who you might locate through the Kauai Museum or Bishop Museum in Honolulu. Most probably, they will tell you to search for a Kuuleialoha Keamoai "Grandma" Kelley creation. "Tutu" Kelley, now in her eighties, is the undisputed master lei-maker of Niihau.

One of her 35-inch five-strand kahelelani leis was priced at $3,900 in The Gallery at the Waiohai Hotel on Poipu Beach. Five strands, five different colors, each a subtle hue of pink to golden maize, each shell perfectly matched in size. A treasure. And a bargain.

There are half a dozen different stringing styles, the ancient techniques among them. The "new" style, introduced at the turn-of-the-century, is called pikake,and is a way of knotting three shells in a cluster to resemble the small blossom. Designs are a family heritage, passed along to the younger lei-makers.

The Niihau trademark is a clasp fashioned from a white cowrie. Avoid leis with the hook'n'eye clasp or the more modern screw-together metal clasps. They are impostors. No self respecting Niihauan would defy the noble momi or kahelelani shell with such trash!

One consideration to temper your on-the-spot enthusiasm: how often will you wear a Niihau lei back home?

You'll get good value at the Kauai Museum whose lei-maker's mother strung leis for Queen Emma. The Gallery at Waiohai, and its related store, Makai Art Village, at the Kauai Surf also have beautiful selections, ranging from modestly priced chokers at $50 to the $3,900 Grandma Kelley beauty. All three stores feature the best of local artisans' works as well.

Did we return to Kekaha to buy the kahelelani five-strand necklace that I fell in love with? No, but Favorite Friend placed it in my Christmas stocking!

The Poke and Prowl Shops of Kauai

Hanapepe has three very special shop stops: the Kauai Kookie bakery and Lappert's Aloha Ice Cream, cheek by jowl on the main highway. Makes for a great rest stop, even if you're not tired. Kauai Kookie (sic) makes a most delectable assortment of buttery, crispy, crunchy cookies, the macadamia nut being our nominee as tops.

Lappert's requires more research before nominating the favorite flavor. But, the ice cream—any flavor—is one of our all-time favorites on four continents. If you don't get to the factory at Hanapepe, you can still experience this add-a-pound-of-fat-for-every-bite-you-eat concoction at the Coco Palms Hotel or the Koloa Ice House ice cream parlor on Kauai, and at Ed & Don's in Honolulu. (Mrs. Lappert's macadamia nut cookies are not as good as Mr. Lappert's ice cream.)

The Station at Hanapepe, named for the converted gasoline service station it occupies, is easily missed, but thousands of overseas visitors have found it nonetheless. Its specialty is original Hawaiian needlepoint design kits, from $5 to $85. Over 100 patterns have been developed over 10 years, and custom designs are made to specification. Catalogs with all Hawaiian designs are available for $3, (refundable if you purchase).

Old Koloa Town at the intersection of Poipu and Koloa Roads is more the place to amble than to do serious shopping, but you have to applaud the preservation efforts of the new owner who practically rebuilt every floor, wall and roof of this old sugar plantation town, the first in Hawaii, retaining its historic flavor.

A meander through the cobblestone courtyard brings you to the old hotel (now a series of small boutiques, some of which got their start as Spouting Horn curio tables), and the old "out house" out back. It was undergoing "refinement" as an open air museum.

If you missed the Hanapepe original, Station Too is on the road to Poipu just past Old Koloa Town. Because needlepoint is usually sold to mothers and grandmothers, you'll find a small collection of little girl things, including locally made plantation palaka pinafores. Cute.

Carla Robinson volunteered that The Stitchery in Kapaa also stocks Hawaiian motif needlepoint. Cheered by this gesture of kindness towards a rival, I inquired "Are you friendly competitors?" "Oh, yes, we go to Weight Watchers together."

Kukui Grove Shopping Center, just outside Lihue, its 55 stores sprawled over 35 acres, is where the locals shop. It claims the best known stores in the state: Liberty House, Sears, J.C. Penney, Woolworth's, Long's. You'll find many of the same souvenirs at Long's that are sold in boutiques around the island, but at better prices.

The Market Place at Coconut Plantation is open seven days a week, offering the only Sunday shopping on Kauai at its 70 stores. It also has a couple of flicks and a Polynesian show Thursday through Saturday at 4PM. The Kahn Gallery is an upscale jewelry and local artist outlet with a perfectly beautiful decor in koa wood, all beautifully lighted.

Princeville. Not to be outclassed by terminals substantially larger, Princeville Airport has its own retail operation. More precisely, Papillon Helicopter has the shop, basically a quality logo shop. They sell just as many T-shirts as they do helicopter rides, and a lot of the more expensive Izod and Haines sportswear aflutter with the butterfly logo. Books, too, are popular, especially after the thrilling sky high ride.

Princeville Center offers limited visitor shopping novelty, but look at your gas tank, especially if it's late in the day. Stations close early around here, and are scarce.

Hanalei. Over the crest and down into the valley of Hanalei, we found a new and delightful shop at Ching Young Village, Pua & Kawika's Place, subtitled on their business card as the "Native Hawaiian Trading & Cultural Center." We were Diana Spencer's first customer in a new location. Not *everything* in the store is strictly Hawaiian, but the majority is.

The unique sales proposition of Pua & Kawika's Place is Pua Kaone, Diana's mother, who conducts Hawaiian quilting classes at the tiny store five days a week for two to three hours, and you are invited to stop by and watch, or sign up for a course.

Conceivably, this sewing circle, in time, could become a cottage industry for Hanalei's quilting ladies. Their tutor's quilts and Hawaiian designed pillows were on display and for sale. A magnificent king sized quilt was priced $3,500; pillows at $75.

Among the dozen stores at Ching Young Village are a backpacking/camping rental shop which dispenses current trail and weather information about the Na Pali Coast.

Maui: Lil' Brown Gal In High Heels

Maui, the "Barefoot Contessa" of Hawaii, is a bit schizophrenic. As a shopping venue, she doesn't know whether to go upmarket or funky or straight. She's done all, seemingly enjoying her split personalities.

And so do her visitors, second in volume only to Waikiki.

Their numbers, ever increasing, create body heat that creates retail competition. Islandwide, except maybe in Hana. Shopping centers, separated only by the width of a sales tag, dot the main drag linking Kahului with Wailuku, the traditional urban centers of the island. Front Street in Lahaina has spilled over to Luakini, one street mauka, and is bulging with multi-story shopping plazas and arcades that keep cropping up like fertilized weeds.

Kaanapali's Whaler's Village has expanded to accommodate more sophisticated boutiques (now over 30), and enlarge its museum space as well. Even Up Country Makawao, having been discovered by us visitors, has a sizable number of strictly-for-the-tourist-dollar stores in addition to the Down Home stores that have always served the community.

The shops at Hyatt Regency Maui (Kaanapali) and Kapalua Bay Hotel have introduced elegance that the Lil' Brown Gal has responded to like any female enjoying being a girl. Collections at the Hyatt Regency Maui (and the wearable art boutique too), and Mandalay Imports at Kapalua Bay Hotel are spoilers, not to mention Bri'oni with its cappucino bar and baby grand piano! That's class. (There's a deli/gourmet food shop at Kapalua that makes dining in very tempting ... dining in on your terrace, that is.)

Over on East Maui, Kihei brings the Brown Gal back into the real world where ten miles of condominiums are punctuated occasionally by shopping centers: Azeka Place (40 shops), Kihei Town Center (it used to be the only game in town), and Rainbow Mall with a baker's dozen shops and restaurants.

However, it's an easy step back into the world of the gracious, onto the sunken grassy village square at Wailea Shopping Village that serves as a stage for periodic performances. Twenty or so shops, including a branch of Carol & Mary's and a very good man's store, Chapman's, which has shops in most of the luxury resort areas around the islands.

The newest shopping experience on Maui attempts, it would seem, to return the Lil' Brown Gal to her agricultural roots. The Hawaii Tropical Plantation is an asset to the state and a joy for the visitor. It's 60-acre plantation, a microcosm of Hawaii's agriculture and aquaculture, is put into even better perspective by the Tropical Market where virtually every product or type of produce made or grown or processed in Hawaii is on sale. There were even a few items we had never encountered.

There were Maui herb teas and Kona coffees, salad dressing and sauce mixes, chutneys, jams and jellies, the gamut of spirits—rums, champagne, wine, liqueurs—all the various chips—potato, taro, banana, coconut—and, of course, the candies and nuts.

There were agriculturally inspected plants and seeds for the farmer in all of us to take and grow at home: orchids, papaya, bamboo, coffee, guava, macadamia nut ... even the sweet Maui onion and woodrose.

There were crafts and handmade replicas of ancient artifacts, expensive quality items and cheap souvenirs. There were the inevitable slogan T-shirts and some apparel.

It added up to a rather extensive, if not complete, showcase of the state's products—the good and the bad. And that's a standard few other operations attempt.

The fruit and vegetable display at the entrance is from the backyard farms of the Waikapu neighbors, and "aunty" at the door is there to explain it to you, if you have a question.

Perhaps the best merchandising gimmick Plantation Market has evolved is a pick-and-pack concept. You get to decide what you want in your box or basket—and how much of each item. That's smart.

Of course they mail.

There should be a Plantation Market on every island for both the enlightenment and convenience of visiting shoppers.

That the growth in tourism is responsible for a greater selection and more interesting merchandise, even in the backwater villages, is a fact that most merchants acknowledge. For competitive reasons, even the smallest boutique, in an unlikely location, will seek exclusive suppliers in the countries on the far west side of the Pacific—Taiwan, Korea, Thailand, India, even China—to woo buyers, residents and visitors alike.

An example. On a recent *SS Constitution* cruise, we hired a car in Kahului to drive to Hookipa, the windsurfing capital of the world. En route, we shopped the tarted-up plantation town of Paia, Maui's newest contender for the exotic merchandise dollar.

I found exquisite beaded dresses from India, and some of the most interesting batik fashions from Indonesia by way of Singapore and California. Really astounding clothes, out of context for the setting.

"I opened Rona Gale two years ago ... barely made enough to keep the doors open. Then, a national TV network crew moved in to film a piece on Hookipa as the 'windsurfing capital of the world,' " Beryl Rothaus confessed.

"That brought the heavier traffic on the highway. I've expanded, and plan to take over space in the back soon.

"The irony is, I have customers from California who come here to buy merchandise I get from California designers."

One reason may be because Mrs. Rothaus, a Brit married to a German who came to Paia by way of Philadelphia and Miami, and her peers in the block-long town have priced their wares reasonably. At least, initially. It's the best way to spread the gospel of Paia.

In addition to a hat store (which had quality Niihau leis at the cheapest price I found on Maui), a couple of boutiques and a rental windsurf store, Paia has Maui's only artist cooperative showroom, The Maui Crafts Guild, with 34 member artists, each of whom had to submit to a jury before being accepted.

Artists being the free spirits they are, the attendant lit a joint of pakalolo as she wrote out receipts and answered customers questions. Up Country, just up the hill, is home for many of Maui's artists—and undoubtedly their private reserves of "Maui Gold."

The Spirit of Adventure on The Big Island

Shopping in downtown Hilo is like shopping in any small town that still has an old fashioned soda fountain with spinning stools to sit on ... or a Chinese store selling preserved fruit in huge glass tubs ... or a Japanese mochi shop ...

The merchants talk to you while they total your bill the old fashioned way, by hand using pen and paper or an abacus. You may miss that familiar computerized voice droning "That will be $34.52. Thank you for shopping with us." But I doubt it.

Oh, sure, it's changing. The newest swank concrete and glass shopping center, Prince Kuhio Plaza, makes the one- and two-story wooden buildings in downtown Hilo seem a bit dowdy, out of place—how do I say it—more personal. Hiloans go "look see" the new stores being phased into existence throughout 1985 at the gigantic compound on the highway to the Volcanoes National Park ... but they go back downtown to buy.

Kailua-Kona. The nook 'n' crannies and myriad arcades in Kailua-Kona have never really turned me on, although friends from out of town tell me I'm wrong. I do enjoy wandering about the Kona Inn Shopping Village, but whether it is because of the shops and oceanfront restaurants or because of a nostalgia for yesteryear when the Kona Inn was *the* place to go for get-away weekends, I don't know.

I do know, as a connoisseur of macadamia nut cookies, that the grand prize winner in the first annual Macadamia Nut Augustfest Cookie Contest is a deserving champion. Chunks of nuts fight chips of chocolate, crowding out all but enough batter to hold them together. And the winner is—ta da—Mrs. Berry's Cookies, adjacent to the pay telephone on the Kona Inn's Boardwalk.

Nearby, the young woman in charge of the Maui Divers' shop, Josie Tampos, is a wealth of information about black coral and will show you a film about how it is harvested, cut, polished and mounted to dramatize the unusual grain and luster.

Black coral is the only other indigenous and precious local jewelry of the islands besides the Niihau shell leis. You'll find a lot of pink coral of all grades of quality, and it is all imported. Jade, too, is found in abundance. Imported also.

Like the Niihau shells, black coral comes from the sea. It looks like a "tree" and literally is the skeleton of a coelentorate sea animal *(antipathed grandis verrill)*. Fishermen knew of its existence for years from branches caught on bottom-fishing lines, but it was only in the late 1950's, with the development of aqua-lunging, that the coral forests were reachable.

One of the pioneer divers for black coral, Jack Ackerman, owns the Maui Divers' shop on the Kona Inn boardwalk. According to Josie, he stockpiled a forest of black coral trees 25 years ago. As that stock dwindles, the price of the finished jewelry increases. I believe it, but another, equally important reason why the price increases is the quality of design and workmanship. My, how both have improved in the past 20 years! Look for jewelry by Boyer, a fine designer.

The Competitive Edge in the Kona Inn Shopping Center has clothes for all kinds of sports, including a "zoot suit" for triatholon athletes—or cyclists, for that matter. Made in Kona of lightweight porous skin-tight fabric—different from the fabric used in similar Mainland manufactured outfits—the zoot suit is customized for Hawaiian and other warm weather climates. It comes in high fashion color combinations that you won't find elsewhere. Or if you want a really tailored to fit zoot suit, call local designer Christal Nylin (329-9453) who lives in Holualoa.

Holualoa. The shopping area that does turn me on is perched above Kona in a village that time might have passed by but for a couple who sought out a place to "do their thing" 20 years ago. Carol and Bob Rogers have revitalized the tiny hillside community, once on the main around-the-island highway, converting the old coffee mill to an artists' classroom and studio, the charming old church to an art gallery called The Little Church Gallery, and the old post office to a crafts store.

Students and friends of the Kona Arts Center and Coffee Mill Workshop have also reclaimed vacated buildings. There's a glass blower, a sculptor, a framing shop and a processor of Hawaiian seasoning that uses the Ti plant.

Studio 7 is such an elegant little gallery that it comes as a complete surprise. So does the artist's work. Morinoue has a decided Japanese flavor in his work; I understand he spends some time in Japan as well as in this superb, quiet mountainside retreat.

The old hotel, still operative and always full, is a collectors' item. You *have* to see it.

The Pineapple Patch, the Big Island's contribution to the art of Hawaiian stitchery, has quilt and pillow patterns as well as needlepoint kits.

Just beyond the center of Holualoa village, heading south, stop by Kimura's Lauhala Shop, the definitive shop for authentic Hawaiian straw bags, hats, accessories and little gifts. Not an import in sight.

Two or three ladies sit in one corner of the room, their sewing machines in humming fugue with their trilling chatter. Laughter peals like cymbals, tying fragments of sentences together. Customers join in.

"How can you sell this so reasonably?" a customer holds up a $23 hand woven purse.

"Because Mama doesn't pay us!" They all howl.

"Are you all sisters?"

Merriment spilled over a floodgate.

"Not all. That's Mama over there."

A young looking mama, Tsuruyo Kimura had a small shop in Kona town for 11 years but "it got too commercial for her ... too many people ... not enough time to finish her work which she brought home every night ... not enough time to enjoy the family."

The daughters, seeking to improve her lifestyle, found the big, airy shop in Holualoa, where they all work and laugh together all day long and spread a lot of love and warmth on everybody who drops by. The shop and its occupants should be named Living Treasures. For that matter, so should the town.

Don't Judge A Book By Its Cover

Waimea. Holualoa is special, there's no denying it. But around-the-island explorers will discover other such art stops, if they keep their eyes open. The shops will vary in mood and merchandise from ultra sophistication to charming provincialism. But, realize that you cannot always judge a shop by its name. Such is the case for Nikko Natural Fabric, on the outskirts of Waimea. It's a superb art stop. Yes, it has silks and cottons from lands across the Pacific—fine quality—but it also has handmade papers, and some fabulous wearable and functional art.

Waipio. There's a shopping as well as a scenic reason for going to the lookout of that broad green gulch of song and international acclaim. It is Waipio Woodworks. The views of the deep green valley, bisected by a silvery ribbon river that flows to a royal blue sea are matched, if you can believe it, by the grace and beauty of native woods smoothed into utilitarian and decorative shapes by Joe Mathiew and his three sons.

The shop is like a small museum. We saw the first piece of the rare kou (not to be confused with koa) we had ever seen. They said the immigrants from Tahiti brought the kou with them for making bows, because of its durability. (Museums refer to it as an indigenous tree.) In any event, it is a beautiful wood, velvety in its highly polish variegated brown tones.

The Mathiews work in all the woods now growing in Hawaii, including macadamia nut, which was also new to me.

Volcano National Park. Another special place to shop is The Volcano Art Center, a non-profit venue for the visual and performing arts. Its location adjacent to the Park Visitor Center in the historic 1877 Volcano House makes it that much more interesting. Marcia Morrison, who is also the art reviewer for the *Honolulu Star-Bulletin* (busy lady), shows and sells the works of the finest artisans on the island. Exhibits change every month. Monthly, she organizes musical concerts or poetry readings, seminars or study classes—or all—in this tiny cultural enclave. Ask for the calendar of events if you plan to stay in the area long enough to enjoy the events.

The Resorts of Kohala. Mauna Lani's Connoisseur's Gallery is exactly that. Mauna Kea Beach Hotel's gift shop almost matches the museum quality of art of the Pacific scattered around the public areas. You cannot go home without 1) seeing the great sitting Buddha atop the majestic stairs outside the main dining room, or 2) without experiencing the luncheon buffet—and those sinful white chocolate-coated macadamia nuts. Order a box to take along.

The Last Word On The Macadamia Nut. Of the several brands available, I prefer the Mauna Loa for their flavor and crispness and because they don't go rancid after being opened for awhile. That assumes, of course, there are left over macadamias which is highly unlikely.

One money-saving idea is to buy shelled macadamias, available in gift shops and at roadside processing plants, and roast them yourself. Our friends, Tojiro and Satsuki Motoki who live on the Kona coast always roast their own.

It is duck soup easy. Just wash the nuts and drain them well.

Salt to taste, throw them in the oven at the lowest heat setting for 30 hours or until crunchy. (So you dine out for a day; that's not bad either.) At $8.00 a pound, it's better than $3.50 per 5-ounce tin, or $11.00 a pound.

Craft Fairs and Flea Markets. At the time of heritage festivals, like the Merrie Monarch Festival, you'll find the art, foods and handcrafts of Hawaii for sale somewhere. Ask. There are Saturday flea markets in Kamuela (waste time) and there *may* be one across from the Keauhou Beach Hotel on the Kona Coast. The qualifier is inserted because Kailua-Kona merchants may be winning support for their contention that the Saturday vendors are "unfair competition" because they do not pay rental or property taxes.

If it is operational, it is a great place for mingling with the local residents. Which is, for a lot of us, a major reason for traveling. We buy memories. While memories can be invoked by an art object or a garment or some other souvenir, the best and most durable memories are of people. Those buys stay in the heart.

7. Once Around Lightly

You can take a limited-passenger, twin-engine airplane from Honolulu's International Airport and see, from the air, all of the principal islands of Hawaii in a day. You'll leave at dawn and arrive back in Honolulu at dusk having landed at three islands, Kauai, Maui and Hawaii and having had a short ground tour on each island. Exhausting, but you will have done it.

If you only have one day, why not?

The better solution, of course, is to have all the time that you want and take an Aloha Airlines jet and spend a week on each island (a month is better), sampling each one to the fullest (as this book has done), and think about moving to Hawaii permanently. (That's how most of us got here.)

Another way is to cruise around the island state, taking a week, visiting each of the islands to choose which island you would like to come back to and spend more time.

That's what 90 percent of the passengers on American Hawaii Cruises' *S.S. Constitution* were doing when we sailed from Honolulu Harbor one Saturday night on this 30,000-ton luxury liner. The majority of passengers, who had never been in Hawaii before, arrived earlier that day, boarded the ship after 2PM, and would fly back to the Mainland the following Saturday, rest on Sunday, and go back to work on Monday.

The week-long cruise provided a chance to see all of the major islands without constantly unpacking a suitcase or making frequent airport transfers. A trouble-free way to go.

American Hawaii Cruises has two ships which circle the islands each week, departing on Saturday evening, returning a week later.

The *Constitution*, our berth for the week, left at 9PM with the lights of Honolulu—big city!—off the port bow and crossed the Molokai Channel. Sunday morning we lay off the southern coast of Molokai which we slowly circumnavigated counter clockwise, then turned south and went down the west side of Lanai, past the south end and up the "Lahaina Roads," the straits between Lanai and Maui, towards Lahaina and, before dusk, swung south for the Big Island. We docked in Hilo Monday morning to spend the day ashore. Then we cruised overnight again. Lullaby sleeping.

Tuesday morning we awoke off the southwestern coast of the Big Island, and that afternoon the ship anchored off Kona. Wednesday we were in Maui. The last two days were spent on Kauai, returning to Honolulu Harbor early Saturday morning.

The *S.S. Independence*, the sister ship, sets out around the north shore of Oahu, circumnavigating Kauai on Sunday. Monday evening, the ship heads for the Big Island, stopping one day each in Hilo and Kona, then spends the last two days at Maui, rendezvousing with the *S.S. Constitution* at home harbor on Saturday.

Cruise prices have been stable since 1983, ranging from $995 minimum for an inside economy cabin to $3,595 for a deluxe outside suite. A prearranged airfare supplement allows a passenger to fly roundtrip to Honolulu economically; from Seattle, for example, for $249.

We enjoyed ourselves.

To a local person the chance to see the islands from offshore is an exciting experience. It was surprising how different the islands look from aboard a ship. You get a perspective of the islands not seen any other way.

The *Constitution's* Captain Wu, trained in the British navy, was a delight. He invited us to the bridge at 6AM to have a cup of coffee and witness the landing in Hilo. He delicately positioned the mammoth vessel alongside the pier without the aid of a tug.

In Kailua-Kona, we anchored off shore because the ship was too big to dock and the local kids dived for coins, just as they did in the days when the *Lurline* and the *Matsonia* were the only links between Hawaii and the Mainland.

Docking at Kahului on Maui and at Nawiliwili on Kauai is quite different from landing at an airport. Docks are made for cargo. Airports are made for people. The atmosphere is different, more adventurous in a way. Finding a free telephone can prove to be a real adventure.

It hardly matters if you have booked an excursion or reserved a rental car. You are met.

In the last two years the cruise line has developed 24 shore excursions covering the highlights of all islands, including some action-oriented tours.

The ship had an arrangement for a $22.95 all-day U-drive,

including insurance and unlimited mileage, and the car was waiting at dockside. Not a bad deal.

Officially, about six meals were served every day. Unofficially, you could eat 24 hours a day, via room service. There were two sittings for the main meals, but breakfast and lunch alternatives were poolside buffets, which we did regularly, resisting the tempting dining room menus.

The wine list was large and most reasonably priced.

There were many cruise-type daytime activities on board, including daily movies and nighttime cabaret shows featuring live talent. The Polynesian show on board ship and the luau at the Sheraton Coconut Beach Hotel on Kauai were adored by the passengers, activities that we tended to treat in a rather ho-hum manner ... forgetting our first experiences with similiar events a couple of decades ago and our own unabridged enthusiastic responses.

Witnessing the first-time experiences of our shipmates—and appreciating their enthusiasm—was one of the refreshing delights of the cruise.

I still break up when I remember the lady at our dinner table saying to her husband who had just used a long Hawaiian name: "Get up and wiggle when you say that."

The American Hawaii Cruises add another dimension to the variety of touring in our islands, and the fact that they are 95 percent sold out attests their popularity and the need for cruise sightseeing and accommodations.

(It also means that to get a choice cabin, i.e. in the middle of the ship, you should make an early reservation.)

As we approached Honolulu Harbor in the early dawn and the golden light flooded over Diamond Head, I felt very nostalgic about our beautiful islands.

The air was so sweet. The clouds over the Koolaus were touched with soft whites and yellows. The tradewinds swayed the palm trees along the shore ... and did I imagine a sweet fragrance from the flowers on shore?

Most of our shipmates would be on planes that afternoon, returning to California and Ohio and Washington and Texas and the rest of the states while we were a taxi ride from home, looking forward to a round of golf or tennis in the afternoon and an evening with friends at the Outrigger Canoe Club.

We all should be in love with the places we live.

We are in love with Hawaii—and we have enjoyed sharing that love with you.

Aloha.

Thank You . . .

We have called on the advice of so many neighbors in Hawaii that we could almost duplicate the telephone book in listing our acknowledgments.

However, we mustn't forget to thank a number of people who scanned different parts of the original manuscript including Marge Stone, David Huffman, Jan TenBruggencate, Carl Lindquist and Jan Selland.

The number of competent and attractive p.r. ladies who helped us included Sandie Allen, Tani Bova, Patti Cook, Lynn Cook, Sheila Donnelly, Mele White Pochereva, Stacey L. Westering, Margy Parker, Karen Murphy, Ruth LeMon Limtiaco, Cheryl Gregorio, Rachel Perry, Leslie Reile, Barbara Brundage, Betty Krauss, Leihua Bissen, Julie Zirbel, Debbie Tauchas, Valery O'Brien, Pauline Wrosham and Shirley McKowan.

Several men, not as pretty but just as handy: Jerry Panzo, David Cheever, Mike White, David Eyre, George Engebretson, Harold Reposa, Roger Coryell, Merle Boyer, David Wilson, and Ron Lopes.

When historical background became obscure, we often picked up the telephone and called Bob Krauss or Edward Joesting or Ed Sheehan.

We owe a special debt of gratitude to Chris Klauschke at Crossroads Press for a patient job in typesetting, John Belt of the same organization for reading proof, and Norma Crowell for her paste-up.

Above all, we thank saintly John Whyland for taking us through a hundred variations of cover layouts and final maps.

253

Index

Aa (type of lava), 47, 148
abbraccio (Oahu), 219
ABC Discount Stores (convenience stores, Waikiki), 221
ABCFM, 32
Accommodations (also see "Hotels" "Bed & Breakfast" and "Condominiums"), 1, 73, 154-157, 169, 186, 187, 191, 196
Ackerman, Jack, 245
Admiral's Barge, 40
Adventures on Horseback (Maui), 82
Agriculture, 75, 85, 103, 107 112, 175, 242
Aiea (Oahu), 40
Aina Haina (Oahu), 15
Airports: Oahu, xviii; Molokai, 67; Maui, 76; Big Isle, 114, 154, Kauai, 172, 203, 205, 241
Akaka State Park (Big Isle), 126
Aki, Charles, Jr., 82
Akina, Allen, 233
Alakai Swamp (Kauai), 175, 188, 190, 204
Ala Moana Center (Oahu), 2, 15,
    22, 24, 28, 47, 213, 216, 217, 231
Ala Moana Park, 22, 41, 217
Ala Wai Canal (Oahu), 215, 217
Ala Wai Golf Course, 3, 217
Ala Wai Yacht Harbor, 3, 4
Alcoholic beverages in public places, 24
Alenuihaha, 104
Alii, 71, 138, 141, 142 180, 199
Alexander & Baldwin, (one of

the "Big Five" companies), 87, 95
Aliiolani (Judiciary Bldg, Oahu), 31, 34
Alion (Oahu), 224, 232
Allterton, John Gregg, 183
Allerton, Robert, 183
Aloha Airlines, xiii, 83, 250
Aloha Dive Shop (Oahu), 41-46
Aloha Shirts (Oahu), 8, 216, 231
Aloha Spirit, xiv, 116, 122, 135
Aloha Stadium (Oahu), 54
Amakapa Pond (Big Isle), 146
Amelia Earhart, 48
American Board of Commissioners for Foreign Missions (ABCFM), 32
American Hawaii Cruises, 250-253
Anaehoomalu (Big Isle), 154
Anahola Bay (Kauai), 172, 201, 202
Andrew's (Oahu), 16, 34
Animals of Hawaii, 21, 66, 73-74, 237, 188, 190
Annabelle's (Oahu), 18
Anthuriums, 80, 86, 115, 122, 123, 124, 127, 237
Antiques Pacifica (Oahu), 227
Apparels of Pauline, 95
Apple, Russell, 127-128
Apple Tour Tapes (Big Isle), 127
Aquaculture, 86, 147, 242
Aquarium (Waikiki), 2, 5, 21, 90
Araki, Tom, 164-168
Arizona USS Memorial (Oahu), 37-40
Arleen Stafford, 219
Army Museum (Waikiki), 6

Art Academy (Honolulu), 2, 16, 217, 229

Art Fence at the Zoo (Oahu), 21

Art galleries (Oahu), 217, 229

Arthur's (Oahu), 17

"Artists in Hawaii" (annual show, (Oahu), 229

ArtLoft (Oahu), 229

Asahina, Dr. Sanford, 15

Asian Art (Oahu), 227-229

Astrolab (ship), 111

Aunty Malia (Hyatt Regency Waikiki), 221

Avocados, 86

Awai, Nake'u (muumuus), 231

Azeka Place Shopping Center (Maui), 242

Azuki (sweet confectionary bean), 56

Bagwells 2424, 10

Bailey, Edward, 83

Bailey's Antique Clothing Shop (Oahu), 215, 231

Baldwin House Museum (Maui), 94, 120

Baldwin, Rev. Dwight, 94, 113

Ballooning (hot air, Maui), 112

Bananas, 61, 86

Banyan Drive (Big Isle), 119

Banzai Pipeline (Oahu), 56

Barbary (sheep), 73

Bay Course, (golf, Kapalua, Maui), 100

Beach House Restaurant (Kauai), 194

Beaches: Oahu, 5-8, 41, 49, 50, 51, 56-58, 62-63; Molokai, 69, 73; Big Island, 127, 132, 138, 146, 150, 151, 152, 168; Maui, 83, 94, 96, 98, 99, 108; Kauai, 188, 193, 201, 204, 211

Bed and Breakfast Association, 193

Berger, Gertrude, xvi

"Bests of Honolulu" (book), 234

Beverages (spirits of Hawaii), 112, 243

Bicycling (Maui), 75-82,

Big Island (island of Hawaii), 114-171

Billfishing (Big Isle), 138-141

Birds of Hawaii, 121, 124, 134, 146, 166, 177, 186, 188, 190, 202, 203, 206

Birthing Stone (Kauai), 200

Bishop Museum (Oahu), 2, 25-27, 53, 167, 229, 230, 231, 238

Bishop, Princess Bernice Pauahi, 26

Bishop, Charles, 26

Bissen, Leihuanani (a former Miss Hawaii), 86

Blanc de Noirs (Hawaiian champagne), 112

Blow Hole (Oahu), 41, 49

Blue Course, (golf, Wailea, Maui), 87

Boats, charters, 138-141, 145, 177

Boat cruises, 92, 96, 98, 177, 179, 198, 209

Bolton, Emily, 232

Bon Appetit (Oahu), 12

Bone, Bob, xv

Books about Hawaii, xi, xv, 36, 61, 182, 183, 190, 213, 224, 225, 227, 234, 241

Borges, Jimmy, 18

Boussole (ship), 111
Brett, Michael, 160, 161, 162,
    167
Brigham Young University
    (Oahu), 57, 58
British influence on Hawaii, 16,
    135, 137, 225, 234
Britts, Barbara, 228
Bri'oni (Kapalua Bay Hotel,
    Maui), 242
Bromeliad, 54
Bronte, Emory, 74
Brothers Cazimero, 18
Brown, Francis Ii, 155
Brye, Bill, 142
Bueno Nalo Restaurant, 51
Burnett, Carol, 99, 204
Burns, Bob, 99
Bus transportation: Oahu, 25,
    47; Maui, 88; Lanai, 96
Buscher, Grace, xiv, 97, 200
Buzz's Steak House (Oahu), 51
Byodo-In Temple (Oahu), 62

Cabarets, (Oahu), 223
Caldera, 84, 129, 130
Cameron, Colin C., 99
Camping, 79, 82, 107, 109, 115,
    130, 168, 171, 198, 207, 241
Canlis (Oahu), 8, 10
Capitol (Oahu), 30
Captain Cook, James, 68, 120,
    134-137, 184, 187
Captain Zodiac (Kauai), 208-210
Car rental, 41, 101, 105, 252
Carol & Mary's (Oahu), 216,
    224, 232, 242
Carriage House (Oahu), 225
Cartier (Oahu), 218
Catamarans, 7, 48, 88
Caves, 107, 108, 132, 154, 159,

182, 197, 209, 210
Cazimero Bros., 18
C. Brewer (one of the "Big
    Five" companies), 85
Chain of Craters Road (Big Isle),
    114, 127
Champeaux's (Ilikai Hotel,
    Oahu), 11
Chanel (Oahu), 218, 232
Chang, Yankee, 35
Chapman's, 242
Char Su, xii
Charlot, Jean (artist), 228
Cheng, Yvonne, 228
Chez Michel, (Oahu) 12, 222
Chez Paul restaurant (Maui), 95
China Friendship Store (Oahu),
    218
China House Restaurant (Oahu),
    15
China Silk House (Oahu), 214
Chinaman's Hat (Island off
    Oahu), 62
Chinatown (Oahu), 17, 35-37
Ching Young Village (Kauai),
    207-208, 241
Chocolates for Breakfast
    (Oahu), 216, 219, 232
Chris Hemmeter, 98, 174
Christensen, William, 28
Churches, 70, 81, 103, 110, 134,
    141
Circle Island Tour (Oahu), 53-63
City of Refuge (Big Isle), 114,
    134, 163
Climate, 75
Clothing stores (Oahu), 213,
    215, 230, 231
Coco Palms Resort (Kauai), xiv,
    200, 239,
Coconut Plantation (Kauai),

201, 240

Coffee, 85, 179, 192, 116, 131, 133, 166, 171, 220, 224, 236, 243, 246

Coffee Mill Workshop (Big Isle), 246

Collections (apparel shops), 56, 221, 232, 242

Compadres Mexican restaurant (Oahu), 16

Compleat Kitchen (Oahu), 224

Condominium accommodations, 83, 87-88, 99, 105

Connoisseur's Gallery at Mauna Lani Bay (Big Isle), 245, 248

Cook, Capt. James, 114, 120, 134-137, 170, 175, 185

Coon's Trilogy (Maui), 96

Copenhagen Cones, 8

Coral jewelry, 245

Cotton Cargo (Oahu), 224

Courtney, Del (Big Band sound) (Oahu), 17

Craft stores, 213, 219, 220, 225, 229, 236, 240, 242, 246, 248

Crafts Fairs, 217, 249

Crazy Shirts, 220

Crime in Hawaii, 3, 49, 183

Croissanterie (Oahu), 17

Crouching Lion (Oahu), 62

Cruiser Bob (bicycle tours), 75-82

Cruises, 3, 40, 92, 96, 98, 209, 250-253

C June Shoes, (Oahu), 220

Damien (see Father Damien)

Danny, Kaleikini, 18

Dan's Dive Shop, 43

Dave's Ice Cream (Oahu), 223

Daws, Gavan, xi,

De Lima, Frank, 18

De Lite Bakery (Oahu), 236

Del Monte Pineapple Experimental Garden (Oahu), 54

De Veuster, (see "Father Damien")

Deep-sea fishing, 15, 138-141

Department stores (Oahu), 229

DeRussy Beach (Oahu), 6, 7

Diamond Head (Oahu), 3, 4, 5, 9, 19-24, 37, 41, 48, 191, 217, 226

Dillingham Air Field (Oahu), 55

Dillingham, Walter, 22

Dillon's (restaurant, Maui), 81

Dim sum, xii, 15, 16

Dining out, see ("Restaurants")

Dinner cruises, 2

Dior (Oahu), 220

Directions, xvi, 48, 187, 193, 229

Discotheques (Oahu), 18-19

Discount shopping (Oahu), 234

Diving, 2, 43-46, 50, 88-90, 92, 95-96, 108, 115, 143, 156-157, 195-196

Dole, James, 55

Dole Pineapple (Oahu), 54, 235

Downtown Honolulu, 3, 6, 16, 17, 20, 28-37, 53, 217

Downtown Improvement Assoc. (Oahu), 28

Dress Hawaii (Oahu), 217, 230

Drives, 47-64, 103, 111, 127, 131, 159-160, 168, 182

Duane's Ono Burger (Kauai), 202

Duerr, Fred, 150

Duke's Alley (Oahu), 215

Duke, Doris, 48

258

Dune buggy rides (Oahu), 51
Duty Free Shoppers (Oahu), 215, 222

Earthquakes, 111
East-West Center (Oahu), 24, 37
Eaton Square (Oahu), 12, 215, 222
Economy, 47, 73, 118, 125, 173-174, 216
Ed & Don's (Oahu), 220, 239
Eisenhower, Dwight D., 40
Ellis, Judy, 170
Elvis Presley, (see "Presley")
Emma, Queen, 52
Entertainers (Hawaiian), 17-18, 59,
Entertainment: Oahu, 2, 11, 18, 19, 22, 56, 214, 216, 218, 221; Big Isle, 155; Kauai, 174; Cruising, 252
Erdman, Pardee, 112
Ethel's (Oahu), 216, 232

Fabric, 23, 220, 226, 245, 247
Fabrications (Oahu), 224
Fagan, Paul, 105
"Fantasy Island" (TV show), 173
Farden, Irmgard, 17
Fast-food, 8, 14, 56, 104, 201
Father Damien (the leper priest of Molokai), 30, 69-70, 74
Fathom Five (Kauai), 195
Feher, Joe, 228
Fern Grotto (Kauai), 198-199
Festivals, 31, 49, 122, 171, 221, 248
Filipinos, 36, 116
"Fisher's Annotated Guide to Hawaii" (book), xv
Fish markets, 35, 119, 234
Fishing, 15, 41, 62, 115, 116, 138-141, 153, 163, 176, 185, 186, 190, 200, 209 245
Fithian, Peter, 136, 140
Flea Markets, 248
Fleming's Beach (Maui), 76, 98, 101
Flowers (shipping), 222, 235
Flowers of Hawaii, 21, 31, 40, 68, 85, 86, 97, 108, 118, 124, 126, 184, 205
Foley, Mike, 59
Food products of Hawaii, 85-86, 243
Foodland, 56, 206, 214
Footprints Trails (Big Isle), 131
Ford Island (Oahu), 40
Fort Elizabeth (Kauai), 176
Fort Ruger (Oahu), 23
Forts in Hawaii, 93, 176
Francis Camera Shop (Oahu), 214
Francis Ii Brown Golf Course (Big Isle), 155
Frey, Mari, 232
Front Street (Lahaina, Maui), 82, 92, 95
Fruit fly, 86
Fruits of Hawaii, 85-86, 166
Fruits (shipping from Oahu), 235
Fujii, Jocelyn, 234
Fujimoto, David Kawika, 163-165
Fumi's (Oahu), 216

Goatfish, 90
Galerie St. Martin (Oahu), 222

259

Galleria (Oahu), 215, 219, 221, 223

Galleries (art on Oahu), 26, 217, 228, 229

Gallery EAS Ltd. (Oahu), 229

Gallinule, 21, 177

Garakuta-do (Oahu), 222

Gardens (commercial), 108, 183

Gaye Pope (Oahu), 220

GBC (Oahu), 218

Geography, viii, ix, 3, 75, 190

Gerrell, Bob, 194

Ghandi, Indira, 21

Giggles (Oahu), 234

Ginger, 85

Gliders, 50, 55, 58

Glossary, xvi

Golf: Oahu, 2, 3, 10, 20, 38, 47, 48, 49, 51, 52, 53, 54, 57, 58, 64, 73, 217; Maui, 83, 87-88, 96-97, 99, 100-101, 104; Big Isle, 115, 116, 130, 131, 141, 154, 155, 156 171; Kauai, 174, 184, 193, 194, 197, 198, 205, 206

Gould, Thomas R., 169

Gray's Beach (Oahu), 5

Green Sands Beach (Big Isle), 132

Greff, Clancy, 208-210

"Grove Farm Plantation" (book), 182

Grove Farm Plantation (Kauai), 179-182

Guava, 72, 86, 123, 166, 178, 179, 211, 243

Gucci (Oahu), 221, 232

Guided hiking/walking tours (Big Isle), 143-154

Guided tours (Oahu), 25, 33, 34, 37; 127, 143-154

Guitars (Oahu), 235

Gunson, Niel, 32

Guslander, Lyle, 200

Haena Point (Kauai), 172, 182, 204, 211

Haiku (Maui), 82, 102

Haili Church (Big Isle), 122

Halau (hula school), 27, 31, 122

Halawa (Molokai), 72, 74

Hale Koikeke Museum (Maui), 83

Haleakala (Maui), viii, 75 -82, 101-102, 109, 111

Haleakala National Park, 75-80, 109

Haleiwa (Oahu), 56

Halekulani Hotel (Oahu), 215, 227

Halemaumau (Big Isle), 130

Hale Poahao, (old prison, Lahaina), 95

Hamabata, Sue & Gwen, 184

Hamoa Beach (Maui), 108

Hana (Maui), viii, 73, 75-76, 83-84, 101-109

Hana Airport, 76

Hana Bay, 76, 104, 106

Hana Kai Resort (Maui), 105

Hana Maui Hotel, 105-106

Hana Ranch, 105

"Hana Road Highlights" (book), 101

Hanalei, 34, 120, 172, 175, 176, 179, 182, 188, 198, 204-210

Hanapepe (Kauai), 172, 184, 192, 239, 240

Hanauma Bay (Oahu), 41-44, 46, 49

Handicrafts, 130, 213, 219, 220, 225, 229, 236, 240, 242, 246, 248

Hang gliding, 50

Hannum, Sherri, 166

Hansen's disease, 68-70

Hansen, Susan, 228

Harada, Wayne, 18

Harrington, Al, 18

Hart & Tagami (Oahu), 229

Hart, Richard, 229

Hasegawa General Store (Maui), 105

Hau Terrace (Oahu), 10

"Hawaii" (book), xi,

"Hawaii, An Uncommon History" (book), xi,

"Hawaii Five-O" (TV show), 35

Hawaii Kai, 20, 43, 48, 49

Hawaii Kai Golf Course, 49

Hawaii Vistors Bureau, xv,

Hawaii Volcanoes National Park (Big Isle), 114, 127-131, 247

Hawaiian Airlines, 83

"Hawaiian Almanac," xi

Hawaiian International Billfish Tournament (Big Isle), 138-141

Hawaiian Holiday Macadamia Nut Company (Big Isle), 162

Hawaiian language, 33, 218

Hawaiian Mission Children's Society, 33

Hawaiian music (himeni), 34, 139

Hawaiian Open Golf Tournament, 48, 54

Hawaiian quilts, 221, 231

Hawaiian Tropical Plantation (Maui), 85-86, 242

Hawaiian Walkways (Big Isle), 144-154

"Hawaii's Super Shopper" (book), 234

Hayward, Peter, 228

Hee Hing Restaurant (Oahu),13

Heiau, 23, 27, 104, 141, 147, 168, 169, 199, 200

Helani Gardens (Maui), 108

Heliconias, 124

Helicopters, 153-157, 203-205

Hickam Air Force Base, 47

High As A Kite (shop), 95

Hiilawe Waterfall (Big Isle), 165, 167

Hiking, 182, 186, 190, 144-154, 162, 171, 211-212

Hiking tours, 111, 144-154, 162

Hilgund at Dawkins Benny (Oahu), 233

Hilo (Big Isle), xi, 34, 114, 116-126, 127, 236, 244

Hilo Airport (Big Isle), 114, 236

Hilton Hawaiian Village (Oahu), 6, 7, 18, 215 221, 222

Himeni, 34

History, 3, 6-8,16, 20, 21, 22, 23, 27-39, 55, 68, 74, 83, 87, 91, 94, 96, 104, 106, 111, 119, 120, 121, 146, 163, 165, 168, 175-176, 184-186, 190, 195, 199-200, 207, 209, 234

Ho, Don, 18

Holualoa (Big Isle), 246

Honalo (Big Isle), 142

Honaunau (Big Isle), 133-134

Hong Kong Menu, 14

Honoapiilani (Hwy-30, Maui), 87

Honokaa (Big Isle), 114, 162, 168

Honokohau Boat Harbor (Big Isle), 114, 145-146

Honokohau (nude) Beach (Big Isle), 145-146

Honolua Bay (Molokai), 76, 101

Honolulu (Oahu), 1-49, 59, 180, 186, 187, 190, 191, 195, 200, 202, 203, 213-235,

Honolulu Academy of Arts (Oahu), 2, 16, 217, 229

Honolulu Advertiser, 15, 18, 182

Honolulu Bookstore (Oahu), 214

Honolulu International Airport, 97

Honolulu Magazine, 10, 18, 19, 230

Honolulu Star-Bulletin, 18, 247

Honolulu Symphony Orchestra, 2

Honolulu Zoo, 21

Honpa Hongwanji Betsuin (Oahu), 53

Hookipa Park (Maui), 76, 102, 243

Hopper, Peggy, 228

Horowitz, Lenore, 201

Horseback riding: Oahu, 64; Maui, 79, 82, 111; Big Isle, 156, 166, 170

Horton, Tom, 43

Hotei-Ya (Oahu), 214

Hotel Hana-Maui, 106

Hotel King Kamehameha (Kailua-Kona), 128, 138, 141

Hotel Lanai, 95

Hotel Molokai, 73

Hotels, 1, 3, 4, 6, 11, 19, 22, 36, 83, 87, 88, 95-97, 99, 106, 128, 141, 150, 154, 155, 156, 169, 174, 182, 201

"How To Get Lost and Found in ..." (book series) xiii

Howell, Mamo (muumuus),231

Hualalai (Big Isle), viii, 114, 148-149, 152

Huehue Ranch (Big Isle), 150

Huialoha (Maui), 76, 111

Hukilau (Big Isle), 120

Hula, 22, 31, 41, 51, 54, 57, 60, 122, 218, 220, 230, 234, 235

Hula Supply Center (Oahu), 234

Hulihee Palace (Big Isle), 141

Hull, Cordell, 38

Hulopoe Bay (Maui), 96

Hunting, 185, 186, 188, 204, 209

Hurricane Iwa (Kauai), 177, 187, 193, 195

Hurtig, Bernard, 227

Hyatt Regency Maui, 97-98, 242

Hyatt Regency Waikiki, 18, 215, 221

Hyatt's Hawaii (Waikiki), 221

Iao Needle (Maui), 76, 83-84

Iida's (Oahu), 214

Ilikai Hotel (Oahu), 4, 7, 11, 12, 13, 18, 37, 221, 232

India Imports (Oahu), 214, 224

Industry, 86

Information sources, xv, 18

Ing, Sheridan, 10

Interisland travel, 236

International Market Place (Oahu), 8, 215, 220

Inter-Continental Maui Hotel, 88

Inzer, John, 50

Iolani Barracks (Oahu), 30
Iolani Palace (Oahu), 28-30, 34
Ironman Triathlon (Big Isle),
142
Ironwood Outfitters (Big Isle),
170
Irwin, Hale (touring golf pro),
100
Irwin, Helene, 100, 105
Irwin Park (Honolulu), 105
Island Adventures (Kauai),
176-179

Jack's Diving Locker (Big Isle),
143
Jackson, Guy, 145
Jacques Bakery (Kauai), 178
Jade, 245
Jameson's (Oahu), 17, 56
Jameson's-By-The-Sea (Oahu),
56
James, Jackie, 43
Jams and jellies, 85, 243
Japanese, 4, 38, 95; shopping
for, 219, 225, 233, 240, 245
Influence of, 88, 116, 119,
155, 161; Immigration, 121;
tourist, 4, 42, 50, 109, 167
Jewelry, 88, 233, 234
Joesting, Edward, xi, 185, 200
Jogging (organized runs), 20,
112
John Dominis (Oahu), 16
John Palmer Parker Museum
(Big Isle), 161
Johnson, Johnno, 151
Jones, Robert Trent, 97, 156
Jones, Robert Trent Jr, 194,
197, 206
JRs Upstairs, 227

Judiciary Building, 28, 31
J.C. Penney, 214, 241

Kaaawa (Oahu), 62
Kaahumanu, Queen, 33, 106
Kaanapali (Maui), 75-76, 93,
96-98, 238, 242
Kaanapali Airport, 76
Kaanapali Beach Hotel, 97
Kaawaloa (Big Isle), 137
Kaena Point (Oahu), 47
Kahala Hilton Hotel (Oahu), 10,
15, 18, 99, 217, 224, 227, 231,
232
Kahala Mall (Oahu), 15, 217,
224, 231
Kahana Bay (Oahu), 62
Kahili, 26, 108
Kahoolawe Island, 75, 83, 84, 91
Kahua Ranch (Big Isle), 170
Kahuku (Oahu), 58
Kahului (Maui), 75, 76, 78, 83,
84, 101, 103, 113, 242, 243
Kahului Airport, 76
Kahuna, 134, 178
Kailua (Oahu), xi, 47, 51, 52, 56
Kailua Sailboard Co. (Oahu), 51
Kailua-Kona (Big Island), 114,
131, 138-142, 143, 244, 248
Kaiser, Henry J., 7, 22, 48
Ka Lae (South Point) (Big Isle),
132
Kalaheo (Oahu), 51
Kalaheo (Kauai) 172, 184, 192
Kalakaua Avenue (Oahu), 2,
6, 21, 216, 217, 221, 231
Kalakaua, King David, 19,
28-30, 52, 113, 233, 234
Kalalau Lookout (Kauai), 172,
188

Kalalau Trail (Kauai), 172, 210, 211, 212

Kalalau Valley (Kauai), 172, 204, 207

Kalanianaole, Prince Johah Kuhio, 48, 175

Kalanianaole Hwy., 15, 48

Kalapana (Big Isle), 114, 127

Kalaupapa (the leper colony on Molokai), 65-71

Kalawao (Molokai), 70

Kaleikini, Danny, 18

Kaluakoi (Molokai), 73

Kaluakoi Golf Course, 73

Kamaaina, 28

Kamaka Hawaii, Inc. (Oahu), 235

Kamakahonu Bay (Big Isle), 138

Kamehameha I, 27, 31, 36, 52, 93, 106, 148, 163, 168, 169, 176

Kamehameha I statues, 31, 32, 34, 169

Kamehameha II, 94

Kamehameha III, 94, 175, 194

Kamehameha IV, 34

Kamehameha V, 236

Kamehameha Hula Festival, 51

Kamehameha Song Festival, 122

Kanemitsu's Bakery (Molokai), 73

Kamuela (Big Island), 161, 236, 248

Kaneohe (Oahu), 47, 52, 61, 62, 229

Kaneohe Marine Corps Air Station (Oahu), 52

Kane, Herb, 154

Kapaa (Kauai), 172, 193, 201, 240

Kapahulu Avenue (Oahu), 13, 14, 53, 217, 225

Kapalua Bay Club, 100

Kapalua Bay Hotel (Maui), 75, 76, 98-101, 106, 238, 242

Kapiolani Boulevard (Oahu), 217, 227

Kapiolani Park (Oahu), 2, 3, 19, 20, 21, 41, 48, 217, 230

Kapiolani, Queen, 233

Kapuna Falls (Big Isle), 126

Kauai, viii, 20, 33, 34, 84, 98, 172-212, 236-240

"Kauai" (book), 200

Kauai Kookies, 236, 239

Kauai Museum, 175, 238, 239

Kauai's Hidden Treasures, 237

Kaumahina State Park, 76, 103

Kaumualii, King (Kauai), 176

Kaunakakai (Molokai), 73

Kaunaoa Bay (Big Isle), 156

Kaupo (Maui), 76, 111

Kawaiahao Church, 33, 34, 37

Kawaihae (Big Isle), 114, 168

Kawela Bay (Oahu), 57

Ka'u Desert (Big Isle), 128

Keahole Airport (Big Isle), 114, 144

Kealaikahiki Channel ("The-Way-To-Tahiti"), 96

Kealakekua Bay (Big Isle), 114, 134, 136, 137

Kealiiwahamana, Nina, 18

Keanae Peninsula (Maui), 76, 103

Keao, Issac K., 70

Keauhou Bay (Big Isle), 141

Keauhou Beach Hotel (Big Isle), 248

Keauhou Golf Course (27 holes), 141

Keawehawaii, Karen, 18

Kee Beach (Kauai), 210

Keeaumoku Street (Oahu), 24, 217, 230, 234

Kekaha (Kauai), 172, 185, 237, 239

Kenai Helicopters, 157

Kennedy, John F. (rock profile), 84

Keo's Thai Cuisine (Oahu), 13

Kepaniwai Park, 84

Kepuhi (Molokai), 73

Kiahuna Golf Village (Kauai), 197

Kiawe, 68, 74, 96, 97, 102, 213

Kiger, Bob, 81

Kihei (Maui), 75, 76, 78, 83, 87, 98, 242

Kiholo (Big Isle), 144, 152-153

Kilauea (Kauai), 172, 178, 202

Kilauea Crater (Big Island), viii, 114, 115, 127, 129, 130, 131

Kilauea Lighthouse (Kauai), 202-203

Kilohana Square (Oahu), 14, 217, 225-227

Kimo's Restaurant, (Maui), 100

Kimura's Lauhala Shop (Big Island), 246

Kimura, Tsuruyo, 246

"King Kong" (motion picture), 178

King, Lt. James, 185

King Kamehameha Hotel (Big Isle), 128, 138, 141

King's Highway (Big Isle), 153

King's Village (Oahu), 25, 215, 221

Kipahulu (Maui), 76, 109-110

Kistner, Adelaide, 25

Kitada's Cafe, (Maui), 81

KK Tei restaurant (Big Isle), 120

Klee Original Art, 232

Knudsen family, 191

Koa, 29, 175, 187, 234, 240, 241

Kodak Hula Show, 22

Kohala Coast (Big Isle), 114, 154-161, 203, 238, 248

Kohala Mountains (Big Isle), viii, 114, 152, 170

Kohemalamalama (Kahoolawe), 84

Kohler, Adi, 157

Kokee Lodge (Kauai), 186, 190

Kokee State Park (Kauai), 172, 182, 185, 186

Koko Head (Oahu), 24, 41, 42, 47, 49, 64

Koloa (Kauai), 172, 193, 194, 195, 239

Komoda Store & Bakery (Maui), 81

Kona (see "Kailua-Kona")

Kona Arts Center (Big Isle), 246

Kona coffee, 85, 133, 171, 236, 173

Kona Inn Shopping Center (Big Isle), 245

Kona Ranch House restaurant (Big Isle), 142

Kona Surf Hotel (Big Isle), 141

Kona Village Resort (Big Isle), 150-151

Koolau Mountains (Oahu), viii-ix, xviii, 51, 64

Kotomori, Amos, 233

Kou (rare wood), 247
Krauss, Bob, 182
Krush, 18
Kua Bay (Big Island), 150
Kuakini Hospital (Oahu), xii,
Kuakini, Governor John Adams,
 141,
Kualapuu (Molokai), 65, 72
Kualoa Ranch (Oahu), 62
Kudu, 73
Kuhio Beach Park (Oahu), 6
Kuhio Mall (Oahu), 215, 220
Kukailimoku, 26
Kukui, 61, 76, 84,
Kukui Grove Shopping Center
 (Kauai), 173, 240
Kukuihaele (Big Isle), 162,
 168
Kukuiolono Golf Course, 184,
 192-193
Kula (Maui), 76, 78, 80, 113

La Dame au Cheval (Oahu), 225
Lady Ann Charter Fishing
 (Kauai), 177
Lake Nine (golf at Princeville),
 205
La Perouse (the explorer), 111
La Perouse Bay, 76, 111
La Mer (Oahu), 11
Lahaina (Maui), 33, 34, 75, 76,
 77, 78, 82, 84, 91-96, 241
"Lahaina Roads" (channel), 75,
 91, 92, 250
Lahainaluna School (Maui), 92
Laie (Oahu), 58
Lanai Hotel, 95
Lanai Island, viii, 95-96
Language (meanings of Hawai-
 ian words), 26, 33, 79, 84, 94,
 102, 112, 164
Lanikai (Oahu), 51
Lapahoehoenui (Big Isle), 159
Lapakahi Village (Big Isle), 168
Lappert's (Kauai), i, 192, 236,
 239
Lappert, Walter, 192, 239
Lauhala handicrafts (Big Isle),
 246
Laulau, 151
Laura Ashley (Oahu), 223
Lava, viii, 49, 52, 79, 96, 112,
 115, 123, 127-129, 131, 133,
 143-153, 155, 157, 159, 168
 197, 229
Lava Tree State Park (Big Isle),
 127
Lawai (Kauai), 172, 183
Leahi (Diamond Head, Oahu),
 23
Leed, Melveen, 18
Lee, David, 228
Lehua, 29
Leilehua Golf Course (Oahu), 54
Leprosy, 68-70
Levinson, Frank, 82
Liberty House, 8, 214, 216, 221,
 224, 231, 232, 234, 241
Licenses, camping, 241
 Fishing
 Na Pali Coast (Kauai), 241
 tramping, 241
Lihue (Kauai), viii, 172-174, 176,
 179, 180, 182, 192, 198, 201,
 203, 240
Lihue Airport, 172, 203, 204
Lihue Shopping Center (Kauai),
 240
Likelike Hwy. (Oahu), 63
Lilikoi, 72, 166, 179, 184, 236

Liliuokalani Park (Big Isle), 119
Liliuokalani, Queen, 29, 233
Lindbergh, Charles, 110
Lindquist, Carl, 106
Little Church Gallery (Big Isle),
    246
Little Circle Island Tour
    (Oahu), xviii
Little Hawaiian Craft Shop
    (Oahu), 219
Loihi (island under con-
    struction), viii
Lomilomi, 151
London, Jack, 71
Longhi's Restaurant (Maui), 95
Long's Drugstore, 241
Lono (Hawaiian god), 135
Luahinewai (Big Isle), 152
Luau, 200, 139, 155, 156, 252
Luke's Hotel (Big Isle), 169
Lumahai Beach (Kauai), 210
Lunalilo's Tomb (Oahu), 34
Lunalilo, King William C., 34
Lurline (ship), 251
Lycurgus, Uncle George, 130
Lydgate Park (Kauai), 198
Lyman, Rev. David, 120
Lyman House Museum (Big
    Isle), 120-121, 128
Lynn, Loretta, 152

Maalaea Bay (Maui), 75, 76, 87,
    88
Macadamia nuts, 85, 118,
    125-126, 162, 192, 235, 236,
    247
Macadamia orchards (Big Isle),
    125-126
Madam Pele, 127, 128, 130,
    157-158

Magnum P.I. (TV show), 35
Magoon's Beach (Big Isle), 149
Mahewalu Point (Big Isle), 151
Mahimahi, 151
Mahukona (Big Isle), 169
Maile Restaurant (Kahala
    Hilton), 10
Maili (Oahu), 63
Mai Pake (leprosy), 68
Mai tai, xiv, 8
Makaha, 57, 63
Makaha Valley Country Club
    (Oahu), 63-64
Makai Art Village (Kauai), 239
Makaikini, Tiny, 105
Makalawena Beach (Big Isle),
    149, 153
Makapuu Beach (Oahu), 50
Makawao (Maui), 76, 78, 81, 82,
    237, 242
Makee, James, 113
Makena Beach (Maui), 76, 88,
    112
Makena Golf Course, 88
Makiki (Oahu), 24, 25
Malia Hawaii (Oahu), 232-233
Malihini, 5
Mama's Fish House (Maui), 102
Manana (Rabbit Island, Oahu),
    50
Mandalay Imports, 232,
    242
Manele Bay (Lanai), 96
Mangoes (fruit), 86
Mano Point (Big Isle), 151
Manuka (Big Isle), 132
Maps, viii-ix, xviii, 67, 76, 114,
    172, 215, 217
Marathons (organized runs), 20
Marijuana, 63, 103, 118, 165,
    183, 189, 244

Marisol (sculptor), 30

Market Place at Coconut Plantation (Kauai), 241

Marlene Sai, 8, 18

Marquesas Islands (see "Tahitian Influence")

Marston, Louise, 207

Martin, Don Francisco de Paula, 36

Martin, Trent, 225

"Masterpieces in the Netsuke" (book), 227

Mathiews, Joe, 247

Matson, xiii, 1, 22

Matsonia (ship), 251

Matteo's (Oahu), 17

Maui, viii, 33, 43, 46, 75-113, 174, 176, 177, 188, 236-238, 241-245

Maui Blanc (pineapple wine), 112

Maui Crafts Guild (Maui), 244

Maui Divers (Big Isle), 245

"Maui Gold" (marijuana), 244

Maui Land & Pineapple Co., 99

Maui Marriott Resort, 97

Maui potato chips, 85, 91, 236

Maui Surf Hotel, 97

Mauna Kea ("White Mountain") (Big Isle), viii, 114, 116, 119, 140, 150, 152, 161, 170, 171

Mauna Kea Beach Golf Course, 100, 156

Mauna Kea Beach Hotel (Big Isle), xiii, 144, 155-157, 198, 221

Mauna Kea Beach Hotel Gift Gallery (Big Isle), 221, 236, 247

Mauna Kea Observatory (Big Isle), 159-160

Mauna Lani Hotel (Big Isle), 155, 247

Mauna Loa ("Long Mountain) (Big Isle), viii, 114, 129, 133, 140, 157

Mauna Loa Macadamia Nut Co. (Big Isle), 125-126, 131, 162, 248

Maunalua Bay (Oahu), 45

McCoy, Lydia, 210

McInerny (Oahu), 217, 224, 232

McNamee, Phil, 43

Meheula Florist (Oahu), 222

Menehunes, 177, 178, 209

Menehune Fishpond (Kauai), 177, 178

Merrie Monarch, 28, 29, 30, 52, 248

Merrie Monarch Festival (Big Isle), 122, 171, 248,

Messengers of Grace, 32

Meyer, Wolfgang, 14

Michaels, Ken, 137

Michel's (Oahu), 10, 12

Michener, James, xi,

Midkiff, Robert, 28

Mid-Night Cafe (Molokai), 73

Mid-Pacific Country Club (Oahu), 51

Mililani Golf Club (Oahu), 54

Mililani Town (Oahu), 54

Military influence, 47

Milolii (Big Isle), 114, 132-133

Mission Houses Museum (Oahu), 33, 34, 230

Missionaries, 32-39, 94, 107, 120-121, 141, 207

Moa (Polynesian chicken),187, 188

Moana Hotel (Oahu), xiii, 8, 200
Moanalua Gardens (Oahu), 54
Moanalua Golf Club (Oahu) 54
Mokuaikaua Church (Big Isle), 141
Mokuleia (Oahu), 55
Mokupuku (Big Isle), 159
Molokai, viii, 30, 41, 42, 49, 65-74, 83, 106, 183
Molokai Airport, 67
Molokai Ranch, 73
Molokai Ranch Wildlife Park, 73
Molokini Island, 76, 88-91
Mongoose (Kauai), 188
Monkeypod (tree), 53, 132
Monuments: Oahu, 25, 31, 37, 48; Maui, 108; Big Isle, 134
Mookini Heiau (Big Isle), 169
Mopeds (Oahu), 42
Morinoue (Big Island), 246
Mormons, 58-61
Morrison, Barbara, 208
Morrison, Marcia, 247
Most popular attractions: Hawaii Volcanoes National Park, 127-131; Polynesian Cultural Center, 58-61; helicopter tour of Kauai, 241
Motoki, Tojiro & Satsuki, 137, 248
Mouflon, 73
Mountain View (Big Isle), 237
Mrs. Berry's Cookies (Big Isle), 245
Mrs. Field's Chocolate Chippery (Oahu), 214
Mt. Waialeale (Kauai), viii, 84, 175, 183, 204

Mule trail (Molokai), 65-71
Mullet, 86, 177
Music, 2, 6, 18, 19, 27, 73, 173, 203, 230, 231, 233
Muumuus, 8, 230-231
M. Matsumoto Store (Oahu), 56

Naalehu (Big Isle), 114, 132
Nahiku (Maui), 103-104
Nake'u (muumuus), 231
Nanakuli (Oahu), 63
Naniloa Surf Hotel (Big Isle), xiii, 118
Nanualele Point (Maui), 107
Napili Bay (Maui), 75, 76, 98, 101
Napili Kai Beach Club, (Maui), 98
Napoopoo (Big Isle), 134
Na Pali Coast (Kauai), 172, 189, 204, 208-211
Na Pali Zodiac Co. (Kauai), 208-210
Natatorium (Oahu), 5, 10, 22
National Car Rental, 101
National Memorial Cemetery (Oahu), 25
National Park Service, 37, 38, 68, 127-131, 134, 168
Nawiliwili Harbor (Kauai), 172, 174, 176-179, 180, 209
Needlepoint, Inc. (Oahu), 225
Nelson, Brian, 162
Nene, 21, 78
Neneuwe Falls (Big Isle), 166
Netsuke (Asian art), 227
New Otani Hotel (Oahu), 10, 20
Nicklaus, Jack, 154
Nickolas Nickolas Restaurant (Oahu), 15

Nick's Fishmarket (Oahu), 11
Nightlife (Oahu), 18-19
Niihau Island, viii,
Niihau leis, 184, 237-239, 244, 245
Nikko Natural Fabric (Big Island), 247
No Ka Oi, IV cruises (Maui), 96
North Shore Fudge (Oahu), 8
Nude beaches, 58, 146
Nuuanu Pali (Oahu), 51
Nylin, Christal, 246

Oahu, viii, 1-64, 72, 175, 176, 191, 203, 213-235
Oahu Country Club, 52
"Oahu Market Island Recipes & Shopper's Guide" (book), 234
Ocean Activities Center (Maui), 88, 95-96
Ocean Nine (golf at Princeville), 205
Ocean Thermal Energy Conversion (OTEC), 147
Ocean View Inn (Big Isle), 142
Ogdemli, Dorothea & Kaya, 228
O'Halloran, Terry, 195
Ohelo (Big Isle), 128
Oheo Bridge (7 Pools, Maui), 109
Ohia, 73, 74, 128, 141
Old Koloa Town (Kauai), 194, 239
Olivine (Big Isle), 132
Olomana Golf Course (Oahu), 51
On The Hana Coast (book), 101
Onomea Bay (Big Isle), 114, 123-124

Orange Golf Course (Wailea, Maui), 87
Orchids of Hawaii, 123
Orchids, 80, 86, 119, 122, 237, 242
Oriental Imports (Oahu), 213, 214
Orientwest (Oahu), 227
Orizaba's (Oahu), 217, 228
Oryx, 73
OTEC (Big Isle), 147
Outrigger Canoe Club (Oahu), xii, 3, 5, 9, 171, 253
O'Brien, Frank, 89

Pacific Book House (Oahu), 224
Pacific Botanical Gardens (Kauai), 183
Pacific Handcrafters Guild (Oahu), 230
Pacific Whale Foundation, 92
Packaged tours, Oahu, 25, 33, 34, 47; Maui, 82, 105, 143-154; Big Island, 144-154; Around the islands, 250-253
PADI, 46, 195
Pahoa (Big Isle), 114
Pahoehoe (type of lava), 148,
Paia (Maui), 76, 77, 78, 81, 102, 243-244
"Painted Churches" (Big Isle), 134
Pakalolo (marijuana), 63, 103, 118, 244
Palaau State Park (Molokai), 72
Pali (Oahu), 47, 51, 52, 229, 241
Pali Golf Course (Oahu), 51
Pali Highway, 51
Palmer, Arnold, 51, 100
Pandanus, 142

Paniolo, 152
Paopao Falls (Big Isle), 159
Papakolea (Oahu), 24
Papaya, 85, 86, 105, 118, 126, 127, 142, 148,152, 166, 235, 236, 242
Papillon Helicopter, 98, 241
Pappagallo (Oahu), 223
Parker Ranch (Big Isle), 158, 161, 236
Parker Ranch Broiler (Big Isle), 161
Parks & gardens, 75-80, 84, 103, 108, 122, 123-124, 128-131, 132, 134, 168
Paschoal, 70
Passion fruit, 8, 86, 123
Patti's Noodle Kitchen (Oahu), 15
Patton, Gen. George, 113
Pau Hana Inn (Molokai), 73
Pa'u, 31
Pearl Country Club (Oahu), 54
Pearl Harbor (Oahu), 15, 37-41, 47, 53, 54, 58
Pearl Harbor cruises (Oahu), 37, 40
Pearl Harbor Memorial Visitor Center, 38-40
"Pearl Harbor Remembered" (book), 234
Pedicabs (Oahu), 218
Pele (fire goddess), 23, 127, 128, 129, 130, 148, 157, 158
Perry, Major Allen L., 3, 41
Petroglyphs (Big Isle), 127
Phallic Rock (Molokai), 72
Picnics shop (Maui), 102
Pihea (Kauai), 188

Piilani Hwy. (31, Maui), 109, 111
Piilanihale Heiau (Maui), 104
Pineapple, 47, 54-55, 61, 73, 78, 81, 86, 96, 99, 100, 112, 142, 234, 235, 246
Pineapple Experimental Garden on Oahu (Del Monte), 54
Pineapple Hill Restaurant
Pineapple Patch (Big Isle), 246
Pioneer Inn (Lahaina), xiii, 92-93
Pioneer Sugar Mill, 92
Pipiwai Valley, (Maui), 109
Plantations: life on, 84-85, 103, 204; (tourist attractions) 85-86, 120 179-182 240-243; (working), 31, 36, 47, 61, 65, 105, 113, 116, 125, 159,
Plants of Hawaii, 86
Plumeria, 234
Poha, 166, 224
Poipu (Kauai), 172, 182-183, 192-199, 238, 240
Polo, 55, 113
Polo/Ralph Lauren (Oahu), 223
Pololu Valley (Big Isle), 170
Polynesian Cultural Center (Oahu), 57, 58, 59, 61, 230
Pomegranates in the Sun (Oahu), 225
Pony Express Tours (Maui), 82
Popo's Bakery (Kauai), 236
Population Oahu, 4; Maui, 97; Hawaii, 116, 158; Molokai, 70; Kauai, 173; Niihau, 191
Port Allen (Kauai), 172
Portuguese, 9, 84, 94, 116, 121, 162, 183

Pottery Restaurant (Oahu), 14
Presley, Elvis, 40
Prides of New Zealand (Oahu), 214
Prince Kuhio Plaza (Big Isle), 244
Princess Kaiulani Hotel
Princeville (Kauai), 172, 182, 203-207, 241
Princeville Golf Course (27 holes), 206
Prison (Lahaina), 95
Protea, 80, 86, 237
Pryor, Sam, 110
Puaa Kaa Park State Park (Maui), 76 103
Pua & Kawika's Place (Kauai), 241
Puamana, 17
Puhi (Kauai), 172
Pukui, Mary, 178
Puna Producers Enterprises (Oahu), 235
Punaluu (Oahu), 62
Punaluu (Big Isle), 132
Punchbowl of the Pacific (military cemetery), 24
Puowaina (Oahu), 25
Pupukea (Oahu), 56
Puu Ualakaa Park (Oahu), 24
Puu Kukui (Maui), viii, 76
Puukohola Heiau (Big Isle), 168

Queen Emma's Summer Palace, (Oahu), 52
Queen Kaahumanu, 33, 106
Queen Kaahumanu Highway (Big Isle), 143, 153, 157
Queen Kapiolani, 233
Queen Liliuokalani, 29, 233

Queen Victoria's Profile (Kauai), 178
Queens' Baths (Big Isle), 127, 146, 147
Queen's Beach (Oahu), 6

Rabbit Island, 50
Rafael, Georg, 99
"Raiders of the Lost Ark" (motion picture), 178
Railroads, 180
Rain, 7, 51, 52, 65, 75, 77, 115, 123, 124, 126, 128, 148, 158, 170, 180, 181, 186, 188, 189, 191, 207
Rainbow Bazaar (Oahu), 215, 222
Rainbow Mall (Maui), 242
Ralph Lauren (Oahu), 223
Ramage Press, 33
Rea Store & Bar (Molokai), 69
Regent International Hotels, 99
Restaurants, Oahu, 7, 8, 9-19, 36, 49, 213, 220, 221, 223; Molokai, 73; Maui, 81, 83, 92, 95, 96, 97, 98, 99, 100, 102, 242; Big Isle, 120, 142, 155; Kauai, 174, 175, 183, 193, 194, 201, 202, 206
Ranching, 105-106, 112, 170
Reyn's (Oahu), 216, 224, 231
Rice, Wm. Hyde, 175
Richards, Monty, 170
Robinson, Clara, 240
Robinsons of Niihau, 191
Rockefeller, Laurance, xii, 109, 156
RockResorts, 99
Rodeos (Big Isle), 132

Rogers, Carol & Bob, 246
Rona Gale (Maui), 243
Ronck, Ronn, xi,
Roosevelt, Franklin D., 5
Rosewood Hotels, 106
Rosey's Boathouse (Big Isle), 120
Rothaus, Rona, 244
RoxSan, (Oahu), 11, 223, 226
Royaks (Kauai), 176-178, 209
Royal Hawaiian Hotel (Oahu), xiii, 1, 215, 227
Royal Hawaiian Shopping Center, (Oahu), 2, 215, 217, 218
Royal Kaanapali Golf Courses (Maui), 97
Royal Lahaina Hotel (Maui), 97
Royal Mausoleum (Oahu), 52
Rumours (Oahu disco), 19
Russian forts (Kauai), 176, 207
Russian influence on Hawaii, 121 175, 176, 184, 207
Ryan's Parkway (Oahu restaurant), 16

Saddle Road (Big Isle), 114
Sailboarding, 51
Sai, Marlene, 18
Saimin, xii
Samoans, 59, 185
Mills, Dr. Samuel, 32
Sanborn, Dr. Kenneth, 145-153
Sandy Beach (Oahu), 49
Sans Souci Beach (Oahu), 5
Sasada, Gen (Molokai), 65
Sashimi, xii
Sato, Todashi, 30
Scaff, Dr. Jack, 19
Scheffer, Georg, 176, 207

Schofield Barracks (Oahu), 47, 53, 54
Scuba diving, 2, 43, 88-91, 96, 115, 143, 157, 194-197
Sea Life Park, 50
Seabury Hall (Maui school), 78
SeaMountain (Big Isle), 14, 132
SeaMountain Golf Course (Big Isle), 132
Sears, 15, 214, 216, 230, 241
Seibu, 88, 112
Selleck, Tom, 10
Serendipity Restaurant (Oahu), 14
Seven Pools (Maui), 76, 109
Sexton, Lloyd, 228
Shaheen's, 230
Sharks, 4, 43
Shattuck, Al, 162
Shave ice, 56
Sheehan, Ed, 213, 234
Shelby's (Oahu restaurant), 11
Shell leis, 200, 209, 236-239, 244
Sheraton Waikiki Hotel (Oahu), xiii, 215, 218
Sheraton Waikoloa Hotel (Big Isle), 154
Sheraton-Kauai Hotel, 252
Sheraton-Maui Hotel, 96, 97
Sheraton-Molokai Hotel, 73
Ship cruising, 250-253
Shirakawa Motel (Big Isle), 132
Shirokiya (Oahu), 214
"Shoal of Time" (book) xi,
Shopping, 1, 2, 14, 15, 28, 53, 56, 83, 88, 95, 96, 105, 118, 138, 141, 143, 161 173, 191, 206-207, 213-249
"Shopping Bag" (book), 234
Show headliners (Oahu), 18
Shrimp (industry), 86

Shupe, Scott, 157-159
Sika, 73
Silkie (antique aloha shirt), 231
Silversword, 78
Sinclair, Elizabeth McHutchinson, 191, 237
Skiing (Big Isle), 161
Skyrovers of Lahaina (Maui), 112
Sloggett, Etta Wilcox, 208
Smith, Ernest (Molokai), 74
Smith, Rev. Lowell, 36
Snark (Jack London's yacht), 71
Snorkeling, 2, 41, 43, 115, 143, 144, 152, 157
Snow on Mauna Kea (Big Isle), 115, 161
"South Pacific" (motion picture), 204
South Point (Big Isle), 132
Spencer Beach Park (Big Isle), 168
Spirit of Windjammer (cruises), 95
Sports, 3, 19, 88, 112, 142, 143, 154, 219, 245
Spouting Horn, (Kauai), 49, 194, 240
Stamper, William, 228
Star Market (Oahu), 224
Statehood, 97, 213
Station Too (Kauai), 240
Stevenson, Robert Louis, 10
Stone, Marge, 5
Stouffer's Wailea Beach Hotel (Maui), 87
St. Benedict Church, (Big Isle), 134
St. Gabriel's Catholic Church (Maui), 103

St. Philomena, (church) 70
St. Louis Florist (Oahu), 235
Submarine Museum (Oahu), 40
Sugar cane, 85, 118
Suisan Fishmarket (Big Isle), 119
Sullivan, Maurice, 56
Sulfone, 70
Sunburn, xiv
Sunset Beach, 56
Sunshine Market (Maui), 80
Sunshine Plantation (Australia), 85
Sunshine Rent-A-Car (Maui), 101
Suntory Restaurant (Oahu), 8
Supermarkets, 56, 174, 224, 235
Surf Meets (Oahu), 57, 63
Surfrider Hotel (Oahu), 10
Susan Marie (Oahu apparel shop), 223
Sushi, xii
Swanzy (Oahu), 62
Swimming, 2, 4, 6, 7, 41, 49, 51, 57, 64, 82, 90, 98, 105, 106, 107, 108, 109, 141, 142, 144, 146, 150, 152, 163, 201, 204, 205,205, 209, 210, 212
Swiss Inn (Oahu), 15
Symphony orchestra (Oahu), 2
S.S. Constitution, 250-253
S.S. Independence, 250-253

Tabus, 107, 134
Tad and Pat (catering), 226
Tagami, Hirosi, 229
Tahiti Influence, 24, 49, 60, 62, 96, 107, 120, 135, 136, 138, 185, 196, 199, 207, 210, 214, 247
Tahiti Imports (Oahu), 214

Takenoya Arts (Oahu), 227
Tampos, Josie, 245
Tantalus/Round Top Drive, 24
Tapa (cloth), 25, 27, 219, 221
Taped tours (Big Isle), 127
Taro, 72, 85, 93, 103, 109, 146,
    151, 163, 164, 165, 166, 185,
    199, 206, 242
Tedeschi, Emil & Judith, 112
Tedeschi Winery (Maui), 112
TenBruggencate, Jan, 183
Tennent Art Foundation Gallery
    (Oahu), 228
Tennent, Madge, 228
Tennis, 2, 15, 20, 21, 22, 47, 48,
    53, 57, 64, 73, 87, 88, 96, 98,
    99, 115, 144, 154, 157, 171,
    174, 194, 206, 211
Teshima, Mary, 142
Teves, Wayne, 166
TGI Friday (Oahu restaurant),
    16
Thaddeus (ship), 120
"The Bests of Honolulu"
    (book), 234
The Competitive Edge (Big Isle),
    245
The French Quarter (Oahu), 225
The Gallery at Waiohai (Kauai),
    239
The Kahn Gallery (Kauai), 240
The Station at Hanapepe
    (Kauai), 239
The Trunk (Oahu), 225
Thomas, Adm. Richard, 16
Thomas Square (Oahu), 16, 217,
    230
Ti plant, 60, 130, 151, 246
Tidal waves, 117
Tokyu (Big Isle), 155

Tony Roma's (Oahu), 10
Tourism, xi, 47, 73, 97, 173,
    216, 243
Tourist newspapers, viii, 18
Transportation, 25, 37, 43, 47,
    51, 83, 88, 162, 203, 237,
    250-253
Travel agents (use of), xvi, 75,
    118
Treasures of the East (Oahu),
    228
Tree molds, 127
Trees, 19, 22, 24, 30, 41, 53, 59,
    68, 72, 74, 82, 86, 87, 96, 103,
    113, 119, 123, 125, 126, 127,
    128, 133, 144, 149, 152, 156,
    159, 163, 164, 166, 181, 183,
    188, 189, 190, 198, 200, 207,
    211, 212, 218, 220, 245
Triathlon (Big Isle), 142,
    245
Tripler Hospital, 53
Tropical Fruits Distributor
    (Oahu), 235
Trout fishing (Kauai), 185, 190
Tsunamis, 117
Turtle Bay (Oahu), 47, 57, 58
Turtle Bay Hilton Golf Club, 57
Turtle Bay Hilton Hotel, 57
Twain, Mark, 132
T-shirts, 231, 240, 243
T. Fujii Japanese Antiques
    (Oahu), 225, 227

Ualakaa Park (Oahu), 24
Ueberroth, Peter, 10
Ukuleles, 235
Ulupalakua Ranch (Maui), 112
"Uncommon Valor" (motion
    picture), 178

"Underground Guide" (book), 201
Up Country (Maui), 80, 113
Upolu Airport (Big Isle), 114, 169
Upside Down Falls (Oahu), 51
Upstart Crow & Co. (Oahu), 224
U.S. Army Museum (Waikiki), 6
Useful addresses/telephones: Oahu, 25, 30, 51; Molokai 72; Maui, 82, 92, 101, 105, 107; Big Isle, 154, 168; Kauai, 179, 182, 191, 210
USS Bowfin (Oahu), 40

Vancouver, George, 106
Villa Roma (Oahu), 216, 219
Village Golf Course (Kapalua, Maui), 100
Volcano Art Center (Big Isle), 128, 130, 247
Volcano House (Big Isle), 130
Volcanoes, viii, viii, 30, 84, 114, 115, 126, 127-131, 133, 171, 190, 224, 244
Volcano Golf Club (Big Isle), 130
Vuitton, Louis, (Oahu), 218

Wahiawa (Oahu), 53, 54
Waialae Avenue (Oahu), 14, 15, 70
Waialae Country Club (Oahu), 48, 54
Waialeale (mountain, Kauai), viii, 84, 175, 183, 204
Waianae Coast (Oahu), 47, 55, 63
Waianae Range (Oahu), viii, xviii,

Waianapanapa State Park (Maui), 107
Waiehu Municipal Course (Maui), 101
Waikapu (Maui), 84-86
Waikiki (Oahu), i, viii, 1-22, 23, 24, 25, 41, 43, 47, 49, 51, 53, 62, 63, 213-241
Waikiki hotels, 1-8
Waikiki Shell (Oahu), 19, 22
Waikiki Shopping Plaza, 215, 219
Waikoloa Resort (Big Isle), 114, 154-155
Waikoloa Airport (Big Isle), 154
Waikoloa Beach Golf Club, 154
Waikoloa Village Golf Course, 154
Wailea (Maui), viii, 75, 76, 83, 87-89, 98, 238, 242
Wailea Kai (cruises), 89
Wailua Lookout (Maui), 103
Wailua Municipal Golf Course (Kauai), 174
Wailua River (Kauai), 172, 198
Wailua River boat tours (Kauai), 198
Wailuku (Maui), viii, 75, 76, 83, 84, 86, 101, 107, 242
Waimanalo (Oahu), 47, 51
Waimanu Valley (Big Isle), 114, 158, 163
Waimea-Kamuela (Big Isle), 114, 144, 152, 156, 158, 159, 161, 162
Waimea (Kauai), 172, 175, 176, 182, 184, 185, 186, 188, 190, 204, 207
Waimea Canyon (Kauai), 172, 182, 185, 186, 188, 190, 204 237

Waimea Falls (Oahu), 56

Waimea-Kamuela (Big Isle), 161

Waiohai Hotel (Kauai), 198, 238

Waiohinu (Big Isle), 132

Waioli Mission (Kauai), 33, 34, 37 120, 207

Waipio Valley (Big Isle), 114, 145, 158, 161-168, 247

Waipio Valley Shuttle (Big Isle), 162-165, 168

Waipio Woodworks (Big Isle), 247

Waldenbooks (Oahu), 219

Ward Centre (Oahu), 16, 217, 223, 228

Ward Centre Gallery (Oahu), 229

Ward Warehouse (Oahu), 16, 217, 223, 234

Warnecke, Carl, 30

Waterfront Fort (Lahaina), 93

Waterfalls, 59, 72, 98, 103, 111, 124, 126, 127, 159, 166, 173, 188, 189, 203, 204, 206, 209

Watumull's, 230

Weather, 54, 75, 77, 83, 84, 113, 119, 128, 129, 131, 156, 160, 182, 183, 188, 241, 245

West Maui, viii, 75, 84-92

Whalers Village (Maui), 96

Whales, 75, 91-92

Whale-watching, 92, 131

Whaling, 50, 75, 91, 96,

Wheeler Air Force Base (Oahu), 47

Whyland, John, 228

Wilcox, Elsie, 180, 208

Wilcox, George N., 179, 182, 208

Wilcox, Mabel, 180, 208

Wildflowers (Oahu shop), 224

Wildlife, 73, 176, 177, 202

Wiliwili, 87

Willows restaurant (Oahu), 17, 231

Wilson Tunnel (Oahu), 63

Windsurfing, 2, 51, 102, 243

Wine-making (Maui), 112

Wisnosky, John, 228

Wo Fat's (Oahu restaurant), 17, 35, 37

Wolfe, Suzanne, 228

Woodhouse, James Hay, 137

Woods Nine (golf course at Princeville), 206

Woolworth's, 214, 224, 241

Wrasse, 90

Wu, Captain Harry, 251

Wyss, Martin, 15

Yim, Lehua, 29

Yoshi, Hisa, 62

Yong Sing (Oahu restaurant), 16

Young, John, 228

YWCA (Oahu), 16

Zoo, 2, 21, 53

Zsalei, 233